Former garden editor of *Country Living*, author of too many books on the finer points of cushions, and previously unacquainted with the world beyond the M25, Miranda Innes now lives on a frequently inaccessible hillside in Andalucia surrounded by olive groves and almond orchards. With her are her partner, Dan Pearce, an assortment of dogs and cats and a changing cast of friends and family.

More information about the author can be found on her website at: www.marocandalucia.co.uk

MIRANDA INNES

Getting to Mañana

BLACK SWAN

GETTING TO MAÑANA
A BLACK SWAN BOOK: 0 552 77098 1

Originally published in Great Britain by Bantam Press,
a division of Transworld Publishers

PRINTING HISTORY
Bantam Press edition published 2003
Black Swan edition published 2004

1 3 5 7 9 10 8 6 4 2

Set in 11/13pt Melior by
Falcon Oast Graphic Art Ltd.

Black Swan Books are published by Transworld Publishers,
61–63 Uxbridge Road, London W5 5SA,
a division of The Random House Group Ltd,
in Australia by Random House Australia (Pty) Ltd,
20 Alfred Street, Milsons Point, Sydney, NSW 2061, Australia,
in New Zealand by Random House New Zealand Ltd,
18 Poland Road, Glenfield, Auckland 10, New Zealand
and in South Africa by Random House (Pty) Ltd,
Endulini, 5a Jubilee Road, Parktown 2193, South Africa.

Printed and bound in Great Britain by
Cox & Wyman Ltd, Reading, Berkshire.

Papers used by Transworld Publishers are natural, recyclable products made from wood grown in sustainable forests. The manufacturing processes conform to the environmental regulations of the country of origin.

To Spigs and Leo, Doris and Ted, Judy and Dan,
with love and gratitude

A view from El Torcal

CONTENTS

PROLOGUE

Four years on, and there is nothing more to build. The cement-mixer has finally rattled off to a new site, and we are poised on the brink of total ownership, peace and privacy. All that awaits us is the pleasurable task of settling in, of assembling the habits that fit the place.

At long last I have a cool blue-grey room in which to work, with its own shaded cloister where roses twine, and I can sit and ponder, looking out onto a paved courtyard with a fountain in the middle and four citrus trees, neat and festive. They fill the air with neroli, the aromatherapy scent of orange blossom. My Alhambra.

Dan has an airy white studio perched at the corner of the courtyard on the edge of a slope, from whose north-facing window he can watch the piebald cloud patterns on El Torcal as he paints. His room looks out expansively, confidently, at the rest of the world; mine is introverted and safely contained.

For my money, this is pretty close to heaven. But the route has not been easy.

1997

1

SOUTHWARD BOUND

'Where are my football boots?' Spigs, in anguish.

'Mum, I need five pounds forty to get to college,' Leo, gravely.

'I've got exactly enough to get to work,' I groaned. 'Not a bean more. See if Spigs can lend it to you.' Deaf to the mutter of grumbling sons, I made a dash for the front door, late for the Tuesday progress meeting at the office.

I slithered over the football boots, thoughtfully placed across the bottom stair, and laddered my tights on the tangle of bikes in the hall. A brief expletive, and I decided to ignore the growing stripe of winter-white flesh in my regulation black legwear. The post consisted of three unappealing sodden brown envelopes. Rain. Where was my umbrella?

Oh, God, I thought. I've had enough of London!

Every day, for what seemed like centuries, I had stepped outside my front door braced for rules, fines, impenetrable and punitive bureaucracy, prohibitions, schedules, deadlines, beggars, tube-train gropers, crowds and rain. Above all, it was the rain that got to me, the heavy grey lid of cloud bringing with it that damp-mac smell, shoals of drying umbrellas, rained-out barbecues, rained-out Guy Fawkes, rained-out weddings, funerals, May Day, school fêtes, the Chelsea Flower Show, concerts in the park.

Survival seemed such hard work in London, and damned expensive for what you got.

In my eagerness to leave the city, I had looked out for suitable country places in East Anglia and around Bath for a year or so, but it gradually became clear that anything I could afford had some major problem of location or construction. Also, the more I looked, the more disenchanted I felt with the prospect of adding to the complexities of English life.

But there must have been something in the stars in January 1997: what had looked one minute like an endless monotonous plain flipped suddenly into a sheer precipice, and within a week my life had changed completely. Until 7 January I inhabited a world of apparent certainties. For fifteen years I had lived in a large house in Highbury with my two sons, Leo and Spigs, whom I had brought up alone. For nine years I had persevered with a low-key relationship with a man who had art-directed a handful of my books. For over a decade I had been garden editor for an upmarket magazine, under two editors for whom it had been a pleasure to work. I had also written a dozen or so books about the meaning of cushions and the joy of curtains that supported us all and paid the mortgage. I was fifty-two, but as sprightly as a teenager. But somehow if you looked a little more closely, things were not as solid as they seemed.

My relationship with Edward was ebbing in a slow and painful diminuendo. Every time I looked there was a little bit less, until finally all that remained was the scowl. I think he saw me as a dangerous and unpredictable wild animal. I hung on, trying to make it work, because that's the sort of person I am, while he tiptoed discreetly towards the exit, leaving his tiger-prod by the door. There was a seam of mutual incomprehension in our affection for each other, an accumulation of no-go areas, questions that were never answered, and it affected me in a simple way. It awakened in me a craving for physical warmth.

Having tried grey for a couple of decades, I wanted to wake up to a blast of sun and tropical colour. Every year, around October, I would debate Seasonal Affective Disorder with my friend Hester, the houses editor on the mag, and we would ponder whether to buy one of those lamps. The debate continued until March, April, sometimes May. We never did buy a lamp, finding instead more exotic ways round the problem of winter gloom: we went to India, Barbados or the South of France on press trips. We got a flash of sun, the magazine got a surprising peacock of a feature about backstrap-weaving in Guatemala or patola-production in Ahmadabad, which had no obvious relevance to jam-making in Guildford but everyone was happy. Then came the day when our editor's own wanderlust got the better of her and she packed her rucksack and left. She was replaced by someone who did not encourage foreign forays.

There was a history to my passion for Spain. My first enjoyable holiday abroad, aged fourteen, had been to Villa Joyosa outside Alicante, in a village with dusty dirt roads hedged with jasmine. Jocasta, my elder sister, was staying at the villa while her husband produced a period film that required multiple galleons to float on the twinkling Mediterranean. I accompanied my parents there on our only family holiday; we stayed three weeks. My inexperience of this kind of trip was reflected in my baggage: I took a checked sundress that made me look like a sofa, and a mandolin. The latter languished untouched, but I fell under the spell of the heat, the dust, the cool expanses of marble in that otherwise humble house, the staccato comments uttered by the village elders unused to seeing a sofa parade in their midst, the solid blocks of sunlight flung through tiny plant-wreathed windows and, above all, the sweet wafts of jasmine. Even that particular sour smell of Spanish plumbing always evoked dreamy nostalgia whenever I came across it thereafter.

Years later Leo and Spigs disappeared every summer to holiday in the south of Spain, staying with their best friends and London neighbours, Kenrick and Kit, in a house by the beach in Conil. There the four boys made their first blushing experiments in the adult world of drink, drugs and girls.

One summer, finding I was unexpectedly wealthy, I rented a house there too and took my boys, a friend of theirs, Paul, and my mother. This was a brave thing to do, since she was beginning to lose her memory. In fact, she was fine with us, but it caused problems on her return flight as an Unaccompanied Geriatric: she refused point-blank to leave the baggage carousel, and indignantly ignored the Tannoy messages put out by my sister, who was on the other side of Customs attempting to collect her. But for three weeks with us her company was a pleasure. She played endless games of rummy with the boys, read the solitary book that had come with the house over and over again – shrieking with surprise every time in the same place – and sat on the beach like an old lizard, sunning herself and contemplating her legs. 'Beautiful legs,' she would muse, as she stroked them appreciatively.

She and my father had once reconnoitred with a view to buying a house near Alicante, but for some perverse reason they had elected to buy a pig farm in Essex instead. Her antecedents were Irish and had settled in Argentina where she grew up, so she spoke Spanish although, unaccountably, with a German accent. She would grandly roll off a convoluted and impressive sentence to some luckless Andalucían waiter or shop owner, who would look at her with incomprehension and alarm. I now know that people do not speak actual *Spanish* in Andalucía, but a laid-back local argot, usually dispensing with consonants and certainly not delivered with clipped Germanic precision. Like me, my mother loved Spain.

The idea of buying a house in the sun had a bit of history for me too. I had already toyed with the fantasy and had had meetings, several years previously, with a couple of slick opportunists posing as estate agents. In each case, my heart had beat faster as they spread out their portfolios of badly photographed ruins, simple white houses, black shadows, tall cypresses, bleached by the midday sun. Both were public-school wide-boys, whose oleaginous pushiness had put me off the places they were trying to sell in the Italian Marches and the south of Spain.

This time, however, my need was acute. So I did what any sensible person would: I went to Manchester, to a property fair, and jostled with blue-rinsed ladies and anorak-clad men in a bleak sweat-and-cabbage-fragranced school hall as they debated the comparative allure of golf courses in Orlando and the Costa del Sol.

The possible choices were France, Italy, Spain, and a motley ragbag of war zones where property was cheap. I dabbled briefly with Turkey, Morocco and Slovakia, then settled on Spain, remembering balmy evenings under the palms watching the sun set over the sea. I pictured a rural *finca*, whitewashed and roofed with old red tiles, standing alone and secluded among ancient olive and almond trees. It became obvious within two minutes that I could never aspire to France or Italy: I didn't have enough money and never would, although those dignified photogenic stone houses with wine cellars, stables and intimate courtyards were fabulous. The Greek islands tempted me, but I could not bear the thought of having to learn not only a new language but a new alphabet too.

I was especially drawn to the south of Spain where the calm, seductive Moorish influence still remained, where raw flamenco music knocked the English primness out of you, and where the food was mostly garlic with judicious and economical additions of pig's ear and chicken's knee, tripe and chitterlings.

The landscape of Andalucía was dramatic and comfortingly domestic at the same time. Great jagged peaks towered over little fields edged by necklaces of white stones, where every inch was cultivated with wheat, olives, almonds and chickpeas. White villages tumbled like sugar cubes down the sides of hills and white houses grew room by room in a puzzle of rectangles, topped by corrugated cinnamon-brown tiles moulded on a man's thigh. I liked the sound of the language and look of the people. I only needed to hear words like *sierra*, *duende*, *flamenco*, *mesa*, *aceite*, *almendra*, *rincón*, *chorizo*, to feel cheered that such things existed. I loved the ladies in their solidly flounced spotty dresses, their shining black hair swept back and studded with roses, the men in their skin-tight, madly glamorous bull-fighting suits of light. I persuaded myself that the streets and supermarkets would be full of people thus clad.

And, of course, the climate, hot, dry and dusty, was like Cairo where I took my first breaths. I spent November screwing up my courage, and December squeezing out my wallet. One of the Manchester agents had given me a thick Xeroxed wad of possible properties, smudgy black and white photos, and Leo, Spigs and I spent hours debating the virtues of each one, and trying to find tiny and probably misnamed hamlets on a map of Spain. We discussed numbers of rooms, sizes of patios, the availability of water and electricity, as though the vague descriptions were the Ten Commandments. I spent hours in Stanford's examining maps and guidebooks.

We brooded over the merits of this muddle of adobe buildings over that, carefully weighing up each snippet of estate-agents' blather. The catalogue was full of tantalizing possibilities: this place had a collection of disparate satellite buildings that the boys could use for rowdy joshing purposes; that one had views down the mountain valleys to the distant sea; another was ready to move into, with all conveniences. Finally we picked out an old property consisting of two sizeable buildings in a valley 'needing improvement'.

The following morning, heart thumping with excitement – and terror – I rang the estate agent and booked a week for myself and Spigs to explore. When I put the phone down, I knew that I had turned a page and was about to stumble into a new story.

2

BESOTTED

On 7 January 1997, a cold, drizzly evening, Spigs and I eventually landed in Málaga, and were whisked to our hideous rented flat in Fuengirola by Robert, the agent. There I spent a freezing, miserable night, wrapped tightly in my solitary blanket, cursing the whole insane idea. Just one thing kept hypothermia away: the thought of a man I had just met, whom I found totally captivating.

I tried to read the improving tome about North American Indians that Edward had given me for the trip, but my attention wandered continually to Dan Pearce, his laugh, his kindness, his generosity, his big square sculptor's hands, and the sonorous confidence of his voice. These obvious merits I weighed up against his well-attested status as a hopeless depressive, and his tenuous grasp of the banal business of surviving. He still believes that the groat is legal tender. It was all there from the beginning, and I chose to ignore what I did not wish to see. He was also the sexiest man I had ever met – always cheering, but especially so when you have resigned yourself to a life of knitting bobble-hats for distantly related babies.

Spigs and I awoke to an endless arc of blue sky and a huge sun that warmed our grateful bones, and when Robert fetched up in his Mitsubishi Big Bollocks it all seemed like a good idea again. We went to the agency, where our eyes were drawn to a fuzzy picture of rambling low buildings huddled on a gentle slope with hills beyond. This was fortunate: Robert dismissed all our homework with the brochure, casually announcing that all *those* properties had been long sold, and any that were still on the market were so because the torrential rains that winter had washed the roads away. We found this to be alarmingly true. Even the brand-new coastal road had large bites out of its six lanes. The Spanish are parsimonious with their cones, as apparently there are only six in the entire country, they improvise with either a white-painted rock or a large stone wrapped in a carrier-bag. Certainly there is no nonsense with cone help-lines.

My idea was to take a crumbly, characterful, cheap old building, and DIY it to make it habitable. Buy a ruin, I thought, put in a bathroom, friendlier electric lighting than the solitary strip of greenish neon that is in vogue with rural Spaniards, and build a kitchen consisting of a bit more than an open fireplace and a bucket of water fetched from the well. Perhaps even fling prudence to the winds and have a roof, functioning doors, windows with glass. We wouldn't need much, I thought, just a few essentials, and we'd keep the rest as it was. A couple of thousand quid should do it, I told myself. I could see us tinkering happily in an arthritic old building, bringing it at last – with the aid of my Black and Decker – to triumphant life. After all, it was the rustic simplicity I loved, which was sadly missing from my London life.

Christina, a big, sensible German woman who had settled down there and worked with Robert, was delegated to take us on our first foray, to the environs of Competa, a bijou little town infested with Brits, Germans and craft shops. The journey silenced even Spigs. We clung to the seats of the car, looking down into swirling mists, and going very quiet when Christina made a run at an escarpment where there had once been a road, but now, since the rains, there was only a vertical cliff-face. At one point I suggested feebly that it might helpfully lessen the load if Spigs and I got out.

'If I go, we all go,' Christina roared. So far she had shown no evidence of a sense of humour, so she probably meant it. When we finally reached Competa's main square we had a necessary drink in the sun by a tinkling fountain, after which we too became charged with devil-may-care courage.

We looked at a house belonging to an English herbalist. It had lots of rooms and land, with steep slopes on which summer grapes were laid to dry. There was a scruffy, dishevelled garden; bougainvillea twined round the terrace.

The house was an astonishing bargain. In an arty part of Andalucía, it had everything up and running – electricity, gas, water, even a tiny, claustrophobic study. There were proper bathrooms, and extra bedrooms with *en suite* showers and a kitchen and a vine-covered pergola outside. Spigs was taken with the quaint directive attached to one of the loos: 'If it's brown, flush it down. If it's yellow, let it mellow.' So what was the problem? It just was not love; and what little the owner had done, I did not like.

Christina gave no quarter. During our afternoon with her, we must have looked at a dozen houses, mostly two-room *fincas rusticas* – simple country buildings – in various states of dilapidation. There was one up a valley looking towards the sea, distantly shimmering, with roses, lavender and a level terrace – level ground is a source of exultation in a vertical country – which was tempting, but tiny. There was another that overlooked the herbalist's house, a minute two rooms, with no cons, mod or otherwise, and a scrap of vertiginous land. What you got for your money varied wildly.

We also checked out a bunch of houses further out, which mostly belonged to Danes and Swedes. They were all very small, and there was something annoying about each conversion. Some of the unconverted places were lovely, down peaceful sandy tracks, the air resinous with sun-baked pine – even in January – but all were *minute*.

Finally we visited a claustrophobic house on the edge of a pretty village in the Sierra Nevada National Park, which we reached at dusk. It had a minuscule internal courtyard stuffed with plants, and to enter some rooms you had to bend double. There was no garden, no space at all, and I felt like a bluebottle trapped in a matchbox. What it was like at midday in high summer I hate to imagine.

That evening we got back to our dank brown flat, damp and disheartened. We wandered aimlessly along the Fuengirola seafront, and had plates of stunningly dull paella – Spigs's was not only dull but grey: I'll never understand why Spaniards douse paella with squid ink. He then braved the night-life, and was accosted by a group of leather-jacketed Spanish boys who intimated that he might like to hand over his money. Familiar with this kind of situation from his secondary school in north London, he returned unscathed with his money intact.

The following day Robert took us up into the hills around Almogia, fifty minutes directly north of Málaga. Again, the journey was terrifying. He drove competently, confidently, and insisted on asking questions. Frequently, answer came there none. The road whiplashed around the furrows and wrinkles in those red hills, and below there was just space – a whizzing empty arc of nothing, with occasionally a mangled vehicle at the bottom. Sometimes there would be a jagged rip where rain had torn a chunk out of the road. Even where the pitifully thin veneer of asphalt was hanging on, there was no defined edge to the road, no barrier, wall or white line. When we arrived at our destination, a little blessedly flat hamlet called Pastelero, it took me a while to regain my composure. I was convinced that if I did buy a place here, I would never, ever, be able to get to it – or once, by some miracle, having arrived, I would never be able to leave.

There were, however, compensations for being marooned there. Tiny white houses were sprinkled fetchingly down clefts and valleys and the countryside was sumptuously sexy, with bosomy hills in all directions, red earth strewn with great blond hunks of limestone, and the Sierra Nevada glittering in the distance on that clear day. Frowning over the lot and close at hand was the wrecked grey dentistry of El Torcal, a mountain of glaciated wind-sculpted limestone, with fantastic stacked piles and tottering peaks of rock. And, as I eventually discovered, among the rocks bloomed the most wonderful spring flora – wild single pink peonies, sheets of little blue and purple irises, verbascum, thistles of every kind, hellebores, wild roses and flowers whose name suggests something rather more beautiful than the dirty pink spikes diagnostic of uncultivable asphodel steppe.

The ground in January was the brilliant green of the west of Ireland. The winter wheat was as rich as emerald chenille, and the breeze stroked it lovingly, making it flatten and glisten like the fur of a pampered cat. Grey-green tufts of olive groves and black winter scribbles of almond trees decked the hillsides, while the precious flatter ground bore seedling chickpeas and broad beans.

Robert feigned reluctance to show us the house we fancied. 'There's no point in showing you *that*,' he said, with consummate cunning. 'It needs a *lot* of money to do up. Too much for you.'

So, we visited three or four little *fincas* on a steep, south-facing slope, wedged in by rocks, jammed up against the bare earth road. They sat on perilous ledges carved from the hill, and we couldn't make any sense of the whimsical layout – rooms led from one to another with enormous drops between them. While negotiating the lurches, you had to avoid clunking your head on doorways three feet high, or getting wedged in entrances eight feet high but narrower than your hips. Haphazard bedrooms opened chummily into the kitchen or each other. Tiny iron beds with red or green cretonne covers were dotted around at random. Most worrying of all were the many unexplained buckets. And if you were unwise enough to step outside, you might hurtle down a perilous slope to land in some farmer's pig yard way below.

The inhabitants, silent Spanish families, watched us

with what I took to be hostility. But I was wrong. Although the sun was shining brilliantly, at this altitude of 560 metres it was very cold, and Spigs and I had dewdrops at the end of our noses. We were very grateful when we were handed one of those leather bottles that have inspired many a hideous key-ring, and motioned to take a slug. Well, to pour a stream of sticky, sweet, Málaga wine all over our chins and down our fronts. But it was warming and reviving, and all of a sudden our silent audience seemed friendlier. Soon we were clapping the owners familiarly on the shoulders, and greeting each house with excited ingenuity. 'We could put the kitchen where the buckets are, make a bedroom out of the pig shed, turn the breeze-block hut into a bathroom, and make the smoke-blackened room into the sitting room. Perhaps put a terrace where the chickens are roosting in the car with no wheels . . .' Spigs and I squeaked, but it was an uphill struggle to envisage the glory of the finished building in every case. We went through this exercise about ten times, until Robert bundled us into his car for lunch.

Paco's bar in the hamlet of Pastelero, to which we repaired, had a chunky palm tree on each side of the entrance, across which lounged a lazy husky with ice blue eyes. Inside, there was the usual deafening clatter of hard surfaces, marble, plaster, metal, a thundering billiard table, a bellowing television. Row upon row of amazingly ugly gilded plastic football trophies flashed on the wall like a full set of gold teeth. Dusty sunlight filtered through nylon curtains, and all was as it should be. Old men fell silent and stared. Serrano hams hung on hooks, exuding something sinister into upturned cocktail umbrellas; rabbits' feet were nailed to a board in testimony to the local passion for hunting. The floor was obscured by a tide of cigarette butts and paper napkins. The neon strip glared, and a couple of huge logs burned in the fireplace. We had more drink, Rioja this time, and a plate of what tasted and behaved like ham-flavoured rope.

While I was discreetly choking, Robert relented. 'OK, the house you saw is just up here, we'll go and have a look at it. But it will need a *lot* of money. It's not right for you.'

Warmed, fed and unaccountably sleepy, we bumbled back into his car, and shot off in a hazardous switchback ride up and down and up, past enraged chained canines and huge rubbish bins leaching plastic bags, apparently going nowhere.

Suddenly Robert jammed on the brakes, and we stepped out into a blinding love affair. This was the house. This was it – and both Spigs and I knew it. In front of us lay a jumble of whitewashed rectangles, with a sagging roof of old pink Roman tiles: fifteen rooms in all, including goat and pig sheds, with tiny barred windows, low peeling doors, and an old stone threshing circle. El Torcal beetled to the north, the Sierra Nevada to the east, El Chorro gorge to the west, and a rounded almond- and olive-covered hill rose between us and the sea to the south. The immediately surrounding land was almost bare of trees, carpeted only with electric green wheat. We can plant trees, I thought, gazing mistily at the only sizeable one, a broad evergreen *transparente* (*Myoporum laetum*), a weed in any right-thinking Spaniard's view, but a handsome one, which cast a protective branch towards the house.

From the edge of the field behind, the buildings

looked like a tiny Moorish village built in the shelter of the tree. We loved the view, the clutter of little rooms, the rough walls, eighteen inches thick. We loved the smell of the place, even the breeze-block animal sheds with their corrugated-iron roofs and little goat stalls.

The house had been empty for nine years, we were told. No-one had a key and we were unable to go inside, so we got overexcited about the stable, the pig-sty and the goat-house. Finally Robert, exasperated by our babble, hustled us into his car. In the pink and fluffy light of love, even Fuengirola seemed charming, quaint, and Spigs's continuing monologue about my parental shortcomings – a surprising number – sounded fair and just.

Two days later Spigs and I went back to have another look. This time Barbara Stallwood – the redoubtable power-house and queen of Almogia real estate who worked with Robert – and her business partner, Juan the builder, came too. This time, we met Mr Alcohalado, the vendor, who had apparently

walked the five miles from Villanueva to open the doors and let us in. In this, he was only partly successful. We congregated in the sun at midday. The doors were so swollen with rain and disuse that keys were useless. I was standing by the holding tank when I heard the most extraordinary grunts and inarticulate shouts coming from below. On investigation the noise came from Señor Arrabal, his wife and sister-in-law, our prospective neighbours, who are all profoundly deaf. This, though, did not deter them from roaring friendly greetings, and proffering vigorous and incomprehensible advice as they thrust Spigs's legs through a small high window. Once inside, he shoved open the front door.

There were six rooms with thick mud, stone and rubble walls and tiny windows; four had a strange patchwork of randomly tiled undulating floors. Two families of Alcohalados had lived in them until they abandoned the house nine years previously. At the south end two solidly and roughly constructed animal rooms had flattish floors of smooth stones and soaring, angled roof beams. Attached to them were two breeze-block and corrugated-iron goat sheds. They were eventually demolished with a single swipe of a JCB's arm.

It confuses me still that south is up the hill, and north is down below, but so it is. To the north, therefore, there were four more-recently constructed rooms, made of breeze-blocks, which were sliding, like an ark, gently down the hill. The floor in this bit, of polished *mortadella*-effect tiles, had heaved, the asbestos roof had shifted and split, the doors and windows were rotted and buckled, the walls had severed, leaving three-inch gaps. I loved it. Demolished and rebuilt, these I envisaged would become one huge cool room with a view of El Torcal.

Most of the old part was roofed with sooty terracotta tiles, laid on bamboo, over wooden beams with the load-bearing capacity of Edinburgh rock after decades of beetle-work. In one room the soaring roof was exposed; elsewhere there were low false ceilings, which generated gloomy forebodings about what horrors lurked on top. I kept remembering my parents' house in Formosa, and their resident rat-catching python in the roof.

Additionally there were two free-standing rooms, casually built with old chipped breeze-blocks and topped with asbestos. Fifteen months later, in April, they served us as bedroom and bathroom, graduating to kitchen and storage when we returned in June. Bees had nested in the roof of the 'kitchen', but they were generally peaceable.

Finally at the top there was the water-holding tank, with its Mexican-looking bucket tower, like a tiny campanile. Cracked beyond repair, it was a fecund environment for a large mosquito population. There were also two, maybe three, wells, inhabited by frogs.

Spigs and I stomped around the too-expensive *finca* muttering appreciatively. Juan the builder then took him to have a look at the wells and the animal houses, and they communicated effectively with body language. God knows how Spigs understood Juan to say, 'We just have to level this off and lay down three inches of hardcore, screed and tiles, and Bob's your uncle,' when his entire Spanish vocabulary consisted of '*Dos cervezas, por favor,*' but I accepted it as a miracle in this land of miracles.

I struggled and panted up the vertical olive and

almond plantation at the back of the house (south), and was knocked out by a magnificent view to the north, of crenellated hilltops crowned by the jagged crest of El Torcal and a wedge of luminous blue sea to the south. The sun was intense, the air crystalline, the sloping fields brilliant green, the almond trees beaded with swelling pink buds and I was lovesick. I took a couple of rolls of photos of the house, mostly showing rooftops decorated with empty beer and vodka bottles, which suggested that there had been riotous chinks in its abandonment. These sorry pictures became my hopes, passions and most precious possessions over many months, and I showed them to anyone fool enough to talk to me for three minutes. Spigs and I were in total and unusual agreement, and told Robert without a shadow of hesitation that this was the house we wanted.

The plan was to raise £1,000 as a deposit, and pay the rest on the sale of my London house. On the eve of our departure for Spain, I had stayed up until four in the morning, painting window-frames and doors in an attempt to transform the house from crumbly to des res for the estate agent to show people in our absence. An offer had been made, but I knew it was worth substantially more. Ah, how different things would have been, had I accepted this first offer.

I was apprehensive at the massive life-changes ahead of me, and bemused as to where they were leading. I had not yet accepted that my partnership with Edward was moribund, although we had been spending progressively less time together. But I had realized that my career had hit a scummy patch, and I was frantic at the thought of writing yet more books about cushions. I was obsessed with escaping. The boys and

I needed some space and distance, and each had said gravely to me: 'Mum, this house is too big for you. You should sell it.'

But something else was about to happen, the biggest thing of all, as I was to discover on my return.

In the early evening of 14 January 1997, Spigs and I returned to Highbury. As we came through the door, the phone was ringing. It was Dan.

3

A CHANGE OF HEART

My relationship with Edward had never been a full-time shared sort of thing. It was more like the visiting arrangements of a divorced parent – I'd go to him on Wednesdays, and we would swap weekends. I would fidget, eat and fall asleep in his flat in Richmond, and he would fidget, eat and fall asleep in my house in Islington.

Given his reluctance to socialize, I had worked up an independent social life, centring mainly on my friends Joyce and Nick, whose generous welcome and support became more and more necessary to me. There was always something happening at their little house in Hackney, no judgement, no criticism, just unstinting hospitality and laughter. The autumn of '96 had had an extra sparkle, due to the frequent presence of a man whom I had previously met long before with Edward.

Dan Pearce, a painter and, as Edward described him, ne'er-do-well, brought flashes of warmth and life to the bleak scrubland that our dying relationship presented. The previous year, Dan's marriage of twenty years had come to an amicable though painful close, and he had left his home and family in Suffolk to seek his fortune in London. Although cast down by his separation from his wife, Elly, and two children, Doris and Ted, things were looking good: he had found a flat, and was doing weekly strip cartoons for *Punch*. Unusually for him, he was earning money.

The possibility of meeting Dan had been embarrassingly magnetic, and I had invented all kinds of excuses to visit Joyce. And if he happened to walk through the door, my knees would tremble and the hairs on the back of my neck would prickle. As a grown-up, you know that this is altogether a bad thing, and can only result in grief, a tawdry peccadillo of the flesh leading inexorably to some Tolstoyan or Balzacian nightmare, culminating in me being hosed off the wheels of a train or joining the mangy queue of Have-It-Away-Day ladies behind London's King's Cross. Yet despite these forebodings, the sun burst out when I clapped eyes on Dan, and the birds sang. I felt warm all over, and transparently excited and wanted to laugh all the time. What can you do?

So, at 7.30 p.m. on 14 January 1997, when I put down the telephone, I said shakily to Spigs, 'I think he's just asked me for a date.'

'Go for it,' Spigs's face said, and I did. And whatever happens, whatever poxy luck or betrayal the gods sling at me or us, I shall never regret it. Dan unknotted his red-and-white-spotted handkerchief and laid out before me warmth, humour, reckless generosity, tenderness, caring, dollops of humanity, practicality, Scrabble, sex, a shared future, shared dreams, and said, 'Take it. What's mine is yours.' Not that he had much. The sum total of his possessions consisted of a chest of drawers and a large mirror.

So we went out together. Whatever uncommitted future Edward intended, he was obviously unaware of how lonely and disillusioned I had become, and the revelation that I had fallen in love with someone else shocked him very deeply – so deeply in fact that eighteen months later he bought the cottage he'd dreamed about in his beloved Cornwall and got married, which he had sworn he would never do. Well, certainly not to me.

When I came back from Spain, buzzing with excitement about the house, Dan's response was to get out pencil and paper and start to plan, using my scrappy back-of-envelope notes as guidance. He joined in everything with heart and head, and even managed to make friends with Leo and Spigs, who were suspicious, gave no quarter, and were going through difficult crises in their own lives. I love most things that Dan says or does, but when he said, 'Your children are my children,' and showed by his endless patience and generosity that he meant it, I felt my passion was well founded.

The ensuing months were a frightening emotional tornado, complicated by paralysing back pain. I think that this was caused by my new and incredibly smart leather suitcase, which I had bought in the Jaeger sale especially for my trip to Spain. The trouble was that I had apparently filled it with rocks, and managed to slip a disc on the return journey. From the moment Dan and I got together, I was in constant and acute pain until 16 June 1997, with no hint of improvement. I know this because some time in April I had entered 'Better or dead' in my diary for that day in June, having been told by a consultant rheumatologist that mine was a standard slipped disc, and would take six months to heal.

I thought my condition out of the ordinary, probably terminal, and I didn't want to go on living if it was going to be that painful. Sitting down was impossible, getting out of a car could lock me into a spasm so painful that all I could do was freeze and weep. I had to write standing up. The silver lining to this particular cloud was that being unable to sit down meant that I lost a lot of weight. It's just no fun eating on your feet.

But my ailment revealed a wonderful side to Dan that I would otherwise never have guessed at or given him a chance to show: I had got used to being bolshy and independent after twenty years of being more or less on my own, with two sons to provide for. Dan was endlessly obliging, patient and positive. I couldn't shop, cook, eat, drive, walk, lie down, get up, put my tights on, bathe, carry anything, lift anything or function usefully at all, and he did everything for me without complaint. I would get stuck on the escalator, in a chair, in my car, or shriek and sweat with pain when a particularly vicious knife twisted in my lower back. Dan helped with everything, and if now he occasionally balks at chopping firewood or picking up his crusty socks, I need only remind myself of those dependent days, and my indignation vanishes. I really don't know how I would have survived without him. The most healing thing of all was his resolute conviction that I would recover – I felt no such certainty.

In the first six months of 1997 whenever I wasn't with Dan, I was visiting an osteopath, two physiotherapists, an Alexander teacher, an acupuncturist, a cranial chiropractor, a rheumatologist, and a sort of reflexologist who massaged my feet while yawning spectacularly, which she ascribed to my stale energy. 'Some people are so bad that I just throw up all the time,' she told me. At least I wasn't one of them. For a while I went to see a psychotherapist because I had a suspicion that there might be a psychosomatic component to my sudden inability to move.

At the time the phrases that ran like a circular mantra through my head were paralysis, ossification, crippled by guilt, stuck in a rut, pain in the butt, pain in the neck. I felt as vulnerable as a hermit crab caught between two shells. There was such a landslide of change going on that jamming on the brakes probably seemed like the best defence, which was what my predicament mimicked. Dan seemed too good to be true, and I kept waiting for the feet of clay to show.

One of the physiotherapists told me that my body was reacting to twenty years of tension, of adrenaline-flooded flight or fight, and that the solution was simple: 'Give it all up,' she advised. 'Ask yourself, "Do I want to do this?" about everything.'

It was the most startling thing anyone had ever said to me, and the truth of it still shocks me. 'You can't live like that!' I expostulated. There is, of course, no other way. Having lived a dutiful grey and anxious life, I now proselytize when I see friends struggling with theirs. I have a missionary need to tell them that as far as I know this is the only life there is, and that every second is precious. 'Grab it by the bollocks!' I want to yell.

Or more politely: *No guardes nada para una ocasion especial, cada dia que vives es una ocasion especial.* Don't save anything up for a special occasion – every single day, hour, minute you live is a special occasion.

I've never really believed in Fate, but something had nudged Dan and me together during a brief moment of change in our lives. I am still incredulous that I stumbled across the only man on this planet who would be brave enough and mad enough to dive with me into my dangerous dream. But there he was, and we were standing on the brink together, beaming at each other and thrilled by the adventure to come.

We were to stand on that brink for much longer than we expected.

4

LOW FINANCE

He waited patiently, but in April Robert, the estate agent, started muttering that he could not keep the Spanish property indefinitely for me and that I must come up with the balance of the purchase price. Once again, I was on the brink of selling my London house, so I asked my other sister, Judy, if she could lend me the money for the two or three weeks between buying the *finca* and selling Highbury Hill. My new buyer was committed, the deposit imminent, and there could be no possible problem. Fatal assumption. Very generously – insanely, actually – Judy agreed, sent me a cheque, and Dan and I went off to Spain, in June 1997, to buy the *finca*.

Even Luton airport could not dampen our spirits. Dan and I kept clutching each other in disbelief. 'It's really going to happen, we're really going to buy the house,' we repeated. We were like a nightmare soap opera that you cannot switch off – air hostesses, shop assistants and passing dogs, they all got to know about the house in Spain as out came the pictures, the drawings, the documents. We bored everyone but each other.

For weeks, close friends had crossed the road rather than encounter our double tsunami of incoherent enthusiasm.

Everything was going so right.

With a little help from our trusty estate agents, Robert and Barbara, and a lawyer, a camel-coated, silver-streaked Marcello Mastroianni clone, who reproved me for my paranoia about the efficacy of the white boundary stones – 'We Spanish are an honourable people,' he said, with lofty dignity – we managed the business of buying with uncharacteristic efficiency.

For the week of the purchase, Dan and I stayed above La Loma, the bar at Almogia, one of the two nearest villages to our *finca*. It was very hot, and my skirts stuck to my bum – I had to walk backwards, lest people should think I was incontinent. The room we stayed in was infinitesimally small and the tininess of the *en suite* meant that you sat on the loo with your feet in the bath. We laughed like successful bank robbers, scorned the tiny problems and, confident that someone benign was watching over us, were entranced by everything from mosquitoes to menu misspellings. We visited the house just once, sat in the tawny wheat-stubble, and watched the sun go down, which it did at nine thirty precisely on 21 June, the longest day. It was Dan's first sight of the house, and fortunately he thought I was brilliant for making the perfect choice. Our neighbour Señor Arrabal's horse pranced about in the field and ribbons of pink oleander flowered far below in the dried river-beds. It was all magic, and we flew back to London smiling smugly, too pleased with ourselves even to babble to the other passengers.

When we got to London, everything fell about our ears. We arrived back on the eve of exchanging contracts on the sale of the Highbury house. We were due to meet at my solicitor's at ten thirty the next morning, and that night, as I did an uncharacteristic spot of tidying, I glanced at a piece of paper that had probably been shoved through the letterbox months earlier. It announced that Arsenal Football Club wanted to pull down my house and another eight in order to expand their stadium.

All-consuming rage and impotence ensued. I rang my buyer, who predictably disappeared from the face of the earth. All our plans ground to a halt, and I had to let Judy down. I could not repay her loan until my house sold.

Dan worked hard on the anti-Arsenal campaign, did posters and cartoons, talked to radio journalists, appeared in the local paper and attended tedious meetings galore. In fact, I have rarely seen him so happy: he had a Mission, and there is nothing that excites him so much as being Superman.

A battle committee had formed of all the local architects, lawyers, professors and vociferous housewives, but after months of being loud middle-class nuisances, we had achieved nothing. We realized that Arsenal could do what they liked, and take as long over it as they liked. We became miserably inured to the situation, and I resigned myself to the conclusion that we would never be able to do anything further with the house in Spain. From being our dream palace, it had become a decomposing albatross around our necks. I felt a hundred years older and deeper in debt – I had been counting on the sale of my London house to pay off all kinds of loans apart from Judy's.

As the year wore on, our bad fortune continued. My ex-husband's wife died of cancer, which was a source of such grief for Spigs that I expected him to go mad. She had been his support and ally, she had encouraged him with his huge, angry paintings, and had listened to him with respect. It was the most agonizing of several deaths he encountered that year.

Leo, my elder son, finished his graphics degree at Brighton, came home, and began a career as football observer with special responsibility for sofa and television.

I was continually reminded of the source of our troubles by the view, from the back of my house, of the stadium in all its megalomaniac turpitude. It loomed malevolently, shutting out the sun, and I turned into Nutter, North London, writing steaming letters to anyone connected with football in any way – rather that than expire from bootless rage.

Although my back was recovering, and Dan was still the best thing since chocolate, my job became more and more demoralizing under the management's new accountant-pleasing regime. The magazine was a phenomenal success, and as such, attracted voracious competition. It was a difficult predicament: it had to be eternally fresh, new and ahead of the crowd, yet the ingredients that the established readers loved must remain unchanged.

Then, on top of everything else, my mother had a stroke. On the day it happened, I dithered over whether to go to the hospital before they had assessed her situation. 'Mum, let's get in the car right now and *go*,' Leo said. I will always be grateful that he is a bully. When we saw her, she was paralysed down one side, but very game. She recognized the boys and made a joke. Gallows humour was always her forte, and she did herself proud, handling the situation with great spirit. She was visibly pleased to have her handsome grandsons visit – always cheered by an entourage of men. Our last memory of her conscious is as the courageous woman she had always been.

The next day Judy went to see her, and she was very low. That night she went into a coma, and died two weeks later. For the first week, the boys had kept up a bedside vigil, and I think the experience of watching someone die peacefully, someone who was ready and wanted to die, was healing for both of them. I am sure that their company – endlessly bickering about the editorial of *90 Minutes*, their football mag – was comforting to her.

She left a small and not terribly desirable property in Essex, and a tiny legacy. This was timely and served to repay some of the money I owed Edward, but nothing more. Although my financial burden was less disastrous, I still owed Judy an unmanageable sum, but she made only a featherlight reference to the house every now and then – as she was compelled to since I was obsessed with it.

Dan did endless drawings of garden and house, planning and changing, adding ponds, rearranging the internal structure, and designing in three dimensions, an astonishing feat for a non-architect. Years of drawing and sculpting showed in the fluency with which he could translate bare numerical dimensions into convincing spaces and seductive views. He could envisage changes of level, how steps would work, and terraces look when clothed with plants. He planned gardens with fountains, rills and terraces, switched rooms around endlessly to make the best use of what we had, imagined sweeping steps and dining-tables roofed by jasmine with views of distant hills, vine-covered pergolas for dappled shade, beneath which to drink strong coffee while the sun scrambled up the sky.

We pondered Gaudi, grand gateways and sinuous mosaic-covered seats by a circular swimming-pool. Dan was enthusiastic about everything from grand conception to piffling detail – he was even positive about Spigs's strange notion of digging himself a well-appointed cave in the mountainside in which to live the life of a stylish hermit. He started, too, to plan his studio, muse on how he would work, and how he could support himself in Spain.

Although we still couldn't move on with our Spanish home, we could dream – we couldn't help it. It was what made being stuck in London bearable. We were going to get to our radiant blue-skied *mañana* somehow, and just in case positive thinking and optimistic imaging might help, we indulged overtime.

1998

5

A SHORT STAY IN HELL

We couldn't keep away from Spain and, after a painfully frustrating absence of ten months, in April 1998 we decided to go for it, to stay in our house for a whole week. What the hell? we thought. We don't need civilized amenities. We've got sun, each other and the joys of the simple life.

While Dan had been designing a million permutations of our house, I had not been idle. I had dreamed up a wonderful name. I thought I had seen somewhere a *mirador*, or viewpoint, called Something Miranda. How witty! 'Casa Miranda' is a multilingual pun, meaning 'house with a view'. Perfect. Not only was I mistaken in my initial premise, but as the years progressed and our programme of renovations became ever more fraught with difficulty, conjuring up a view of imminent bankruptcy, the name came increasingly to mock me.

To keep our spirits up at the sticky end of making a home, Barbara was anxious to show us a *finca* that had already been converted. Dan was bonding with Juan the builder over glasses of fino in La Loma, so she took me on my own to visit Ken and Olive's house, just outside Almogia on the edge of the main road, beyond which was a precipitous ravine. The site made me feel a little nervous, but the building itself was a handsome two-storey *finca*, almost a *cortijo*, which had miraculously retained some of its original character. Many new buildings in the area have one or more features from a repertoire that might have been taken from the Irish building classic, *Bungalow Bliss*, with wiggly crenellations, redundant towers, metal-framed windows, moon gates and white plastic doors as startling as perfect glittering teeth in the mouth of an octogenarian.

Two floors is pretty grand around there, and this house had a wonderful airy open space upstairs, unspoiled, whose low windows looked out over the dizzy gulf and distant mountains, with a great wooden arch like a rainbow spanning the whole floor. Ken was in residence, frantic to get the wiring and plumbing finished before Olive's arrival the following day. The most important item of furniture, her magnificent organ, had already been installed. It dominated the ground-floor room like a small, baroque altar that had been teleported from another time and place to fetch up beside the telly and rose-patterned sofa. Ken, who was altogether as uxorious as any woman could possibly want, paused briefly in his panic to show us the finer features of the house: shiny kitchen, bathroom, electrics, hideous tiles, imposing staircase, then returned to his task of cajoling the builders and sweating. I was intrigued by this loving flurry, and looked forward to meeting Olive. Unfortunately fate intervened and I never did.

Our house, by contrast, looked unprepossessingly

sad, skittering with motley wildlife. Things with scaly tails disappeared round corners at the approach of a human, distinctly snakish wriggles parted the grass outside the 'bedroom', and bees were still buzzing in the roof. Dan was stung in the middle of his forehead – briefly he resembled a Cyclops – as he banged a length of metal into the wall from which to hang a hammock.

There was no water, no electricity, no lavatory, no sun, and I found the fact that there was no flat ground singularly distressing. Everything was either an uphill slog or a downward slither, and both induced a twinge of my back torment. Thank God, I did not have the vaguest idea of quite how primitive the next couple of years were going to be.

Positive was our *mot du jour*, however, and we weren't going to let a little thing like living in the Stone Age dent our optimism. In our minuscule hired Ford Ka we made a bold foray down the serpentine track into Málaga, and bought a load of necessities from a huge aircraft hangar of a supermarket: dodgy enamel cooking-pots that burned everything, a camping gas-stove, an air mattress, two deck-chairs and an assortment of plastic containers intended to keep marauding creatures out of our food. We were proud of ourselves for having fitted all the essentials of life into a sardine tin.

That afternoon I spent hours plying a broom, trying to make the house less of a health hazard, but I did not have the courage to tackle the windowless room whose floor was littered with telltale torpedoes. I took one look by torchlight, then shut the door firmly.

I am not houseproud. In fact, I hate housework passionately, and two decades of living with boys made me realize that it is a Sisyphean task anyway: no sooner have you cleared a respectable space than a tide of socks, football magazines, videos and dirty crockery rushes to fill it. But here I lusted for the housewife's kit of Squeegee mops and Dettox, dusters and Pledge, sponges and hundreds of clean tea-towels. Above all, I longed for running water.

The water we had came from the cute little holding tank, with a length of cord and a rather feeble plastic bucket: the trick was to chuck the bucket in face down, so that it filled up properly. I did not mind hauling up the water, because I felt it was doing my pecs a power of good, but I did mind the fact that it writhed with mosquito larvae and other noxious things. That was before we spotted the dead cat in the bottom of the tank. I wanted to boil everything I touched and worried for the world about Weil's disease, psittacosis, tetanus, brucellosis, dysentery, malaria, leishmaniasis and bat-bites. Apart from the sunny first day, which fooled us into expecting a heatwave, we were unable to use my cunning 9.99 YHA Solar-powered Shower – a plastic bag that you filled with (wriggling) water and left out in the sun to heat. By the time we went home we had become so thrifty and clever that we could scrub the dishes, brush our teeth and do an entire body-wash with a small saucepan of boiled water.

We used the tiny room that is now our bathroom as a kitchen, and slept in one of the decomposing outhouses, where I was convinced that a lizard – or worse, much worse – was tunnelling through the wall and about to eat my nose. Our inflatable mattress was as soft as an old balloon that first night. We had made the purchase smugly – how very clever to get a double bed into a Ford Ka. How disappointingly stupid, though, we thought, only to semi-inflate it. It slopped around like a half-filled hot-water bottle, and the smallest movement set up shock waves. If Dan turned over, the mattress convulsed and threw me out of bed. In effect, we ended up sleeping on the bitterly cold concrete floor like wet fish on a slab. I wasn't going to have any of that the next night – oh, no – so, thanks to my bullish efforts with the foot-pump, the mattress was as unyieldingly corrugated as roof tiles. This time, if you turned over, you fell into the next valley. The whole thing was as hard as a fridge top and just as inviting.

During the course of the week we managed to get it to a satisfactory compromise in terms of softness, but that did not make it any warmer. The cold from the cement floor came blasting through it and chilled us rigid as we lay, not daring to turn over because of the rubbery backlash and creakings. I have never known nights as long, I have never known thoughts as dark, I have never known cold as paralysing. And it *was* cold, intensely cold, with a relentless west wind that shivered my timbers, and from which I did not warm up once. Dan has functioning circulation, but mine is amateurish and intermittent – it never made it to toes and fingers.

During this and our next visit we discovered that the simple life is anything but simple. Candles blow out, spatter wax, don't give enough light to do anything by, can't be found or lit when you need them, burn down with astonishing speed and shatter ceramic holders. Paraffin lamps leak, require the dexterity of a brain surgeon to get them going, burn the wick but not the fuel, make clouds of acrid black smoke for a short brilliant flash, then go dark. Washing-up was a trial too. I would collect the water from the well, put it to boil on the stove, forget about it, top up the remaining inch of water, heat that up until it was too hot to use, pour it into the washing-up bowl to cool down, forget about it, and finally, usually in pitch darkness, wash a mountain of dishes, glasses, cups, pans and cutlery unsuccessfully in tepid greasy water with nowhere to stack anything. Happiness, during that long week in April, was paper plates.

I had a similar lack of success with washing things by hand, which I'd always thought resulted in brilliant whites. We couldn't find ordinary pillows in Spain, so we bought a bolster and a rather classy self-striped white case for it; within a week, it was a distressing cocoa colour. When I could stand it no longer, I donned my Marigolds and floral pinny, heated a pan of water and whomped up a bowl of suds. Trilling away, I scrubbed and squeezed, and scrubbed and squeezed until there was a Sierra Nevada of foam. Triumphantly I drew the pillowcase from its snowy hiding place. A long cocoa-coloured snake emerged.

Never mind, I thought, I have another trick up my sleeve. I filled a huge enamel pan with water, lugged it to the wobbling gas ring, shoved in the unattractive article and brought it to the boil. Having left it simmering slowly for a respectable time, I looked, simmered it for a further half-hour, had another look and gave up. It was noticeably smaller, and the cocoa had concentrated in streaks. OK, I thought, the sun will do it. It took a while to find a spot where the sun could smile upon the bolster case but visitors could not. It had taken me practically a whole day's work. And the result? An undersized patchy brown pillowcase, smelling strangely of soup, and curiously stiff to the recumbent head.

And then there was cooking which, far from being the pleasure it has since become, was an act of kamikaze courage.

Preparations for dinner went like this:

1. Buy food we cannot ask for or identify, in quantities we cannot specify, from local shop.
2. Ponder long and hard on how to transform eight unidentifiable bits of chicken and four courgettes into something delicious. If you buy a chicken in Spain, the shopkeeper will ask if you would like it cut up. And if, unwisely, you say yes, he will attack it like an axe murderer and smash it to bits.
3. Fiddle at length with the dubious controls on gas bottle and stove balancing on teetering table; attempt to light gas with wax matches that either fling blazing heads onto your front, bend and burn your fingers or fail to light at all as dangerous quantities of gas escape from both cooker and valve. This stage takes some time and involves feisty use of *language*.
4. Chuck some oil into one of the Continente enamel pans, remembering too late that they are all heavily coated in grit, and put on stove.
5. Remember that the chopping board (a small and unsatisfactory lump of pine that came with some inedible cheese) and Opinel knife need washing.
6. Trudge off in search of bucket. Dunk it in holding tank and fill larger enamel pan with water, ignoring the wriggling life therein.
7. Repeat stage three with second burner for water pan.

8. Remember oil pan too late to rescue pan or oil.
9. Wash up knife, horrible plastic plates, chopping board, etc., in boiled no-longer-wriggling water.
10. Start stage three again, with new pan and unburnt oil. Throw in large quantities of garlic, chicken, tomatoes, courgettes and red wine, stirring with a screeching metal fork in the absence of a wooden spoon. Burn fingers. Swear.
11. Snatch a glass of Rioja. Smell burning.
12. Kitchen now saturated with darkness. Impossible to tell by candlelight whether or not food is cooked. (The kitchen was the last room to be connected to the electricity supply, and for months we were cooking by candlelight or kerosene.)
13. Spend valuable minutes trying to light oil-lamp, which extinguishes itself every time its glass hood is lowered, and suffers from all the previous match problems, plus having an unreachable wick.
14. Smell burning, rush into kitchen, snatch red-hot pan from cooker, ignore smell of singed flesh, fling pan onto table, stumble around in darkness to find plates, cutlery, salt and pepper. Remember too late that had meant to cook rice.
15. All tribulations salved by Dan's rapturous hunger. And his offer to wash up.

One evening Juan visited us in our twilight squalor, and we had a convivial glass of wine together, while he observed our plucky attempt to live *al fresco*. On his return to the office, he talked to his electrician, Paco.

For five nights that April we had squinted at things by guttering candlelight, and the tricksy glimmer from a pair of recalcitrant Czechoslovakian oil-lamps. For about ten minutes this was romantic. Then we realized how hopelessly dependent we were on electricity, and how unappealing was the prospect of turning in at dusk. The morning after Juan's visit we were stumbling about in our enseamed mire when Paco dropped by and flipped the trip switch. Hallelujah! There was light! It had been there all along. Our four lightbulbs sprang into 20-watt life and a whole world of possibilities opened up – reading, seeing what we were eating, avoiding lizards, snakes, scorpions, spider's webs and rats.

Until the advent of light, putting bare feet on the ground had been hazardous; I expected to encounter the crunch of spider-legs beneath my toes or the sting of wasp on my hand as I picked something up. I was convinced that beneath every stone there lurked something that had stored up a lifetime's venom in the hope, one day, of meeting my ankle. In fact, the worst that happened to me was that one morning something snake-like, but very small, shot out of the way as I had a pee.

Flies arrived in droves with no other objective but to annoy. Round and round and round the ceiling they flew, like planes lining up at Heathrow. They plodded about on the rim of my coffee cup, puddling in a good assortment of unsavoury footprints, then returned to the patch of bare arm where they had previously mooched around, tickling. At first they made me hysterical, and Dan and I used up a great deal of very focused energy finding fly-papers. We located them in a hardware store after a complicated charade. Triumphantly we hung two from the middle of the low sitting-room ceiling. Touchingly, Dan empathized with the first fly to fight for its life on the sticky strip.

Within a day or two both were covered with its unmourned cohorts, with an additional aura of my hair, since I caught it every time I sat at the table. Exactly the same number of flies still circled the ceiling.

During that week, strange cats assembled every evening at six thirty sharp to sit expectantly on the sloping terrace. The first time this happened, there was just a very plain ginger one with a pinched Dickensian face. I gave it something to eat, and congratulated myself on having acquired a rat antidote. The next evening there were nine cats, all of whom, by the look of it, were closely related. This was alarming, and the thought of a daily exponential increase of this magnitude kept me in panicky calculation all day. Nine times nine is eighty-something, I thought. I could visualize the hungry multitude all too easily. That night, however, there were only two. The ginger cat stayed constant, its likely companions a pretty tortoiseshell or an occasional tabby.

Each morning we awoke to a cheery bird chorus. I'm hopeless at birds, so I didn't know what they were, but I did recognize a wood pigeon whose throaty burble sounded very out of place. As did the cuckoo – I recognized that too. And at night there were owls, which seemed to emit a pettish shriek, rather than any to-whit to-whoo. Chickens and cockerels prattled all day in the surrounding farms, and the peacock that lived in someone's gorgeous little orchard down the hill screamed peevishly every evening, presumably performing the function of a watchdog with added glamour. Vultures cruised in gangs over goat corpses. Little crested brown birds marched perkily up and down wherever the earth had been disturbed. Kestrels hovered above the valley, lazily observing the quotidian business below, and Dan was thrilled to see a pair of eagles floating languorously above the hill, one of which carried a huge snake in its talons. 'Grass snake. Completely harmless,' he asserted. Unconvincingly.

What amazed me most that April was the flora. Huge banks of different wild flowers, mauve and pink and purple, drifted by the road's edge. Forty-eight different flowers, excluding anything yellow, of which I disapprove. Our field was dotted with gladioli, while handsome eryngiums and milk thistles edged the track. On our hill, Hangman's Hill – infested with ghostly miscreants or heroes from the Civil War, depending on who was trying to frighten you – there were silky pink cistus, and phlomis with silver-grey leathery leaves, fan palms and constellations of daisies and marguerites. Dan and I braved a gale to climb to the top. I insisted we take his brand-new expensive little camera in order to record the flowers, and he dropped it on a rock halfway up and broke it. After a week of hell, this was not a good moment, and he very nearly lost his temper, very nearly wagged an admonishing finger.

At the end of our first week in the house, Dan and I allowed ourselves a moment of jubilation. We had survived! We jumped up and down and hugged each other in celebration, each thinking privately of how wonderful it would be to get back to Highbury where baths, central heating, lights, music and functional cooking equipment were standard.

We looked forward with some apprehension to June, when we were due to return.

6

ARSENAL TO ANDALUCÍA

It was an interview with a ninety-six-year-old ceramicist from Poole Pottery that opened my eyes to the necessity of a brutal course of action. She was lean and spry, and had made scones that she served with her own strawberry jam for tea. The little pots containing clotted cream and the elegant teapot from which she poured our Earl Grey had been made and painted by her own hands back in Poole's heyday in the 1930s. She had total recall, was as sharp as a razor blade and funny with it, and the interview was going swimmingly when we heard the front door burst open, then slam. A shadow crossed her face, but she continued to tell me about glazes and biscuit and so on. We heard heavy footsteps in the hall. I had just asked about her floral designs when the kitchen door crashed open and a man, seventy if he was a day, stomped up to the fridge, flung open the door and gazed mournfully within for several minutes. 'What's to eat?' he asked, not bothering to turn round. The scene had an uncanny familiarity, except that the players were a decade or five ahead of me and my sons.

So, when Dan came into a chunk of money in 1998, enough to get building started, we decided to move out of Highbury, leaving it to the tender mercies of Leo and Spigs who were by now twenty-five and twenty-two respectively, and old enough, I thought, to consider getting places of their own. For some time I had felt that one of us should go – either the boys or me – and since the boys seemed reluctant to leave home, the onus fell on me. I hoped that I was thus preparing them gently for independence, which would be foisted upon them should Highbury Hill ever sell.

The prospect of moving seriously into our house in Spain and starting the building work was unbelievably exciting and Dan's sketches multiplied – every bus ticket or phone bill had window details, floor plans, stair sections, and garden layouts scribbled on it. The house required planning and ingenuity, because the site was a steep slope and the north-facing rooms were six feet below the southerly ones. With a view to future letting possibilities, I wanted it to function as two self-contained units, each with its own kitchen and bathroom.

We envisaged big, empty rooms opening out onto terraces. We pictured the house surrounded on all sides by paved sitting areas, with flights of shallow steps from one level to another. I was still pretending that we could fidget with the house as it was – just fix the roof, lay a few terracotta tiles outside, and level the floor within – and got very indignant when Juan suggested that the best way to proceed was to knock the whole thing down, flatten the site and start again. 'But I love *this* house, you can't change it. I don't want a *new* house. I just want this one to work,' I told him.

He smiled wearily, and adopted the cunning ploy of

knocking it down and building it up bit by bit, so that I didn't notice. It seemed to cost rather more than I had expected but, then, finance has never been my forte.

I was dubious about how we were going to survive financially. For ten years or so, when the magazine was in its infancy, being garden editor had been the best fun in the world. I was paid to visit the most gorgeous gardens I could find and interview their creators. Gardeners are an endearing breed and there is nothing finer than sitting out in someone else's carefully tended garden, sipping their wine and enjoying the fruits of all their hard work. But I was suffering from a passion to *live* the life, not write abut it. Recently Dan's weekly cartoon for *Punch* had been swept aside by its new editor, and I felt in my bones that my own job could not last for ever. If, or when, it finally ran its course, nothing on earth would induce me to go back to a regular besuited job.

After some thought, however, I managed to tailor my work logistics beautifully. I did most of my work at home and spent just one day a week in the office – a wasted day as far as I was concerned since open-plan offices are hopeless for anything requiring concentration, especially if you are incorrigibly nosy. I put it to the new editor that if I worked in the office for an entire week each month, coming in every day, in effect I would be in the office more, not less. It had a sort of logic, and she agreed to let me try it out. I thought it worked brilliantly but, as it transpired, she thought otherwise.

The plan was that we would move most of our furniture and ourselves to Spain, and I would return to England for a week each month to go to the office. I was longing to clear out of Highbury Hill, which was still blighted by Arsenal's dithering, and still unsaleable. By now I hated the place – it reeked of disappointment and frustration, and the stadium loomed, dark and menacing, symbolizing the bloody-minded ruthlessness of the Arsenal big-shots.

Dan and I were stuck. We could not afford to complete the Spanish house until Highbury sold, we could not sell it until Arsenal made a decision, and until that happened I had to remain in my job, no matter what. So we worked on Casa Miranda piecemeal whenever we could lay hands on any cash, were in permanent trouble with the bank, lived on a bracingly squalid building site, and I travelled back and forth feeling deracinated and mad most of the time. It was like having a passionate and clandestine affair with a married man: when I was in Spain I was in a permanent swoon about the Turneresque sunsets, the changing colours of the landscape, the twinkling brilliants in the night sky; when I returned to England I shrank, kept busy, yearned and phoned. There was a yawning Dan-shaped gap at my side, and grey ugliness everywhere I looked.

I am not suited to be a nomad since the thing I need, whatever it is, is always in the other place, and for these long months I was definitely a person of no fixed abode. Superstition and homesickness gave me a leaden heart every time Dan took me to Málaga airport for my monthly stint. Doom-laden phrases like 'That was the last time I ever saw him alive' swooped about my head like a hungry gull. I would leave the most beautiful place in the world, dotted with silver olive trees, gilded by a veil of slanting sunlight, and travel to the grim solitude of Gatwick. Then I would be emotional tumbleweed for the week or ten days of my stay. That's what deracinated feels like to me: untethered and prey to the moods of others. Of course, I was constantly on the phone.

Joyce, who had brought Dan and me together, Judy, my generous sister, and Hester with whom I worked, were my solidity. Over the next eighteen months, the lists and timetables that were my anxious mantra increased tenfold.

We had decided to let the Highbury house to Leo, Spigs and two of their friends. I thought that the four of them could cover the mortgage between them, which would be one less thing to worry about – a daft idea for reasons that were plain to everyone else, but I maintained a credulous faith in my boys.

The house was big – five bedrooms, an attic and a cellar – and every inch was crammed with stuff. Suitcases bursting with jumble-sale booty teetered on top of wardrobes, long-unexplored boxes filled the attic, rusting pieces of machinery and gardening gear festered in the cellar.

If I ever doubted my elasticity, my ability to stretch wide and vague then snap back pithy and mean, the weeks leading to our departure from Highbury Hill on 11 June 1998 should have convinced me that Bungee is my middle name. The prospect of sorting and packing up twenty years of hoarding was so scary that I did nothing. In fact, I panicked. Well, I did more than panic, of course. I bought books called *Organize Your Life*, and *Household Lists*, which I read carefully, underlining things in red. But apart from that, I carried on going to the office, ignoring the mighty juggernaut that was roaring and honking straight at me.

It came in the form of Mark and Chris from the company we had chosen to move our furniture.

The pair had never been to London before, might never have crossed the borders of Warwickshire, but late on the evening of 1 June 1998 they fetched up in Highbury, having seen most of London unintentionally in their frantic navigation of the city.

'There are no street signs! It's crazy! We went round Trafalgar Square three times,' they said. Trafalgar Square? On arrival they looked wretched, and their faces lengthened further when they saw that nothing had been packed. Not one thing. I offered them beds, dinner and a few glasses of wine, and they cheered up. Beds, in particular, were good news: they had been resigned to sleeping in their cab.

Huge, gentle and, as we discovered, incredibly efficient, they were an odd duo. Mark had waist-length glossy brown hair and had worked for the Forestry Commission. Chris, the driver – big, lugubrious and mute – was devastated to be parted from his wife and little girl for a single night, and ached to get home. The van was due to go back up north, and then Dave, the owner of the removal company who had done this route many times, was going to drive it to Spain a fortnight later to meet us at Casa Miranda.

So, fresh and perky, we assembled on that sunny June day and started packing. We intended to take just the basics and personal things, leaving indestructible or ready-broken furniture for the boys and their friends. I'm always hopeless at decisions, and that day involved several thousand. Mark, poised with crate and newspaper, would hold up a slightly burnt lampshade or a chipped casserole and ask, 'Are you taking this?'

I would prevaricate.

Dan said, 'No, chuck it,' about everything, which galvanized me.

'Yes, we want that!' I would say, and Mark would wrap it carefully and put it into a crate.

There was stuff piled on stuff, and as soon as one room looked decent, I would notice a huge pile of more stuff behind a box or balanced on a television set. Objects bred before our eyes, boxes emerged, long-forgotten, and turned out to be full of Leo and Spigs's childhood drawings. And everything looked so tawdry. Pictures ripped from walls left picture-shaped gaps. Cupboards revealed unpainted walls behind them. Unspeakable things dropped out of drawers and sofas. Even the lightbulbs that Mark wrapped so tenderly were dusty. I have never felt so ashamed.

Then, just as we thought the bulk was done, we discovered a massive cargo of forgotten stuff in the attic: my collection of antique tins, little leather suitcases stuffed with love letters, and curious bits of sports equipment.

'Chuck it,' Dan thundered.

'Keep it,' I squeaked.

Dan stood over me, breathing heavily with a passion to discard, while I pleaded for this box of letters, that satchel of old postcards or basket of photos. In one particularly random pile of papers I found a grant cheque for £68 dated 1969, when I was doing graphics at the Central School of Art and Design, and which I probably mistook at the time for a bill. That was real money then. All this stuff had been hoarded against the day when I would have time enough to sort it and enjoy it all, and finally that day was imminent. And Dan wanted me to chuck it! Rather than sort it then and there, I imperiously overruled him on every count. Every letter, bill and blurred photo came to Spain unedited. He might have sneaked the odd box into the bin before I noticed, but I don't think so. It doesn't sound so bad but believe me, it was awful. I thought Dan was a Nazi, and he thought I was a shambling soggy sentimentalist. We each saw the other in a new, unflattering light.

Lest packing and moving should not prove arduous enough, I had arranged to go to Modena for three days on behalf of the magazine. On my return, prior to packing up my elderly car and driving down to start our life in the south of Spain, we had decided to have a Farewell Highbury Hill party.

The prospect made me very gloomy. I hate parties, particularly my own, and I expected to spend the evening surrounded by mountains of Doritos, knocking back cheapo bevvies in solitude. It would be a golden opportunity for everyone to show me how much they didn't love me. And driving the car, laden with stuff, to the south of Spain was not good either: car too old, roads too fast, and all on the wrong side. The trip to the garden festival at Modena? Crazy. Where had my brain been, I asked myself in the early hours of several mornings, when I decided that this would be a good idea?

I can recommend Modena, though. The Italians are lucky in that their wealthiest period coincided with brilliant architects and town-planners. The centre of Modena could well have rung to the rude taunts of Montagus and Capulets, and the garden festival was a revelation. If you've been quizzed and frisked like a dangerous criminal on attempting to enter the Chelsea Flower Show, then queued for half an hour for a tepid drink and a desiccated sandwich and been told by an officious man with a 'No Entry' sign that you are walking the wrong way ('Want me to wobble my bottom, then?'), you may share my distaste for it. The organizers are complacent for no obvious reason, it reeks of rules and regulations, and it always rains.

But Modena was a different world. It was fun. The sun blasted down all day, babies and dogs swarmed all over the displays and nobody shouted at them, attempted to put a parking ticket on them or sentenced their guardians to community service. You could walk round the show gardens, peer closely at the planting, bury your nose in the lilies, feel the texture of leaves; Georgina, my colleague from the office, and I took masses of surprisingly good photographs for the magazine, arriving at dawn and snapping away until nightfall. There was wonderful Italian food in the evening provided under canvas by Modena's best restaurant, and while we ate ricotta-and-roast-aubergine-filled ravioli, a Prada-dressed young chanteuse sang Thirties love songs, while wafts of white jasmine and rhinospermum filled the night air. There were necklaces of fairy-lights strung about the darkly mysterious gardens, the stars twinkled above, and platoons of unexplained white geese stomped about ruminatively.

After a three-day truancy I got back to Highbury at three in the afternoon, having travelled since five a.m. The party was due to start at eight. Dan and the boys had worked incredibly hard – the house looked clean and tidy, there was loads of interesting food, and they had sorted out some good music. The evening was memorable for the echoing spaces where furniture and massed junk had been.

Loyal crowds turned up, caroused as they should, and I felt such affection for them. I did not have to eat all the Doritos. It was sad, giggly, and definitely the end of an era for the boys and me. We had lived in that house for thirteen years, from when my now giant, brooding sons had been uncomplicated little boys who liked to be read to before they went to sleep. So many things had happened – the full spectrum of celebration, tears and arguments. So many pets had come and gone. What kept striking me, as I wandered from empty room to empty room, was how wonderfully improved it was without my baubles and gewgaws, most of which were crammed into the car. Before and after was like the contrast between the stifling fuss and fidget of a high-baroque Austrian church, and the serene emptiness of the Matisse church near Vence, whose only decoration is jewelled light from the windows.

Dan can genuinely do without things, and feels no need to overprotect what he does own and love – like the sumptuous woollen rug he and his daughter Doris bought excitedly for Spain, all sky blue and sea green on a cream background, across which he clomps happily with mud-encrusted feet. His clothes get strewn on the floor, his half-completed paintings are stacked under cups of coffee, his few possessions are piled and stuffed and shoved. But I can't do it. I know it's all trivia, but I love my Shaker boxes and Guatemalan baskets, naïve painted wooden birds and Indian printing blocks.

We had had my middle-aged Citroën checked over, asking the garage to pay special attention to the tyres and the spare, then we had crammed it with possessions packed solid. Jammed as tight as a Rubik's

Cube, it hunkered down very low on its suspension. We had tickets for 11 June at 5.21 a.m. on the Eurotunnel from Folkestone. We set off into an unseasonal monsoon with high hopes.

Our new life was about to begin.

7

LAST EXIT TO PASTELERO

France was in the grip of a tropical rainstorm as we careened blindly southwards. Our first stop for petrol was stimulating. The sharp young man who filled the tank pointed out that our front nearside tyre was showing metal and, on inspection, so was the other front tyre. One of the rear tyres had a great rip in it, and the other had a gash within. Even the spare was a different size and had DEATH etched on its thin and dusty rubber. It was a sobering moment, and a vertical learning curve. As the attendant did a graphic enactment of the imminent 'BOUM', I sussed my brand-new mobile phone within two minutes – under normal circumstances this would have taken a week – and rang the garage in London. They claimed to have checked the tyres, and had certainly charged me for doing so. I stood in the rain on the forecourt and gave them hell.

Their response did not inspire confidence. 'Yeah, well, the guy who checked your car, we sacked him. There's no-one to shout at.'

It was a demoralizing start to the long, overloaded

journey through France and Spain. Wads of cash sorted it, and we set off with a full tank and four virgin tyres.

Rain. We explored French rain – the thin and misty, the big and blobby, the horizontal and the half-hearted – until we got past Clermont-Ferrand. After that the sun shone, Dan drove fast and confidently, I slept, and we fetched up at my friend Sophie's house near Uzès at golden dusk in time for an icy plunge in her swimming-pool. We were in the south at last, among the heat and dust and oleanders, surrounded by white- and blue-painted plaster, terracotta roof tiles and olive trees. *Yes.*

Sophie is one of life's great showmen, and she had prepared a feast, with the heterogeneous bunch of people that foreigners rustle up when entertaining abroad.

'You'll love Pierre,' she told us. 'He's drying out, but he's *frightfully* handsome. The couple over there have just moved into the big house at the top of the village. A bit D-U-L-L. He's a landscape architect. I thought he might tell me what to do with my flotilla or whatever it's called – you know, that big tree that drips sticky stuff on the car. You've met Didier? He's my new French lover – well, Henri couldn't stay sober for more than three minutes – and he's rampant. *Rampant.* You know, he just follows me around, drooling. *Rather* flattering. Fixed my drains without a murmur. Was *grateful* to do it.'

An estate agent, a writer, an ex-heroin addict, a retired bank manager and a pair of grizzled hippies were the assortment that night. Despite the challenge of finding conversational common ground, it was a wonderful evening, made unforgettable due to the presence of a slim blonde crop-haired girl, a Swedish opera singer, who sang Mozart to us, unaccompanied, making my mascara run because she was so slight, so brave, and her voice was like the sun sparking rainbows in crystal. This was a powerful moment for Dan and me. Between two worlds, two lives, we would have been felled by practically anything, but this was like being given a tiny glimpse of Paradise.

The next morning we headed south, and spent the night, jubilant to be in Spain and speechless with exhaustion, in a less than lovely hotel in Tortosa. The following evening we arrived at our new home, having driven fast through heat-blistered plains and one-goat towns where we were the biggest thing since Franco did the foxtrot. We had seen a variety of hills, mountains, crags, nuclear processing plants bang next to populous beaches, industrial smog rising from the Costa Brava, troglodyte cave houses with lace curtains and plastic garden furniture, and a tiny pine-thick valley that might have been airlifted from Switzerland, prettily adorned with gushing streams and sunlight twinkling on conifer needles.

And at our journey's end, a rock-strewn desert awaited us. The site had been massacred and was pocked with piles of sand and breeze-blocks. All we could take comfort in was the rough cement foundation of our minute bathroom, the only flat area of our sloping home, where the sun was getting ready to slither behind El Chorro.

We sat there in the last golden rays, tired and dispirited, and Dan terrified me by weeping quietly.

'I miss Doris and Ted so much,' he gulped, from his perch on the damp cement, the tears trickling down his cheeks. And his ex-wife Elly, I thought. This

misery would never have assailed him had he stayed in Sudbury. Oh, God, what now? I have since learned that Dan is a drama queen, but fair is fair: on that unforgettable night in June we had no food, no beds, no comfort, no water, nothing to sit on.

But even then, at our utter nadir, when our lunatic courage had evaporated, leaving just the grutty dregs of our dream, there was a spectacular sunset and the sound of goat-bells and cicadas. The golden view of dusky wheat-fields was unsurpassable, Juan and his men had built a mighty metal and concrete basket for our swimming-pool, they had demolished the old kitchen and put down the foundations of our new bathroom, and Dan and I had each other – sort of.

That night the air mattress deflated quietly, sneakily. We were awaiting the delivery of our own furniture just a few days later, and the mirage of a real bed kept us struggling with our tormentor. We made it, just, through the first night, though when we awoke we were lying on a collapsed soufflé. The second night we had to get up just before dawn to repump. The third night it was a despairing exercise at four in the morning, the hour of the wolf, and that was how it settled with ever-increasing nocturnal swearing and pumping until our very own, shamefully ancient, charmingly flat mattress arrived several days later than promised. Dan is a man who needs his sleep. In normal circumstances his head hits the pillow, and narcoleptic chat and laughter ensue. I've never before met a man who laughs in his sleep, but Dan obviously attends intoxicated revels in his nocturnal life. And feels grumpy and bereft if he has to miss them.

We barely slept, each of us buried in our separate gloom, and awoke to a cloudy grey day, feeling no better. The removal lorry was due to arrive the next morning, so I scuttled about trying to prepare for a houseful of furniture to be dumped on our Spanish rubble heap. Some of the housewife gear I had bought in April had been filched by a houseproud thief – I'll know him when I see the polish on his doorstep – but I toiled away with broom and dustpan, moving the dust from one corner to another, and in doing so distributing it generously everywhere. After a bit of this I gave up and plodded up the hill with a book and one of the rainbow hammocks Leo had brought back from Mexico. I slung it between two olive trees overlooking the valley under a grey sky, abandoning Dan to his misery.

The lorry failed to arrive, and this, I'm afraid, was the pattern for the next four days. The weather was cold and grim, and Dan and I were well over our noses in a pit of despair. I thought he was a wimp and he thought I was a psychopath. Maybe I am – his tears and mournful sighs usually elicited an abrasive answer from me. I spent as much time as was seemly in my hammock up the hill strung between the silver leaves, reading and worrying about whether I had an extra Y chromosome.

It was during a solitary foray that I received an offer that might have changed my life. I had climbed the hill behind the house and was stationed on a warm flat rock gazing lugubriously out to sea, having succumbed to the call of the wild. The little wedge of Mediterranean was twinkling hazily and I breathed deeply, enjoying the peace and silence and, above all, the absence of Dan's groans. But not for long. One would have thought that Hangman's Hill would be safe from intruders, but the sound of approaching goat-bells indicated that I was about to have company.

First the nimble goat-leader pranced over the sky-line, swinging her udders in a most unseemly way, followed by half a dozen others similarly burdened. Then a small wizened man came into view, chewing something. On seeing me, he spat engagingly and sauntered casually in my direction.

'*¡Hola!*' he barked, as though he were slapping a parking ticket on my criminally parked vehicle.

'*Hola*,' I replied demurely, hoping that he would saunter away again. The conversation that ensued, brilliantly translated, went as follows:

SWM: 'You're pretty.'
MI: 'Thank you.'
SWM: 'How old are you?'
MI: 'None of your business.'
SWM: 'Got a husband?'
MI: 'Yes. He's big and jealous and just down there.'
SWM: 'I don't do this for a living, you know, herd goats. I'm just here because it's Sunday.'
MI: 'Oh!'

SWM: 'I've got a Mercedes.'
MI: 'Oh!'
SWM: 'I've come up for the day from Málaga, where I live.'
MI: 'Oh.'
SWM: 'You can come and live with me there. I'll be at the Pastelero bar at three.'
MI: 'Thank you. But unfortunately I can't. Goodbye.'
SWM: 'Goodbye.'

Small wizened man regrets missed opportunity to kiss someone eighteen inches taller than himself, spits in preparation, then advances, lips pursed.

I was gone.

This kissing is a Spanish forte. The secret lies in the element of surprise. A few days later I was driving along the rutted track in the old Citroën when I happened to find myself alongside another ancient goatherd, the regular weekday one. He waved and signalled that he had some urgent piece of news for me. Like a sap I wound down the window, all concern and interest. And blow me, if he didn't stick his head in and kiss me on the lips. Bleucch!

As I swept the house and attempted to disguise the crud of ages, I discovered small treasures that augured well or ill, depending on my paranoia level. The faded picture of an overdressed Virgin Mary in a *Playschool* hand-made frame was neutral to good. Ditto the saucy photo of Miss Almogia *circa* 1969, wearing nothing but a pout and a crocheted bolero. Eight hand-knitted carnations in scarlet nylon seemed like a positive thing, though difficult to find the perfect setting for. Mr Alcohalado's as yet unused funerary urn was equally tricky to place, and made a somewhat depressing partnership with the carnations. Eventually I could bear them no longer and threw them out. The tiny tattered passport photo, cruelly stapled top and bottom, of a young man in soldier's kit was definitely bad news – pictures of young soldiers are always poignant, but this one was doubly so: it had faded to a cloudy and uneven sepia, and the soldier was definitely dead by whatever cause. There were unequivocally benign things too: a tiny pair of gold, pearl and fake-emerald earrings that once adorned a young bride's ears, and a minuscule hoard of nineteenth-century coins, paper thin and worth nothing, but terrific *feng shui*.

To pass the time until we could set up home with our furniture, I also did a spot of decorating. I was still attached to the notion that we could just gussy up the old part of the house as it stood, so I made the acquaintance of Cal. This is the Spanish version of limewash, and Mrs Paco, who ran the village shop in Pastelero, sold it by the sack – as well as gas bottles, surreptitious petrol from an old barrel, Californian Poppy lipstick and lavatory brushes.

Cal comes in white lumps. You add it to water, and it turns to magic whitewash, conveniently distasteful to insects. The traditional covering for those rough walls – ideal for disguising the ravages of age, marauding beetles and cracks – it makes a soft white finish, cosmetically smoothing imperfections, and has to be renewed with some frequency as it comes off on your shoulders if you happen to brush past. Most Spaniards prefer vinyl, but then the increased insect population is very noticeable.

What you need to know about Cal is that you add

water to it, but not in a plastic bucket, which will melt. A dramatic chemical reaction takes place between Cal and water: the whole bucket boils and spits and you need to make sure that it can't reach your eyes or skin.

If you are a sensitive creature, you should skip this paragraph. Unless you want your home to smell of boiled shit, hardy spirits should know that the ideal container for mixing Cal is not the galvanized bucket that has become the loo, however well scrubbed and rinsed. This was the penetrating aroma that infused our bedroom for a day, and unsettled Juan visibly when he visited on some building errand.

Then, if you don't want your plaster to emulate an expensive-looking crackle finish that flakes off the wall as soon as it dries, you should let the bubbling – and, in this case, fragrant – mass subside and cool. Some people say you should leave it to mature for a couple of days before using it, but I was a woman in a hurry. Enthusiastically I slapped it on creamy, swooshing it over lumps, old wallpaper and cracks, not bothering to sand down or in any way smooth the surface. In other words, it was a real slob's job. As I applied it, the wall looked a complete mess, with all the crud glowing through the wet surface.

As it dried, however, a magical transformation took place. All the old gruts disappeared, and I was left with the sculptural, undulating white walls familiar from Greek postcards. I also discovered that I could tint the thick soup with ice blue and ochre. In most places I stripped off the original wallpaper roughly, ripping it away in satisfying ribbons. Papering these walls originally must have been quite a feat, since they were a vertical rockery. The Alcohalados had elected to use a grey paper, patterned with darker tangles that cleverly mimicked the pubic-tuft effect of a gaggle of harvest spiders, with which the house was infected.

Over that summer, harvest spiders caused me a certain amount of grief and soul-searching. I had never met them before, but Dan said that that was what they were, and in matters of fauna he is generally right. A congregation of them lived in the little room called 'sitting room' for a bit. They looked like daddy-long-legs, with a brown bead for a body, and eight whiskery legs upon which they bounced in a manner both solemn and perky. They liked nothing so much as lurking behind a piece of furniture or a picture with all their legs knitted together in a sociable mob. Consistently dense on whitewash days, during which they courted genocide, they would suss wherever I was about to paint and huddle there in a dim suicidal throng, awaiting the glop-laden brush. Most of them – the girls, I think – functioned knotted together in a throbbing clot, but there were one or two outriders, slightly larger, which would scuttle off across the wall to find new territory, and unfailingly make the wrong choice. They'd rush back, quivering with achievement, and lead their harem straight to the patch I was about to paint.

But I chivvied off the spiders and, ignoring the dandruff crackle effect, slapped on the Cal, and quickly nailed up a load of paintings of fruit by Mary Fedden and Dan. I painted six rooms like this, and we basked in their glowing whiteness until Juan demolished them shortly afterwards.

While we waited for our furniture we also decided to investigate the market in Villanueva. I had high hopes, expecting to find gorgeous local produce beautifully arrayed, as you might in France. I pictured home-made cheeses, ham, organic olive oil, herbs, with a sprinkling of charming peasant pots and maybe woodwork.

Apart from mountains of knobbly veg and fruit, what we found, however, was *hideous* furnishing fabric in a variety of man-made fibres, Crimplene dresses, shapeless pinafores, sub-Fortuny wrinkled nylon sacks, trousers whose legs you could zip off in case you suddenly needed to reveal your knees, and quantities of socks and underpants. There were Top Life jeans for a paltry £6, T-shirts proclaiming 'Natural Attitude Simple Is the Best', trainers called Abidas, Beppi and Wind Sports, a cookery stall that had brass pestles and mortars, doughnut dippers, special double frying-pans for tortillas, triple mouse-traps and galvanized buckets. My favourite outlets were the small and very specialized stall that sold only goat-bells, the tool van, which sold everything from umbrellas to tripods for cooking over an open fire, and the dried fruit, nuts and honey stand, which also stocked useful herbs '*para gases*'.

There were a surprising number of old men in jaunty straw hats. It took me a while to realize that they were not there to do some shopping and help her-indoors, but for the ogling opportunities, the discreet bottom-pinching under cover of the mêlée, and the odd sneaky kiss.

It turned out that Dave had had better things to do than drive the huge lorry crammed with a lifetime's collection of wobbly tables and chipped crockery down the – to him – familiar route to southern Spain. So the benighted duo, Chris and Mark, had been conscripted for the trip, the two lads for whom Warwickshire was adventure enough.

Dan was busy mourning his comfortable ex-home and non-Nazi family, and now he had something new to worry about. Were Chris and Mark OK? Would they make it in one piece? I'm afraid I didn't spare them a thought, but Dan put in a lot of hand-wringing and brow-furrowing on their behalf, and eventually it paid off. We were expecting our movers on Thursday. The following Tuesday, when we went down the rutted and vertiginous track to the village for a loaf of bread, we stumbled across them. There, outside Paco's bar, was Chris, debating how to top himself. London was bad, but Spain was hell. He hated us, the job, Spain, and everything about abroad. Mark, who had Soul, was making friends with a horse whose owner was in the bar.

Dave had sent them off without money, directions or hope. They had survived with his credit card, forging his signature. Mark, who wasn't doing any of the driving, was young enough to enjoy the adventure. Chris had done all the driving, and he was exhausted and frayed. We found the big man sobbing, chest heaving, in the dusty main street of Pastelero. He missed his wife and little girl. I handed him my mobile. He phoned home, and felt a tad better. It turned out that Dave had told them to find Castelero, instead of Pastelero, so they had visited every castle, hopefully, *en route*. Spain, of course, bristles with castles, and they had worn their tachometer to an illegal crisp tilting at spectres. It had taken them two days to find their way out of Málaga. It was a miracle that they had made it to Almogia, and that, having arrived, they had gasped the magic words 'Barbara

Stallwood'. She had been found, and had directed them up to our village.

Seeing that the expected tragedy had been averted, Dan immediately revved into Captain Invincible mode. He had a Role. There were Things To Do. From the vile Slough of Despond arose Superman, and he took charge. Chris flatly refused to drive his van up our track, convinced – correctly, though I did my best to persuade him otherwise – that it would get stuck or turn over, and that he would be marooned in Spain for the rest of his days. So Dan persuaded ancient Miguel, the manager of the Almogia knickers factory (purveyors of fine knickers to M&S, according to rumour), to ferry stuff from one end of the track to the other in his old Mercedes van. Back and forth he went, stacked up by Chris and Mark at one end, unstacked by Dan at the other. At one point Miguel became very grey and asked to sit down for a glass of water. Sit? Glass? Water? We did our best, fetched him a box to sit on, a tin cup to drink from, and some tepid Coca-Cola. He owned up to a heart condition.

Finally, after a day of intensive furniture-shifting, we were the proud owners of a fully furnished hillside, with cupboards and tables sprinkled at random up the slope. Chris and Mark got right back into that cab and set off for Warwickshire. We waved until the van was a tiny blip on the coastward road.

Then we walked back along the rutted track to our nicely appointed field. Hot, dusty and overexcited, we watched the stars come up from the vantage-point of an *al fresco* mattress, and whispered about the house where all this furniture would soon have a home.

8

INTREPID EXPLORERS

Having been residents for all of a week, we decided to make a shopping foray to the village. We needed basic food, drink and cleaning materials and, with the aid of the dictionary, wrote a pretty convincing list. Pastelero, our nearest point of civilization and a ten-minute walk away, was a little hamlet bounded at one end by Antonio's new bar, and by Paco's shop at the other. In between there were sundry dogs, small houses with hybrid tea-roses growing out of ingenious but hideous piles of old car tyres, Paco's bar, the village dustbins and a glass-recycling container.

As Dan and I neared our destination, there were no clues to tell us that we had indeed stumbled up the cinder path to Paco's shop: no name over the door, no Nescafé in the window, no check-out lady in a nylon uniform filing her nails. In fact, as we peered cautiously into the semi-gloom beyond a rainbow chain curtain, we realized that there was no-one there at all. Mrs Paco's dozen or so cats gazed at us languidly, in between scuffling with each other. We stood and shuffled our feet for a bit, admiring the

Aladdin's cave of consumer delights that festooned every surface: real fruit, veg, eggs, honey in juice bottles, all produced locally, a startling revelation in terms of flavour and none conforming to EU anything, Hurry'Up bars, Wipp and Colon washing-powder, Bonka coffee, Wi-wi hand-cream, hams so mature that you'd need hyena's teeth to masticate successfully, buckets of vile margarine but no butter, crates of wild asparagus, salted sardines in wooden kegs, fly swats, exotic soap that looked like brawn, and brawn that looked like soap, undrinkable wine that cost 30p a bottle (excellent for clearing your drains and keeping your *septico* sweet), and single cigarettes.

Eventually, hoping we were not being rude, we poked our heads into Mrs Paco's television shrine and shouted. In the time it took her to emerge we could have made off with half her stock. She glared at us severely as we struggled to formulate our wishes, and the transaction was further complicated by the arrival of the old man with three teeth who lives at the end of the track. They puzzled over our list together as though we were not there, dismissed it and segued into a shouted discussion of the weather. While we tried shyly to point out some of the things we wanted, Señor Three Teeth was occupying centre stage, ruminating about whether to push the boat out and buy two sardines, or just the one.

To pass the time until we should have Mrs Paco's full attention, we amused ourselves by comparing the clarity, design and visual qualities of the eleven manufacturer's calendars on the walls, mostly depicting bottling factories or transit vans. Dan riffled hopefully through the plastic flowerpot that held foreigners' post. Native Spaniards kept theirs in a banana box.

Mrs Paco was shoulder-high, stoutly middle-aged and aproned, and bore the surprising name of Encarnación. I suppose it's no weirder than Jesus (a common Spanish name), but it was difficult to use in a chummy sort of way, so she was known generally as Mrs Paco. She had a confusing identical sister, who was always being greeted effusively by complete strangers. At least, she was – until Mrs Paco had chemotherapy and sported a jaunty black wig for a while. I am delighted to say that she recovered, and her own hair grew back, thick, brown and glossy, but curiously punk.

Two sardines safely wrapped and stowed in Señor Three Teeth's jacket pocket, Dan and I re-entered the fray. Mrs Paco continued to frown ferociously, then finally signalled to us to take what we wanted from her laden shelves. She smiled broadly at this solution, and we realized that the frown was not of disapprobation, simply of mystified concentration. Having collected our perquisites, two interesting ceremonies ensued. With great solemnity, Mrs Paco made a scribble of indecipherable marks on a tiny scrap of paper with a very blunt pencil, her hand hovering like a predatory eagle over the tangle of maybe numerals. Then, after much contemplation, she seized a figure – ludicrously low – at random from the air. Then, as we counted out the pitiful *duros* she asked for, she gathered handfuls of sweets and nuts and stuffed them into our bag. We bade each other farewell like old friends, and resolved to do all our shopping there in future.

Courage bolstered by this successful transaction, we decided boldly to drink the delights of Pastelero to the very lees by calling in at Antonio's bar for lunch. Its opening, more or less when we moved in, had caused a bit of a furore because the village already had Paco's bar, where I had nearly choked to death on the rope-like Serrano ham. As we strode in through the swing doors and I attempted to ignore the frank appraisal of ten pairs of masculine eyes, we discovered that Antonio worked to the usual Spanish formula slightly updated: recessed spotlights replaced neon strip-lights, while wooden chairs with cushions, tablecloths on the tables, and wood panelling took the place of the more generally favoured noisy reflective plastic and Fablon surfaces. He did not have a clattering one-armed bandit but quiet electronic darts, and the sound was turned way down on the obligatory television showing transvestite slapstick.

We settled ourselves self-consciously at one of the tables, and a pretty young woman, who looked as though she had stepped out of a 1950s cookery book so shinily bobbed and slender-waisted was she, sashayed up and introduced herself as Antonio's wife Antonia. She beamed and handed us a menu, which read:

Lean with tomatoe
Moorishs spits
Chine's skewer
Sirloin to the green pepper
Liver on iron
Stuffing potatoe

This was a difficult choice: I inclined to the spits, Dan favoured the liver on iron. The smell of frying garlic from the kitchen awakened real hunger in both of us, so we ordered soup to start with. Mine, *picadillo*, was a flavourless milky mystery, but preferable to Dan's choice. His large bowl of *callos* (pron.

chaos) appeared to be made from chickpeas and the parts of a pig you'd rather not think about. It had a surprisingly delicious flavour, but fell down in the texture department. Antonio, overweight, terminally anxious, with a day's growth of dark beard on his dough-pale chin, brought us our main courses and stood fretting over us until we'd forced down a couple of rather too hot mouthfuls and pronounced it all delicious.

The food in both establishments was consistently good: people came from miles around to eat in our hamlet and we soon found that because everyone wanted both Antonio's and Paco's business to prosper they patronized their establishments alternately. In Spain four people can eat and drink simply but well for about twenty quid, probably less than one would spend on fancy food and folderols if one were to cook at home, and definitely a different league from going out to eat in England. I love it – it's very New York, and makes meeting people much more relaxed. And both Paco and Antonio are very obliging. When an exacting friend of ours demanded garlic butter, '*Surely* you know how to make that? Just take some butter, mash some garlic into it with a handful of chopped parsley. It's so *simple*. You *should* know how to make it', Antonio's missus did not slap her round the head with a fish slice for being so patronizing, she pottered off to the kitchen and made about half a pound with real butter – an exotic rarity in Spain. Both Antonio and Paco *demand* that you have multiple liqueurs on the house.

Walking down to eat at Pastelero, as the setting sun turned the rocks to gold, became a frequent pleasure whenever we needed respite from the gritty demolition site that was our home. We'd amble to one or other and take a table outside by the palm trees. The familiar paper tablecloth would follow with a bottle of Rioja, olive oil, a basket of freshly hacked bread, and a hefty terracotta platter piled with meat, fish or *calamares*, chips and a token lettuce leaf with *alli-olli* on the side. It was always the same, always good. In summer there would be a barbecue out front beside the road, occasionally enlivened by a passing herd of inquisitive goats.

Both bars had an unchanging cast of customers. A typical midday at Paco's would consist of the old man, connoisseur of sardines, with the bottle-glass specs and huge smile of very gappy teeth. If he was unaccompanied by his long-suffering English girlfriend Elspeth, Paco White Pantaloons – whose signature white jeans had a phosphorescent glow as he strode, fast and purposeful, across the parched brown hills – would be trying to terrorize some hapless foreign newcomer with tales of the perils of life in the *campo*, his long black ringlets electric with passion as he watched his victim's eyes widen to saucers. Paco Goat Man – the uninvited kisser with whom I had had a close encounter a few days back – would be standing tall in his flat cap, gazing calmly into the horizon, his ancient furrowed face giving him the serene look of a wise village elder and belying some distinctly opportunistic behaviour with tipsy English women. Mr and Mrs Paco's teenage son, uniquely not named Paco, would be blushing, playing pool and trying to look cool.

There might be an alarmingly pink English couple sitting outside, being pestered by inquisitive dogs. Paco himself – whose bar boasted not only the world's largest display of gilded plastic football trophies but two large prints of fluorescent lovers dallying respectively by a waterfall and on a beach and a huge poster of a Ferrari – would quick-step between the tables bearing armloads of hefty terracotta platters loaded with *calamares* and *lomo en salsa*, stopping briefly to lay an affectionate hand on one's shoulder as he recited the menu. On Tuesday evenings, 'English night', there would be a rabble of unruly expats sitting at a long table, shouting, drinking too much, playing darts or knitting imperturbably. On Saturday evenings and Sunday lunchtimes we would occasionally see one of our builders, almost unrecognizable without his flat cap, his hair slicked down with Brylcreem, sitting surrounded by wife and children. Off-site the builders were always effusively friendly, and drinks whizzed back and forth between the tables. Their wives tended to glower at us, having heard who knows what tales of Dan painting clad in air, or me spending a morning with a cowpat of henna on my head. They took one look and saw a pair of dangerous Bohemians.

We had reason to spend much of our time away from home. Casa Miranda was undergoing major changes. At first I thought the builders were continually fighting, and would peer nervously through our tiny windows to make sure I wasn't going to have to have a word with them in my nanny voice. But that's just how they talked – aggressive shouting, with the occasional burst of flamenco *cante*. I never lost my amazed respect for Spanish builders. That summer they *ran* about the rocky site in temperatures of up to 40 degrees Celsius pushing wheelbarrow after wheelbarrow of wet cement over crevasses on narrow plank bridges. They began work on the dot of eight a.m. and finished on the dot of six p.m. They had a siesta for exactly one hour, sometimes on the floor, in their car, or side by side, snoring companionably, in our swing seat. As the winter drew on they would arrive in darkness, shuffling like penguins, buried in woolly layers, mufflers, balaclava helmets with tweed caps or pork-pie hats jammed on top, which they peeled off as the day progressed. In the bitterly cold east wind slicing like frozen razor blades from the Sierra Nevada, they staved off hypothermia with a bonfire, and the boldest would have a tiny nip of *anis dulce* in his sweet black coffee – mostly they were very abstemious. They worked solidly, dependably, with punctual breaks for tins of tuna fish, *bocadillos* and yoghurt. And they had generations of skill and fluency with things like laying tiles, making brick edgings, constructing archways, effortlessly arranging shapes and patterns that would have taken me hours of drawing and thought. They worked in gangs of three or four, and during the course of construction we must have had about thirty in our lives.

Outdoor loos were one of the worst difficulties of this period. They required much digging and led to costiveness – there's nothing like waiting all day for the builders to leave, finding a discreet spot, poking about hopelessly in the compacted earth with a bendy trowel, moving on in search of less cement-like soil, then realizing that the entire population of the hillside across the valley is in full view, and vice versa, to make one give up on the whole idea. Living *al fresco* certainly helped me overcome one or two inhibitions.

This was when the plastic-bag shower came into its own. We discovered that after about five hours of blazing summer sun you got enough tepid water to shampoo your hair but not quite enough to rinse it. The only place we could put it was hanging from a low doorway or, in full view of the *campo*, from a branch of the *transparente* tree. Dan favoured this option, but I preferred the relative privacy of the doorway, even though it necessitated sitting bare-bottomed on a low and very scratchy chair throughout the procedure. Out in the open. A surprise for passing Spaniards.

However, very soon we had mains water that we could drink straight from the tap. Only in the bathroom, to be sure, and only during the unpredictable times of day when there was mains water – half an hour here and ten minutes there – but I was awed by the luxury of being able to turn on a tap and have water gush out of it. And with bathroom walls and plumbing, at last we had a proper loo.

We had no other rooms, though, so our furniture stayed where it had been put. Things grew roots where they landed – no matter that it made no sense to have my wardrobe by the pig-sty, or Dan's drawing-board in the windowless stable. For three months, until we had a suite of proper rooms with floors, walls, doors and ceilings, all our possessions were on show and open to the elements.

The other thing our builders did that June was get going on the swimming-pool. This was unquestionably my first priority. Let the rest go hang, I thought. We need to be able to splash about and cool off in the simmering heat of summer, and if our children braved the journey, a swimming-pool would be the least we could offer them by way of amusement. Tomas, the JCB wielder, had dug a massive circular hole in the old threshing floor, and Pedro and his mates had spent their days constructing a vast basket of iron poles, brick and cement. The days grew steadily hotter, and they sweated down in the pit clad only in shorts and wellington boots pouring cement, but they persevered. It was thrilling to watch.

One particularly flawless day, we just had to get out. We had to see the sea, escape the building site, the random furniture and the drone of the cement-mixer. Barbara had recommended St Julian beach so we headed south, with our cossies and towels in the back of the car. The temperature rose, and our bottoms stuck to the seats, with additional unattractive sweat-slicks down our backs. Part of the problem was that the very effective heater could not be turned off. We followed the signs from Málaga, and found ourselves in a midge-ridden swamp, dead flat arable land, where potatoes were being harvested by teams of women. There was an extraordinary overcast sky – it was like being submerged in milk – and the place had a sad, tawdry air. It was Mardi Gras, though, compared to the beach when we finally found it. Under the oppressive white sky, which hid the sun and the planes that we could hear but not see, there was a vast wasteland of brown sand, ribbed with sunbathers. Diggers and huge lorries trundled from one end, grinding past the bodies, to dump their cargoes of sand at the other end, miles away, in some mysterious Sisyphean labour. Behind us was a solitary box-like windowless building – a multi-storey torture facility if I ever saw one – and in front of us out to sea was something like an oil-rig. It was *The Red Desert* crossed with a vacant coned area of the M40.

However, we had come here to be beside the seaside and have *fun*, so Dan swam and I lounged under the low white sky on a sun-bed, rather too close to a couple whose child was forever either too near or too far away, either of which required a great deal of shouting.

Eventually Dan and I decided that what we needed was food, so we found a little beach restaurant and ate grilled sardines elegantly speared on bamboo sticks to look like an undulating cloth of silver. Actually I can't stand sardines, but they did look good. After this, the sun peered wanly through the white sky, Dan persuaded me to swim, and we had a wonderful time, bouncing and splashing in the water like a pair of elderly Labradors. We played the hallowed games of joshing, snatching trunks, splashing water in faces, diving for each other's legs, pinching bottoms and giggling. St Julian was suddenly fine and, buoyed by this success, Dan suggested that we go up to the lakes.

According to the map, these are many-fingered reservoirs, miles away behind the El Chorro gorge. I did wonder if we could handle two adventures in a day but, hell, we were on holiday. An intrepid old man thumbed a lift and accompanied us for most of the way, and we rattled him about in the car with mutual incomprehension but smiles of encouragement all round. Hitchhiking seemed the usual means of transport for old Spanish blokes – they flagged you down imperiously, jabbered something incomprehensible that did not sound at all like your destination, then several miles later commanded you to stop at a precise point in some stretch of road with no sign of human habitation.

We headed north on the motorway, and climbed for a bit. Then we came through a cleft in the mountains, hit the plain beyond and were smacked in the face by the sun. The heat was like warm syrup. It was hard to breathe it was so thick and hot. The plain spread out for shimmering miles, every inch carefully tended, with costly irrigation equipment throwing a veil of engineered water over the sunflower fields. The land was obviously rich and fertile, and the people who lived here took care of it; it afforded them handsome two-storeyed *cortijos*, enclosed in compounds, tufted with tall palms and cypresses. Here was a different league of farmer from the hillbilly subsistence peasantry among whom we lived. But the price was suffocation in the frying-pan of Spain.

We drove for ages, breathing thickly, and fell gratefully into the only air-conditioned café we passed, which was attached to a garage. Cooled and fortified we journeyed on, along an arrow-straight road, until we came to a turning to the left, towards some little hills. Unsignposted, no clues. OK, we thought, as we poodled through cooler air, along meandering dirt roads, climbing, with the sun still clear and strong but no longer out to kill us. We crossed a dam, and suddenly we were in a landscape I had dreamed of: rounded, toffee-coloured rocks tumbled down to the dark green water's edge, umbrella pines crowded the slopes, growing from cushions of wild rosemary, *santolina* and thyme. There was not another human being within sight or earshot. It was empty and beautiful – a wild contrast with the morning's industrial beach. Fish popped the surface of the water, the air was resinous, the sun slanted through the trees, the rocks were smooth and warm. We swam blissfully, languidly, and there was but one tiny snake in Paradise: bony things beneath the surface that grabbed at your ankles – presumably the skeletons of bushes that predated the flooding of the reservoir.

We fetched up on a little sandy isthmus with a pine-dotted hillock at the end. We strung our beautiful Mexican *hammoco matrimonio* between two shady umbrella pines, and I lounged in it reading Rohinton Mistry while Dan hurled himself into the water again. Later, dubiously, but with increasing confidence (ropes held, trees did not tumble down the hill), we stretched out side by side. Life does not come much better than lying in a gently swaying hammock with your chap *du jour*, caressed by light warm breezes, reading a great book, listening to the *chirr* of crickets, and gazing occasionally through a fringe of susurrating pine needles to the flawless azure above. Paradise was ours for the price of a fifty-minute tooth-rattling drive through bucolic Andalucía. As the sun drifted lower, we sat on a rock by an emerald green baby pine and gazed at the cloudless sky reflected in glassy water.

Reluctantly we dressed and drove on, winding between great boulders and pines. Suddenly rounding a corner, we saw a shock of water, the most improbable turquoise, like an unconvincing hand-painted Fifties postcard. A little café faced it, tucked under vines and massive eucalyptus trees. We stopped and had some coffee, admiring the lock-keeper's tiny beautifully tended formal garden, all neat geometric-clipped box and cypress trees. A poor man's Alhambra, I thought. We got back into the car and, just when there could not possibly be anything better, we drove round a handsome house at the lake's edge, and beyond its gazebo stretched a long slice of brilliant aqua – we had been gazing at a mere rivulet where ducks puttered, and just round the bend was a view as sumptuous as the strange hills on the Yangtze. We stopped briefly to gasp. Life has nothing to show more fair, I said to myself, for the second time that day.

It was mid-June. Summer did not officially start until the 24th, when every Spaniard would cast off his cardie and head for the *campo*. The lake was empty but for three slithery handsome boys with ponytails, gold nose-rings and taut, tanned six-packs.

As we drove on beyond the lake towards home, we came to a dream landscape of Japanese perfection – patted, rounded rocks, through which snaked the road, high and winding, under a tufted canopy of pines. Finally we came to the gorge itself, El Chorro, a 600-foot vice of fissured rock through which the road trembled, and to whose wrinkled side a perilous wooden walkway clung; it had been put there in 1921 so that Alfonso XIII could test his vertigo, and unrepaired since. Dan was delirious with excitement – he has a passion for anything vaguely rock-like and geological and this was the mother of them all.

Our return home was low-key in comparison with what we'd just seen – we curved southwards into neatly husbanded valley country, everything tranquil and cared-for, cross-hatched with citrus orchards and striped with vines. Finally, really tired, we reached the scruffy lion's pelt of our own wheatland. It had been a day to remember: a moment of calm before the breathless heat and dust of the summer to come.

Home-made insect repellant

I douse myself with this every summer. Sometimes it works, sometimes not, but I loathe all the commercial ones.

Plunge a sprig each of thyme and rosemary into 300ml boiling water and leave to soak overnight, then put the infused liquid in a spray bottle and spritz on.

9

THE DRAIN IN SPAIN

As we progressed through different degrees of summer, from the blue-skied sunny perfection of June to the foot-searing, mind-numbing heat of August, when we had to spray ourselves at night with water to get any sleep, Dan and I were living in the four oldest rooms of the house with thick walls of rubble and mud. I had painted the outside with Cal, and planted a jasmine and a *dama de noche* in pots to lend a waft of something other than sewage to the evening air.

My plant care at this time was intermittent, and Dan, though brilliant at planting trees and shifting rubble, was forgetful when it came to watering. At this point I was smitten with a surprising infatuation for succulents. I have always been snobbish about them, dismissing them as a kind of suburban paving you cannot comfortably walk upon. But I can only respect and admire any plant that survives – nay, *thrives* – on total neglect. While all the things with fancy flowers fell foul of drought and creeping cement, the succulents soldiered on, fattening up and occasionally astonishing me by throwing up a great spike of Day-Glo crimson flowers. And their strange subtle colours – verdigris, copper and pewter – exerted a charm that made my usual palette of pink, orange and scarlet look, frankly, violent. I began to feel intimations of maturity, and wondered nervously whether good taste was about to replace happy-go-lucky vulgarity as my *Weltanschauung* for that season. I need not have worried, for at the Monday market in Villanueva the plant stall had a blinding collection of geraniums in the whole clashing Pucci spectrum, plus a scented magenta *Mirabilis jalapa*, a cacophonic outburst which framed the front door for quite a while.

During this frustrating time when no patch of bare earth was safe from builderly depredations, pots were all we could manage, but we had great ideas for covering the slopes with cypress and olive trees carpeted with rampant purple perennial morning glory, swathing pergolas with passion-flowers, vines and jasmine, and filling beds with herbs and vegetables. Herbs in particular were happy in our dusty clay soil. The spindly basil plants from the supermarket grew into knee-high bushes, rosemary became a small dense thicket, given enough time, and thyme sowed itself: it sprang up in purple-flowered aromatic tufts in the most surprising places. Vegetables were more temperamental, and our only real successes were with courgettes – which also covered a gratifying weed-depressing acreage – and delicious sweet-sour yellow cherry tomatoes, which grew with admirable determination in a heap of rubble. My masterplan was to plant as many trees as we could, envisaging a cool, leafy oasis on the side of this baked hill. Dan plodded out regularly with his mattock, and made huge holes into which tiny cypresses, olives, pears, apricots, eucalyptus, grevillia and false pepper trees were dropped to grapple with the inhospitable environment. Many were engulfed by weeds, never to be seen again, but a surprising number survived, and were joined by two vigorous self-sown *transparente* seedlings that attained six feet in two years. I just wish they'd consulted me about where to put themselves.

In accordance with my bizarre directives, Juan was demolishing Casa Miranda one room at a time. First he built the swimming-pool at the top of the site, then the bathroom at the bottom, and then, bit by bit, the rooms between, with Dan and me perennially in the way, the human equivalent of harvest spiders. Pipes, electric cables and extension leads, machinery, formes for the two circular windows, lengths of timber, iron rods, wheelbarrows of cement, buckets and boots made an adventure playground of the route to anywhere.

Camping on our Spanish building site was a trial,

and we tested our endurance and each other to the limit. Dan was Eeyore, especially before midday, and I was Nurse Ratchet. As walls fell about our ears, ceilings crashed about our feet and thick clouds of grit coated everything, I wrote two or three articles a month, and Dan painted for a forthcoming exhibition. We had nowhere sensible to work, with Dan in the tiny all-purpose sitting room–kitchen, having plates stacked on his palette and being constantly tidied up or otherwise interrupted, while I tried to write professional-looking garden features with one of a frustrating series of malingering and captious laptops balanced on a chair, a crate or a rock.

Let me take you on a guided tour of our residence at this time. Duck cautiously through the low metal front door unless you wish to be trepanned, and you will find yourself in a small, squarish cell lit by a tiny recessed window. Had you wanted to, you could have made generous curtains for our entire residence out of one table mat. None of the three windows in the four rooms had glass, but it was a simple matter to foil mosquitoes with half a metre of netting. On entering you will be immediately confronted by a small pine sideboard bearing a *mille-feuilles* of vital documents, cheque books, passports and airline tickets, which regularly blow onto the floor whenever the door is opened. Turn sharp left and you will bump into a rickety blue-painted table, a legacy of the Alcohalados, which tends to be similarly laden with papers, Spanish dictionaries and phrase books, Scrabble, plates and my Mac Powerbook. Apart from beds and the floor, these were our only horizontal surfaces. Edge carefully round the table, avoiding the defunct cooker that serves as pan rack and washing-up stand, and there are the two dwarf rush-seated chairs that came with the house, so low that when seated, your nose rests on the tabletop. There is also a small sofa, wedged in against the wall, behind the chairs.

The fridge is in the furthest and most inconvenient corner. A macramé of electric cables festoons the floor, which is a fetching piebald of black and white plastic tiles, with a random mélange of red and cream terracotta taking over where they evidently ran out. This sumptuous parlour has the benefit of a single bare 60-watt bulb over the table. (When Dan's son Ted came to stay, he and Dan were forbidden to be in this room at the same time; it caused gridlock and if they stood by the window the place would be plunged in darkness.) This is our public room, in which we receive visitors, work, and parley with the builders about their missionary passion for PVC.

In the corner opposite the fridge there are two doors, neither of which shut. One leads to our bedroom, where the low bed is beautified with a magnificent Pakistan patchwork *rilli* in cinnabar, ochre, white and sludge green. Romantic lighting glimmers from a bare 20-watt bulb above. There is no room for anything else – and if Dan has left his clothes in a heap on the floor, as he invariably does, one or other of us will fall over them on going outside for a pee.

The other door leads to another bedroom, whose paperback-sized window faces west, drenching it all with Venetian red and golden light when the sun sets. The light in Spain is so bright that a pinhole could illuminate a cathedral. I love this room – especially since our trusty movers Chris and Mark provided it with a real bed. I retire into this private haven to regain my composure after some particularly harrowing inability to understand something simple in Spanish, or when I have been shopping and, for a chicken casserole, have demanded a headless penis. This is easily done, since the words for chicken (*pollo*) and penis (*polla*) are dangerously similar.

I have put Dan's rug on the floor, his paintings on the walls, a milliner's stockpile of hats on the wobbly hat-rack that was thoughtfully left by the previous owners, and lounge on the bed feeling calm and cocooned.

Leading from this room is another where my clothes and girlie knick-knacks are stuffed into collapsing plastic wardrobes. It has no window, but three plaster shelves have been hollowed from its massively thick walls, and all our other possessions are crammed into them, our only storage space. This is our safest and most private room, and contains the galvanized bucket that will serve me as a loo until our *septico* has been completed.

Dan had no compunction about using the whole world as his smallest room, but I was paranoid and coy, and dreaded the necessity of bodily functions. The arrangement was horribly insecure: the door did not shut properly so a builder might stroll in at any time, and a bucket is not conducive to comfort. Neither does it instil confidence. The loo paper was always somewhere else and there was no water. I'm glad to say that it was Dan, not me, who was caught with his pants down by Paco *eléctrico*.

At the far end of this room there was a low door, maybe a metre high, leading down some vertiginous steps into some kind of beast-house. The lizards, whose demesne this house had been, were reluctant to clear off, not that we wanted them to, although their tails, left hanging absentmindedly in view when they hid their faces, had an unnervingly snake-like quality. Lizards are welcome to stay, and I have it in mind to paint an outside wall with a huge lizard, as they do for good luck in Africa. Geckos, too, are benign residents, at home behind the paintings, hanging in there with their prettily spatulate fingers.

But then I became aware of little black torpedoes in the plastic-wardrobe-and-bucket room, suggesting a less charming cohabitant. The spectre of Weil's disease haunted this otherwise inoffensive place – I didn't know what Weil's disease was, except that it was nasty – and for several days after their appearance I could not enter without a great pantomime of banging pot lids and rattling doors. This was especially inconvenient, since my clothes were in there. I once had dealings with a rodent operative in London, who lauded rats for their intelligence, then confided approvingly that they preferred not to attack humans but when cornered they went for your throat. After a bit of a talking-to from Dan, I overcame my fears. Bravely I cleared the room and gave it a good sweep.

Then I started to come across sticky black things. When I moved the bed in the back room to get on with the whitewash, I came across a little froth of ants eating something that looked animal in origin – possibly a bird's head, I thought, brought in by something bigger. It made me feel a bit queasy, but I swept it up and continued with my work. Another sticky black thing lurked beneath the sofa in the front room.

Later I went into the plastic-wardrobe room, in search of some bijou or other, and there, beneath one of the plastic wardrobes, was *another* sticky black thing, with flakes of black stuff around it. Skin, I thought. There was another beneath the other wardrobe, with a curious litter of straight whiskers. At this point I stopped being brave, and shrieked for Dan. We peered, hand in hand, and realized that the sticky black things were not avian spare parts but plums from the elderly tree outside the kitchen. And the whiskers were not the remains of a rat's short back and sides, but had been nibbled from one of Dan's paintbrushes, leaving just a neatly trimmed stub.

But plums were too big for mice to transport, unless they ganged up like the ants and worked in teams. That we were cohabiting with rats was confirmed by the neat little squirrel-like footprints in the dust. The thought of rats filled me with paranoia, and I screamed at anyone unwise enough to leave a crumb of bread or cheese uncovered in the simmering shack we called 'kitchen'. But the feeling was mutual, and once they had decided that we were permanent, they moved to less populous quarters.

Our tribulations were nothing compared to the war of attrition suffered by our friend Clive. He stayed in his little *finca* down the hill whenever he could afford to, which unfortunately was not often. He did, however, manage a week in Spain that summer. He arrived at his house late at night, tired and desperate to sleep, dumped his stuff and made for the bedroom – where horrors and devastation awaited. He found a rats' nest in his bed. They had attacked the large teddy-bear, a beloved relic of his late wife, and in the most sinister fashion had eaten just its eyes. He was spooked, but too tired to do anything except drag the stuff outside and sleep in an untainted spare bed.

The next morning he tottered into the kitchen to find droppings in his cutlery drawer, on the work-top, in his saucepans, cups, teapot, everywhere. He put his food supplies into the fridge, and wearily, methodically, set about scrubbing and sterilizing everything. To cheer himself at his lonesome task, he put on some music. Gradually he became preoccupied by the strange tinny sound of Bob Marley. He seemed to have lost his woofers. On investigation Clive discovered that the rats had eaten just the bass connection cables. He fixed them and continued with his gloomy labours. He put the rescued sheets in the washing-machine, turned it on – and nothing happened. The rats had not only eaten the wiring; another nest was delicately balanced on top of the drum.

When all else fails, there is food. He opened the fridge, and was puzzled by the lack of chill that greeted him. The light was on, but cold it was not. The rats had fastidiously selected the motor wiring as a superior snack, disdaining the lighting wires. That evening when he came round for dinner he was very low, and copious quantities of £2 Rioja and one of Dan's chicken casseroles barely lifted his spirits. It was a caprice of bad luck – but such things happen occasionally and made you feel very *alone*.

But Clive's was not the only tragedy that summer. A few weeks later, I asked Barbara how Ken and Olive were doing in their new house.

'Oh, I thought you'd have heard. Ken's dead,' she told me.

I was shocked and sorry: I had admired his conscientious scurrying and had hoped to see the results. Apparently, just days after Olive had arrived at the house, they were sitting down to a cup of tea and Ken had had a heart-attack. Understandably, she and her organ returned immediately to England. The house stood empty for a while. Driving past always gave us a chilly frisson.

That August my psychotherapist friend Suzy came to celebrate the inauguration of basic plumbing and our pool and, at the same time, Dan's children, Doris and Ted, who lived in Sudbury with their mother. Doris was tall, brown-eyed and strikingly good-looking, with a shiny swatch of straight chestnut hair and expressive eyebrows. She had emphatic opinions about everything, usually expressed in a parade-ground voice, which quite often made me wince when it concerned my family or friends. She had just taken her A levels, and was planning to go to the London College of Printing to do graphics. We were told that there were 5,000 applicants for a very few places. She got one of them, but then decided graphics was the wrong choice; ditto the London College of Printing. 'I want to be the person directing the designers not do it myself,' was her gallingly confident remark as she coolly relocated to Colchester to read art history.

Ted, also tall and good-looking, with black hair and a dimpled chin like Dan's, had to be tortured from his habitual silence by card games or an urgent need to imitate someone's idiosyncrasy of speech. He was an astoundingly good mimic, and while we laughed till the tears ran, it was with the uncomfortable thought of how prattish we would sound when quoted for the benefit of his friends.

That summer, Ted was easily the most desired Englishman at the Cadillac dance-hall in Almogia, head and shoulders above the competition both literally and figuratively, and for months after his stay our trips down the hill to the bank would be enlivened by bevies of ludicrously beautiful Spanish girls sighing, 'Eduardo, *donde está* Eduardo?' as we passed.

During her visit Suzy managed to look impeccably elegant, even painting her nails sky blue to match a dress. The rest of us looked like hairy, matted castaways – Robinson Crusoes in sarongs. We did not have a kitchen, and although the bathroom nearly worked properly, it had a problem in the stink department. Casa Miranda became briefly famous for its smell of sewage. Some people still ask if we have sorted out our drainage yet. The shameful answer is that I don't know. It seems to have moods: good days, and days when there is a definite waft of something that is not pine-scented.

There we all were, sprinkled about our crumbling rooms surrounded by a curious mixture of inappropriate furniture, cooking extremely simple meals on the wobbly camping stove. We lived under Dan's huge yellow parasol – eating, drinking, reading, playing endless competitive games of Scrabble and working – on the only cemented terrace, which was fine except that it sloped at an uncomfortable angle, so that chairs, tables, plates, oil-lamps and glasses slid inexorably towards the part of the house that was sliding inexorably down the hill. The slope had an extra frisson factor, thanks to a cat's cradle of trailing electric cables that provided light, music, and power for the droning cement-mixer. The Spanish are wary of gas cylinders – you have to sign seven documents to get hold of one – but they are casual about electricity: they join wires by splicing the live ends together, or poking them into sockets, then covering them with a curved roof tile or wrapping them vaguely in a plastic bag if rain threatens.

They are so casual, in fact, that Dan nearly died.

Months later Miguel, endlessly helpful, was working on the house when one of the cookers arrived, and offered to connect it. He managed to get the butane-gas rings to work, but left before he'd fixed the electric oven. For a while we just used the rings. Then one day we decided to put the oven together, which involved wiring up the heavy-duty plug and reaching behind the cooker blindly, with long, flexible arms, to jam it into the socket. There was a loud bang, and Dan shot backwards across the room. Miguel, we realized belatedly, had had an original take on which wire should go where.

I decided that no life-loving rodent would square up to the formidable Doris, so allotted her a chastely undersized bunk bed among my clothes in the rat room. Ted had the adjoining west-facing room with a proper bed, and we put Suzy with the lower half of the bunk into our bedroom. We decamped to the donkey shed: it had a certain rustic charm, and was certainly well ventilated since it had no door, no glass in the window, and not much of a roof. It was a casual piece of *ad hoc* architecture, with no electricity, a handy multi-functional manger, a rudimentary fireplace – haunt of lizards – in one corner and sagging roof beams. I had assembled all my precious things in here. The bedside table (a kitchen table, actually, and rather too large for its new role) was piled with cameras, jewellery, my computer, Dan's paints and all the other bits and pieces we wanted to keep an eye on. I'm not quite sure why we felt that this was a secure room, really. The rest of the furniture consisted of a large wooden trunk in which I had most of my clothes, and a small cupboard in which Dan had his. Dan had tacked a length of canvas to the rotten beams over our bed to prevent the small tickly insects that lived there from falling on our sleeping faces. The floor was made of hummocky worn rocks, through which weeds sprouted. We laid flattened cardboard boxes down on an original flooring material advertising our removal company, over it. I tacked a theatrical curtain of brash scarlet turban fabric from Delhi across the entrance for a modicum of privacy.

The first night that Dan and I retired to Mon Repos, looking forward to peaceful contemplation of the stars through the holes in our bedroom ceiling, there was an almighty cacophony of squeaking and scurrying. It took a while to find matches and candle. We had been told confidently that mice and rats cannot coexist, but the sea of little faces in the manger and on the table suggested that they were, and in large numbers. When we lit the candle they fled. What I cannot forgive is the casual nip one gave to my Indian necklace of tiny cinnabar beads, which now showers beads around like designer dandruff. On subsequent nights, at the first hint of any bellicose business, Dan and I sat bolt upright, and made loud cat noises.

That summer continued in the grand tradition of fiestas. One of the best – if most clichéd – things about Spain is that everybody is always having fiestas. From the first sunny Sunday in January and on saints' days, of which there are 365 per annum, Malaguenians drive up from the coast in throngs to picnic among the olive trees, with the full panoply of tables, chairs, barbecues, music and candelabra. At Easter the streets are full of impeccably dressed families, enjoying themselves politely at the bejewelled altar of religious excess. On New Year's Eve, the town hall dispenses champagne and grapes to sober Spaniards gravely observing in their Sunday blacks, and to the inebriated English, who racket and puke in an acrylic rainbow.

Shortly after we were installed, I was in Paco's bar rambling on to Juan, our builder and by now a trusted friend, about flamenco dancing – I love the nose-flaring intensity of the dancers, the bare, basic, thrilling rhythm and, of course, most of all, the Barbie-doll frilly dresses. The blur of leathery hands in a frenzy of crisply syncopated clapping, the air of high passion and awesome seriousness. Flamenco dancing is the perfect tempestuous affair between charisma and kitsch. Juan listened kindly, and invited Dan and me to Monterrosso the following Saturday for an evening of flamenco.

'What time should we come?' I asked, tremulous with excitement.

'Oh, around ten,' he said, and ambled off to buy more drinks.

Well, it took all week to decide what to wear, and on Saturday evening at ten I was still in a quandary about shoes – Doc Martens were less than perfect with the white bias-cut dress I had finally chosen, but anything racier would have been suicidal on the rocky and unpredictable terrain.

Dan was fretting. 'Come on, we'll be late. We'll miss the contest. Just wear what's comfortable. The boots look fine. No-one's going to look at you anyway.'

Wrong tack, as any woman could have told him. Forty minutes later, boots on feet, high heels in bag at the ready, we set off. We were not really talking to each other, but he managed to hiss that we had probably missed the whole show and that there was no point in going.

Monterrosso is a crumpled-pocket-handkerchief

village, strewn up a steep hill. We parked at the outer perimeter among quite a throng of cars, and climbed to the village centre, where I did a discreet shoe-change. Chairs and tables were neatly laid out on the sloping red dust, in front of a raised stage. Alongside it was a long bar, at which a crowd of men were shouting jovially at each other. There were no women to be seen, and we were the only non-Spaniards. There was no sign of anything in the flamenco line. We wondered if we had missed it.

Sebastian Moreno, a short, powerful, middle-aged man with an air of authority and a very gappy grin, motioned us to join his table at the front. Juan was there as well, along with two others I did not know. Juan demanded to know what we would drink. '*Tinto de verano*,' we chorused – a safe, long, summer drink of red wine and lemonade with ice and lemon. It is a lot better than you might imagine. However, he disdained to get us anything so mongrelly, and came back with two glasses of fino. A long and earnest discussion ensued, requiring many more glasses, about the astounding merits of fino. We admired its purity, its colour, its flavour and its miraculous anti-hangover properties. We continued in this way for *two hours*, until the mayor scrambled onto the stage, made a lengthy speech introducing Paco the hairdresser – an etiolated, pale, knobbly man who might have wandered out of an El Greco painting (except he doesn't often wear a pink dress) – whose skilled extemporizing on the guitar transformed what followed into music.

What we were attending turned out to be a flamenco *singing* contest. There were no fiery *señoritas* flouncing in frilled and spotted skirts, no sexual chemistry between undersized but testosteroneous men and rip-snorting Junos, and not a solitary castanet. There were just six men and one woman, one after the other, clapping and yodelling as they related their marital difficulties, or their shopping lists, or whatever. It could have been in Chinese for all we understood, though the word for 'heart', *corazón*, came up regularly. To start with I was bitterly disappointed: I wanted bejewelled dancing girls, not singing farmers in their Sunday best.

However, as the empty fino glasses multiplied, the music grew on us. By about four a.m., the village square was full. Stout, moustachioed ladies in pop sox dandled children on their knees, a few lissome bare-midriff girls chattered near the bar where their prospective partners were showing off. Occasionally there would be a respectful moment of silence as one of the singers itemized a particularly poignant shopping list, but mostly everyone in the audience bellowed at each other without giving the singers a second thought.

Dan and I realized that we were very honoured. Not only were we the only *extranjeros*, but we were sitting at the judges' table. Juan, Sebastian Moreno and their two *compadres* were awarding marks out of ten. I never got the hang of it. Antonio, who has Down's syndrome, sang a song without end, and was finally shuffled off the stage mid-trill, kindly but firmly, by the mayor and the hairdresser. I thought he'd done very well. Juan gave him a perfectly circular zero. Similarly the woman, who sang beautifully and with passion, was discounted altogether for being a woman. The boring guy who meandered on and on about potting compost and rubber grommets got top marks. But by this time I had my dancing boots on, and was grooving on down, careless as to whether the best person won. Finally, as we lurched towards our car, Sebastian called us back, and invited us to come and eat paella with him the following day. We felt like celebrities. We got home with the yawning sun, and can confirm that, indeed, fino does not give you a hangover.

Two o'clock he said, and Dan, as you may have guessed, is cursed with punctuality. At two o'clock on the dot we were there, in Monterrosso. Alone. There was no sign of Señor Moreno, and we wondered if we had misunderstood his invitation. We had – we were not the only guests; it was a party for the entire local population. By three, people had put out chairs and tables along the village paths, and Señor Moreno had built an impressive fire – the sort that used to toast heretics, Moors and witches – and was tipping washing-up bowls of prawns, chicken, garlic, tomatoes and peppers into a monstrous pan like St Brendan's coracle but three times the size. He beamed like a picket fence when he spotted Dan, and dragged him over to stir the contents of the coracle with a huge wooden paddle, while he poured in buckets of water and binfuls of rice.

Dan was as happy as a bouncing dolphin – stirring, tasting, advising, lifting, fanning and serving. By this time the whole village was sitting out – including some who had not stuck to the wondrous fino, judging by their furrowed faces and the blackness of their sunglasses. Jugs of wine were on the tables, dogs were sniffing around cautiously, the ladies clattered with gold jewellery. I was rather shocked by the way they picked at the food, eating just the chicken and prawns and leaving the rice.

We ate everything that was put before us, and conversed in a limited but energetic way with Manolo *metálico* and his fearsome wife, a Hillary Clinton double. The sun shone, and below us the olive trees whispered silver in a light breeze. It was a great day, and a great paella, and in a surge of confidence about our house, some parts of which were almost habitable, we decided to give a paella party ourselves, and invite all the builders and some of the Brits.

We had come to the end of Dan's money, Suzy, Ted and Doris were still with us, the concrete-mixer had moved on to another site, and it seemed a good time to say what we hoped would be a temporary adieu to our builders. We were still severely handicapped in the kitchen department – with just the camping stove and water from the mosquito breeding-tank – but our priorities were impeccable. We had a terrace with a hammock and a stone seat under the shady *transparente*, we had a functioning loo and a swimming-pool. In short, we felt the need to celebrate.

We were thrilled with our swimming-pool – I couldn't believe we actually owned one. The previous month, as it had slowly filled for the first time, Dan and I had bounced and splashed, screaming with undignified laughter as we attacked each other with water-pistols or dive-bombed our inflatable erstwhile bed, which had become pool fun. Swallows and swifts swooped over the water, and we debated whether they were drinking or catching insects, a point we have not established satisfactorily to this day. We wittered on about how the marine blue reflected the sky blue, which was given depth by the blue mosaic, and flying back from England that summer, I practically combusted with excitement, because I could see the unmistakable round blue eye of our pool *from the plane* as we prepared to land.

Juan gave us a long shopping list with all the paella ingredients, and the next morning we roared down to the Málaga supermarket and filled the car with what he had specified and crates of red wine. He arrived later with a couple of huge paella pans, and Dan stripped down to scrub off the ancient patina of paellas past. We passed the afternoon peeling prawns, washing the vegetables in water hauled from the tank, and cutting them into the particular sizes and shapes that Juan recommended. He was a bit concerned that we did not have the correct Airplane brand spices, but made do with alarmingly generous handfuls of my precious saffron. Failing a proper stove, he built a fire in one of the walled plant containers on the terrace.

In order to look ravishing for the occasion, Suzy, Doris and I slathered our faces in sulphurous black Dead Sea mud, and sat in the sun until it had set in a solid, painful crust. I had unwisely put it in my hair, as recommended on the packet, and had a pre-party panic trying to get it off. We had a proper shower now, no longer had to wash our hair in the bidet, but the gas was apt to run out at inconvenient times, and did so during the lengthy dislodging of the Dead Sea. There was nothing for it but to scream a bit and carry on picking out clods of mud in the icy water. The bathroom had another tiny fault: the taps appeared to be connected to the electricity in some mysterious way and we would hear little shrieks from people unused to getting 15-volt shocks from the taps as they showered.

Dressed to kill, from the ankles up, and sporting sensible walking shoes below, we assembled for an evening's carousing. Of course it did not rain. In Andalucía you don't need your cardie and umbrella just in case. But as the sun set in its usual splendour, a small violent gale blew up. A light sanding of Saharan grit coated our perfectly made-up faces and made our eyelids puff up unbecomingly. Dan's huge yellow parasol took off – it took a while to spot it upside-down on the roof. The salads, which we had washed to remove all traces of their native soil, were newly dusted with a fine crunchy film, and paper plates and napkins rose into the air like a flock of starlings, to land wherever was inconvenient. No matter, by now we were clinking our gritty glasses and cared not a jot.

Juan slaved away over his hot flower-bed, and people started to arrive: our English neighbour Annie, looking polished but without her Spanish lover; Barbara Stallwood, as glamorous as a film star, and Chris her husband, with a carful of food and drink; Chris's mother Mabs and her husband Tom, who used to be chief superintendent for the Rugby division of Warwickshire; Helen and Tommy, nice, funny and incomprehensibly Glaswegian, with Tommy's nonagenarian mother; and the men who had worked on the house and pool – sexy young Pedro, Miguel, Manolo *metálico*, Paco *eléctrico* and the moustachioed pirate who had laid the terrace tiles and built the flower-bed stove.

Michael Stallwood, son of Chris and Barbara, elected himself disc jockey – not a popular move as he has an unfathomable passion for Queen and Meatloaf, foggily interspersed with Enya. But he also made vats of incredibly alcoholic sangría that must have distorted our hearing to the point where we lost our critical edge. It contained fresh fruit, red wine, sugar, lemonade, fruit juice, vodka, gin, red Martini, Cointreau and ice. The procedure was as follows: drink. Tell life story to complete stranger. Fall over.

The paella was a great success, but Juan floored us by asking for the meat and fish to follow. And Barbara wanted to know where the bread was. 'The Spanish can't eat anything without bread. And where's the beer and the whisky? They have to have whisky.' We hadn't known, and felt like utter failures. How could we be so ignorant? Barbara despatched Michael in the car, and he returned miraculously with several chickens, lots of fish, some chops, whisky, beer and some acceptable CDs. An unlikelier candidate for the loaves-and-fishes trick would be hard to find, but he rescued us that night.

After the resolution of this crisis, events become a little blurred. Suzy bonded fondly with Tommy's mother, talking far into the night, and Manolo showed me how to do a simple flamenco step. I flamencoed nimbly until I fell into the fire, and then decided I'd had enough. Not a serious injury, but a blow to pride and bottom.

Gradually everyone danced or talked themselves into exhaustion and left, until only Michael remained, curled up in a snoring ball in a deck-chair. Nothing could shift him. 'He'll be fine,' Barbara said. 'He often falls asleep where he lands. He'll be in exactly the same position when he wakes up. We'll collect him in the morning.' We manoeuvred the sleeper onto our collapsing air mattress, covered him with blankets, and there he slept, next to the pool. Fortunately he did not turn over.

Yes, we did curse the sun for being so infernally

bright the next day, and the birds for being so raucous, and Michael, who woke up his usual maddeningly perky self, despite drinking as much as us, and sleeping on the instantly deflating mattress.

The following night, still feeling fairly fragile, Dan and I picked our way cautiously by candlelight to the donkey room. We caterwauled as usual, to encourage the resident rodents to bicker elsewhere, and sank gratefully into our bed. We talked companionably for a while, agreeing that the summer had been unrelentingly hard work but absolutely worth it. In peace and quiet, except for the distant barking of farm dogs, we snuffed the candle and, within minutes, were fast asleep.

I woke with a shriek. My face was wet. So were the bed and the floor. Raindrops the size of gobstoppers were hurtling through the roof, trickling down through our canvas awning and onto the candles and matches beside the bed. I could hear water splashing in twenty different places in the donkey room, and did a panicky inventory of which precious thing was where. It was pitch black, about four in the morning, and I could not rouse Dan. I felt like Grace Darling as I stumbled into the teeming blackness to locate buckets and washing-up bowls in which to collect the rain, judging the location of leaks by ear. I bundled the electronic stuff and my jewellery into the trunk, sprinkling earrings all over the floor then crunching over them, only to discover that the trunk had a crack across the top through which water seeped. Found some bubble-wrap, and a couple of carrier-bags and wrapped everything up. Not only was Dan not helping, but he kept shushing me, deeply embroiled in one of his nocturnal cocktail parties and dreamily oblivious to the surrounding disaster.

Suddenly I remembered the electric cables, and freaked: the entire hillside might become lethally charged. Feeling my way along the walls, I found the sockets and nervously unplugged them. Needless to say, none of the lights worked now as the cables were all soaked. Then I scurried about in the darkness, trying to recollect what damageables we had left out. We had become so used to constant sunshine that we lived outside, and an old ghetto-blaster, which rumbled with Ted's hip-hop all day, was beside the pool with his tapes. I'd left some gardening books out too, and the usual bundle of towels was littered about. I had a nasty feeling that my camera was there somewhere, but no idea where. The trouble with the middle of the night is that it is ideal for worrying but not much else. I fretted indecisively for about three hours, moving bits around, dropping them, tripping over cables and eliciting fresh groans from Dan. At length I just gave up on the crisis. What did it matter? Who needs cameras anyway? Certainly not me: I have never managed to take a picture that did not lop off the top of my subject's head. Finally an Irish-looking dawn diluted the inky black to a gloomy grey. Daylight, even of this variety, made the problems bearable, and having cast a loss-adjuster's eye around the devastated donkey room I fell back into our clammy bed, to another volley of groans from Dan.

The rain continued well into the day, and we were all out of sorts. It was not a dramatic, bonding sort of rain with thunder and imminent disaster, it was the dull, grey sort that evokes Llandrindod Wells on a Sunday afternoon. Suddenly there were too many of us and the house was too small. We all felt cold. Overnight winter had come, and we wanted woolly things to wear, soft carpets underfoot and blazing fires. The swimming-pool in which we had larked but a day earlier looked both uninviting and inappropriate.

Shortly after this excitement everyone returned to England leaving Dan and me to reacquaint ourselves with each other. We had our annual tiff, followed by a brief peaceful and impoverished hiatus until October's clutch of royalties meant that we could put our heads into the lion's mouth again, and invite the builders back.

This was not unalloyed good news: the first thing they did was demolish the trio of crumbling rooms between the doughty old part of the house and the bathroom. A thick layer of dust, like cocoa on tiramisu, covered and penetrated everything, and Manolo, Pedro and Miguel gained an intimate insight into our bathroom habits – we had to cross the rock-strewn no man's land that was their new field of action whenever we wanted to use the loo. As building progressed, the loo was frequently out of bounds altogether because of wet cement or newly laid tiles on what would become the floor of our sitting room. Even

within, door locked, one was not guaranteed absolute privacy. For one thing, the builders frequently wandered past the window, and glanced inside casually to meet the surprised gaze of whoever was sitting there. Then a bold gecko moved into the bathroom and picked choice living quarters above the medicine cabinet. If you wandered in, he would look at you for a minute or so, then scuttle out of the window via the hinges – somehow he could flatten himself to squeeze through a crack the thickness of a tissue. He was very fastidious and could not abide the proximity of human bodily functions. As soon as you left, he would straighten his tie, clear his throat, and return to his pad beside the light fitting.

We were living in just bearable discomfort in the most beautiful place. We had intermittent water and electricity. In the evening, after the builders had gone and wonderful peace descended, we would collect a couple of glasses of Rioja in preparation for the nightly sky show: every evening summer and winter there is a spectacular sunset, rippled, ribbed, washed with cloud and colour – orange, turquoise, indigo, azure, scarlet, apricot, magenta – the heavenly legacy of Turner played out for our benefit. Banal matters like no-one telling us that Tomas was coming with the JCB, and that it would make sense to move our bed out of the donkey room because he was going to knock it down, were swept from our minds. No matter the chaos and discomfort, Dan and I were putting down roots. This was where we belonged.

Juan's Shellfish Paella: our party
Serves 8

6 unpeeled jumbo prawns
12 unpeeled medium prawns
3 tablespoons extra-virgin olive oil
2 onions, peeled and chopped
3 medium tomatoes, peeled, seeded and finely chopped
2 heads garlic, peeled and chopped
a large pinch each of saffron threads and cumin
2.5 litres water
1 stock cube
1 tablespoon sweet paprika
chopped fresh chilli to taste
225g dried butterbeans, soaked overnight and drained, or frozen broad beans (optional)
salt and black pepper
600g Spanish paella rice
1 large red pepper, finely diced
12 mussels, scrubbed and debearded
225g frozen peas

Heat a large paella pan or sauté pan over a medium heat, add a spoonful of the oil and the prawns and sauté for 5 minutes, then remove and set aside. Heat the rest of the oil and fry the onion gently for a few minutes. Add the tomatoes and garlic and cook for a few more minutes. Toast the saffron in a small dry pan over a medium heat for 1 minute, crumble into 2.5 litres water with the stock cube, paprika and chilli, and pour over the tomatoes. Add the soaked beans, season with salt and pepper to taste, and simmer until reduced by half, about 45 minutes.

Stir in the rice and red pepper, increase to medium heat and cook for about 10 minutes, adding the mussels halfway through. Discard any that do not open. Stir in the peas, place the prawns on top of the rice, reduce the heat to low and cook for a further 10 minutes. Remove from the heat, cover with a clean dishtowel, and cool for 20 minutes. Serve from the pan at room temperature.

10

THE WITTER OF OUR DISCONTENT

As the days grew shorter and occasional downpours turned our surroundings to mulligatawny sludge, our precious 'civilized' haven started to look like the mildewed interior of a Neanderthal cave. Setting foot outside to go anywhere, 'kitchen' and bathroom included, required planning, wellington boots, umbrella and torch. None of the old doors fitted, and there was still no glass in the windows. Plane tickets, banknotes, chequebooks and Juan's estimates riffled off their perilous piles and scattered our future on the floor to be trampled on.

It got colder, and our heroic builders started work in darkness, making bonfires to warm their frozen fingers. I wished I knew them well enough to join them at the pyre of doors and old beams. They were so muffled and miserable that I always took them sweet black coffee in the morning, with a slug of *anis dulce* on particularly vicious days. The east wind from the Sierra Nevada blew for weeks at a time, as cold and cutting as the icy wind from the Urals that made winter in Cambridge so bracing.

We were still living in the old southern part of the house as the northern walls were demolished and replaced, the new ones occupying almost exactly the same positions but being thrillingly vertical and much higher – we did not want to crouch beneath the low, cramped ceilings of yore. As the days lengthened the walls grew, until one watery spring day nineteen chunky chestnut beams barcoded the sky as the preliminary skeleton of the sitting-room roof. Big square terracotta tiles were laid on the vast empty expanse of floor. When the builders had gone home, we would tiptoe in and gloat in the echoing emptiness. Scale played scary tricks with us: spaces that looked tiny when they were just walls laid on a rubble of broken breeze-blocks and the remnants of the builders' morning bonfires suddenly assumed airy expansiveness when neatly floored and cleared of rubbish. Then the roof diminished them again, until the furniture went in and they expanded once more.

I had to spend a lot of time at the office in London, and being alone at Casa Miranda was not heaven for Dan. He was marooned in the old building as it was demolished around him, with no windows, warmth or company. The new building was also windowless, and bone-penetratingly damp from the drying plaster. He tried desperately to make some part of the house habitable before my return and achieved miracles, but at painful cost to himself. Furniture removal for one thing – everything huge had to be taken from wherever it was gathering dust or getting sodden with rain on the hillside, and assembled in our new rooms. Then, the minute doors were in place, the remaining furniture had to be moved out of the old rooms so that the roof could be taken off. Pronto.

He had daily battles with the builders, who tended to make up their own minds about where to put the windows and doors. In an attempt to forestall their draconian decision-making, he did detailed drawings of the fireplace we wanted, complete with accurate measurements.

'You don't want that. It's ugly,' Juan said.

We did not think so, but Juan knew better. On his instructions Miguel built a fireplace that looked like an HGV bursting through the sitting-room wall. We were dismayed. I succumbed to a dark moment of despair, and rang Babara.

'Don't worry,' she said. 'Just tell them to redo it how you want it.'

Without a murmur Miguel dismantled the HGV and constructed a magnificent altar to Vulcan, with a hot-seat upon which to park one's bottom.

We had another run-in with Juan about skirting tiles, which he thought essential. 'How will Miranda clean the floor?' he demanded.

This was not a problem, since I intended to try the No-Clean method of housework, so Dan instructed the builders to ignore his ideas.

Juan countered with much lip-pursing. 'The trouble with Dan and Miranda,' he once said indignantly, 'is that they know what they want.'

To prevent any future misunderstandings, Dan built a perfect miniature of the house from cereal packets, which the builders copied reverently to the extent of making doorways asymmetrical – they itched to paint a scarlet K across the kitchen wall. We would see them, knee-deep in rubble, spherical with knitted garments, apparently playing doll's houses with great solemnity. Everybody loved that model – it made sense of the complicated building for the blokes who were working on it, and for a while it housed an itinerant gecko.

Dan's darkest day came when the builders had finally put up the walls, doors and even the windows, with glass and the obligatory bars at our north end of the house. Spaniards have a fearsome paranoia about Moors or gypsies or roving underwear salesmen, and put bars on anything that will hold still. We did not as yet have a bedroom, so our bed was the first thing to greet the surprised visitor coming through the front door. I was still in England so Dan rang me with excitement to tell me about the kitchen, the sitting room, the new improved fireplace and the wood-burning stove. November brought spectacular rain outside and sweating newly plastered walls within, so he was eagerly awaiting the delivery of firewood to hasten the drying process.

Finally, on a particularly evil day of horizontal sleet, Pepe the woodman brought a load of logs, with which Dan could at last make a fire and get *warm*. His big four-wheel drive stopped outside the house, then slid gracefully sideways down a mud ramp, and would have continued to the bottom of the hill, had it not been halted by the fig tree. Dan sprinted out under the bruise-black sky and helped shift a small mountain of logs, paid Pepe, and waved him goodbye. Then, soaked to the skin, he saw the front door bang shut with the key on the inside. Thanks to Manolo *metálico*'s absent-minded failure to provide us with door handles, he was locked out. The rain got heavier and the night got darker as Dan walked round the house. Apparently every door and window was locked and barred, except one – the kitchen window. The builders had not yet bothered with putting bars on this one as it was plainly unreachable. Barely big enough for Dan to get his head through, it was a good three metres from the ground. In the teeming darkness he constructed a ladder from scaffolding poles, climbed up perilously, fending off prods from the plum-tree branches, smashed the glass and wriggled tightly through the tiny window to flop gratefully into the sink. Typically, there was a power-cut because of the rain so he had to stumble around in darkness.

That evening he discovered that the back door was unlockable, and he could simply have walked in. At the grim nadir of all this he rang me from Paco's, hoping for sympathy, and instead got a wigging for being needy. I seem to remember saying that I couldn't always be propping him up emotionally. Oh, the shame of it.

When I arrived home, having been away for two weeks of shopping therapy interspersed with bouts of work, the fireplace was up and blazing, and the wood-burner belted out comforting dry heat. Our bed was still the first thing to meet the eye on entry, but then – oh, joy of joys – my desk, all set up with electric points for my Apple Mac and printer. Dan had moved book-cases and filled them with our curious library of tattered novels, *Teach Yourself Spanish*, self-help manuals and gardening books.

The only missing link was the one between cooker and gas bottle: the highly unpredictable Repsol man failed to materialize for months, so we were still concocting meals on our wobbly camping stove.

But I had a blissful frenzy of washing in the new washing-machine, and dishwashing in the new dish-washer. I washed and washed, often tripping the electricity, and felt like all those ads where housewives in tightly waisted pinnies have detergent orgasms as dust and dirt disappeared. Behold! there were my strange Oxfam garments and Dan's jeans freed from the mud of ages.

He had arranged lamps, a sofa by the wood-burning stove, dressers and cupboards, the rocking chair, soft rugs underfoot, pictures on the walls, a proper table with chairs, all warm and inviting and looking, at last, like a home. A miracle, in short, as I have come to expect where Dan is involved.

Juan kept an eye on the house and its inhabitants, and was shyly intrigued by Dan's paintings and drawings. He kept leafing through the pages of sketchbooks, or cocking his head to one side to get a better view of a painting. Finally, after much shuffling around the subject he summoned the courage to ask Dan to draw a portrait of him. Dan was delighted, and arranged for a sitting the following morning. Juan arrived at eight – rather earlier than strictly necessary – and allowed Dan just forty minutes, during which he smoked, talked, fidgeted and finally fell asleep. Despite this, Dan managed a rather fine big pencil head and shoulders. It was an accurate likeness, did not make Juan look like Antonio Banderas, and has not been seen since.

Whenever there were problems, such as when the sitting-room roof leaked in twenty places or the chimney belched industrial smog, Juan would be round on the dot of eight a.m., his pockets bulging with sweets as he battled with his smoking habit. He would turn up on his moped, helmeted and jacketed, and follow one of his builders around the disaster area, his hands clasped behind his back, soberly taking in his version of the story. He would compare it with ours, then make judgement. We were always satisfied with his decision, and so, apparently, were the builders. They never grumbled about taking down a wall they had just spent three days putting up, and Antonio did not begrudge a horrible day spent snorting soot in our malfunctioning chimney or being swallowed up by a mudslide while sorting our water pipe. Juan looked after his men and his clients with equal seriousness and kindness.

As a result, when he asked for money we jumped to attention and drove ourselves mad trying to fathom the vagaries of the Spanish banking system. At Christmas, in response to Juan's urgent request that his men have enough money for a proper carouse, we went into Málaga where the Banco de Santander claimed to have a reciprocal arrangement with my UK bank, the Royal Bank of Scotland. The drive took an hour each way, and as we repeated it over the next four days we discovered three things: that the Banco de Santander did not open on Nuestra Señora de la Esperanza's day, that it closed on the dot of one on Saturdays and, finally, that the cash transfer we wished to make was impossible for obscure bureaucratic reasons. On one occasion we terrorized Señor Velazquez Romero, our reluctant guide in these transactions, with our discovery that the Royal Bank of Scotland had just acquired the Banco de Santander. His pallor, always impressive, became almost phosphorescent over the next twenty minutes, which he spent on the phone trying to get to the bottom of this potential disaster. Eventually on Christmas Eve we managed to extract enough money for the builders, only to find on our return that their office was shuttered and padlocked for the holidays.

The office might have been locked, but Juan's house was open. Every Christmas without fail, he invited a crowd to eat with him in the adventure playground that was his stone-built country house, paying blithe disregard to who was on nonspeaks with whom. Lovingly constructed by his own two hands, it was situated within easy walking distance of his town house in Almogia, but it was country by virtue of having leeks, tomatoes, potatoes and chard in its garden, and an unnervingly transient cast of animals, which might be pets or dinner, depending on his whim. Juan's wife Maria never graced these gatherings because, according to him, she had a townie's suspicion of the countryside.

The house looked as though Ivanhoe had had a hand in its rugged dark battlements and beetling turrets. In lieu of arrow-slits, however, Juan opted for white plastic windows, and there was a white plastic door where you might have expected a drawbridge. Inside, there were no walls or doors: he would show you proudly to the area officially demarcated 'bathroom', tracing the projected walls with his feet and drawing your attention to the glittering sanitaryware, but it was uncomfortably exposed for anything more intimate than blowing your nose.

The kitchen consisted of a wide stone fireplace at which Juan stood, warming his bottom and beaming at his guests, and a wood-burning baker's oven the size of an old-fashioned telephone box, from which emerged trays of succulent lamb braised slowly alongside herbs and vegetables from the garden.

Juan's guests sat on plastic garden chairs around a wobbly plastic table, while he and Barbara exhorted them to eat and drink more than they meant to. Juan's grasp of English has never progressed beyond pointing out the 'toolie' (toilet), asking for 'moonie' (money), and his triumphant 'Wassa matter?' a two-word phrase that suited most social occasions. But my Spanish was good enough to understand and appreciate his habitual gentlemanly greeting '*Guapissima*'. That Christmas, purple-faced with warmth and whisky, people who shouldn't determined to dance and, with their paper hats at increasingly rakish angles, lurched ungracefully around the exposed pipes and piles of bricks, ignoring the virtual walls, occasionally collapsing on the loo seat to get their wind back.

Dan and I were not sufficiently drunk to enjoy this part of the event, so we bade a remarkably sober goodbye to our friends and builders and went home to a rousing game of Scrabble.

December had been like an English summer, though the days were short. We had sat sleeveless in the sun writing Christmas cards and fretting that we were sending them off too late. That Christmas, Pastelero – along with every other village in the country – put on a display of lights. Its one street was littered with light-bulb boxes until the wind chased them away. Somehow the twinkling tiaras exhorting Yuletide cheer just emphasized the emptiness of the village, but the general sense of bleakness suited us fine. Our previous Christmas had been appalling: Dan had returned to his marital home to see Elly and the children and felt as ghoulishly estranged as people do on those occasions, however fond everyone is; I had been the lone cheerleader at Highbury in a battle-zone of bottles, ashtrays and an Amaretti tin that some juvenile reveller had used as a handy vomitorium. My boys had not surfaced until afternoon was drifting into evening, with hangovers so severe that speaking was outlawed. This year I had declared a moratorium on Christmas and the boys were fending for themselves in London, Leo having a year out after getting his graphics degree at Brighton, and Spigs home from Ipswich where he was doing a course in spatial design.

Dan and I decided not to have Christmas. Well, there was an embarrassment of cards festooned around the kitchen, and I did sneak out and buy a string of fairy-lights and draped them in a minimal frill around one of our small trees. But we didn't have presents, and lunch was a festive spag bol. No crackers, no parties, no family, no door-slamming, no tears, just an overwhelming sense of relief. I had a brief twinge of missing the boys, whom I rang on Christmas Day, but they both sounded fine, and it passed wonderfully quickly.

After lunch we dragged ourselves reluctantly from the fireside and braved the grey and cold to climb the peaks at the top of El Torcal, which looked like a Disney mountain, with ectoplasmic ghouls of mist winding around the rocks. We got lost, night fell, and I was resigned to spending Christmas night sleeping on a rock when we heard the unmistakable sound of stiletto heels clacking on stone a few feet away. We followed the sound, and came upon a sophisticated party of designer-dressed Málaguenians having a hundred-yard Christmas totter from the car park. We had done a complete circle, and were within spitting distance of our starting point. But at least we had seen glacier-green hellebores, Christmas roses, flowering wild.

* * *

During this time Dan and I put our new and insecure relationship through a severe testing. My heart sank every time Barbara told me of some couple who had come out here and split up because of the pressure of losing all their familiar friends and habits, and living full-time with a partner whom they had previously only seen in short bursts. I had a premonition that we would eventually be that couple. Dan and I didn't really know each other, not under duress of this kind: he was exiled from friends and family in a country whose language he did not speak, and I was still masquerading as the efficient breadwinner and resenting it, trailing back to England every month. Every time I left the sun-gilded olive fields to board a plane alone it was a violent wrench.

Dan was often homesick, and would lie, sometimes for days, on the sofa mostly groaning, often snoring, occasionally weeping quietly. It is not that he is work-shy – on the contrary, he's never happier than when he has a job to do. He is a natural painter, effortlessly turning out magnificent landscapes, and a talented illustrator. The problem is that he is defeatist. He can accomplish the most stupendous achievements – move a mountain of rubble, build a dry-stone wall, paint a terrific landscape, invent a new life for Oscar Wilde – but unless work lands in his lap (not a safe assumption when you have moved to the wilds of Andalucía and have told no-one of your change of address) he gets demoralized and depressed. I had hoped that the general splendour of Spain would induce him to become permanently perky. It was not to be. Slowly we built a *modus vivendi*. Painfully we learned where each other's exposed nerves were. Gradually the days of welling tears or blatant hypochondria lessened, and my snarling rabid dog stayed in its kennel.

But we were perennially on the brink of chaos at the beginning of our residence in Spain, and remembering where things were was vital. I can't count the number of times I scrabbled frantically in my bag, heart racing, adrenaline pumping. There was always someone waiting, tapping his feet impatiently, as I went through this performance. Dan developed an irritating relationship with the man on the ceiling at the start of our stay proper, casting his eyes heavenward about thirty times a day, after an exchange that went like this:

D: 'Where are the car keys, house keys, passports, maps, socks, *dineros*, playing cards, little saucepans?'
M: 'Try looking where you saw them last: on the table, on the fridge, in my bag, under the bed, in the drawer.'
D: '*You* had them last. You *must* remember where you put them.'
M: 'Nope.'
D casts eyes to ceiling, and M reminds herself to book a one-way ticket to London.

I found this routine incredibly undermining. I never applied for the job of Custodian of Small Things, but because women cannot help but be the beasts of burden, with an unwished-for talent at Pelmanism, that's how it turned out. Handbags, ladies, that's where we go wrong. While you tote a handbag, you are signalling to the world and your man your willingness to shoulder piddling time-wasting responsibilities. There is a peculiarly depressing scientific theory that the brains of men and women over millennia have evolved differently to suit different tasks. Men have gone out and slaughtered things, so their mental development has been to do with cunning, opportunism and finding their way home. Women, on the other hand, are conditioned to be the guardians of the daily minutiae, finding things mainly, and therefore tidying, cleaning, ordering, filing.

Those activities require a lot of RAM. At the beginning there were certain things that we *had* to remember, keys being the most vital. If we went out, there were three doors to lock. (That was in the good old days – now there are ten.) I was forever losing keys and chequebooks. And having to hang on to twenty-seven fussy details used up more memory than I had to spare, with the result that I usually could not recall our telephone number, my name or the word for 'post office'.

My role as keeper and finder of vital bits and pieces made me very tetchy, and the fact that I did it so *badly* made Dan tetchy too. My idea in leaving London had been to shed responsibilities, not acquire more. True, early on we had nowhere to keep anything, apart from the fatal handbag (back-pack, actually, because of the slipped disc). Eventually I ended up carrying so much that I needed a wheelbarrow. We had also set up a formula for successive autumns. As the last summer visitor left, Dan and I had a short, bitter argument, trashed the previous few months and each other's relatives and friends, and started planning a spinster/bachelor future. As my sister Judy's partner, Hubert, says, 'Guests give great pleasure when they arrive and particularly when they leave.' Having visitors – whom we had sincerely longed to see – under these circumstances simply meant that for months we never had a private conversation, never had a chance to discuss things, reach agreement, share tasks. We each felt needy, unloved and unlistened-to.

There was a particularly horrible day that winter when we were about to return to England together. Dan was deeply enmired in gloom and could not bring himself to get out of bed until midday. It was overcast and cold, and we were isolated in our own personal doldrums.

I had decided to go to Antequera to buy some beautiful big swirly bowls for Hester, and I'm ashamed to say that then I was still too cowardly to drive. I bullied Dan into taking me, and we mistimed our arrival to coincide with the siesta. The town was eerily empty. There were no cars, no pedestrians, no dogs, and nothing was open. Blank shutters shiny with drizzle covered every door and window. That was how it remained for three hours, while we bickered over an indifferent meal in an overpriced restaurant. Dan thought buying bowls was a waste of time and money, and I was determined not to go back to London empty-handed. I bought more bowls than I wanted or had any use for, and extra large ones, because I was as self-righteously sulky as only a fourteen-year-old should be. We did a perfunctory food shop, forgetting all the necessary things, and drove home in silence.

Our peevishness was compounded by the fact that we had agreed to go to Paco's bar that evening with Clive, who was keen to get away from his rat battlefield. His invitation was more generous than he had intended since he found himself in the company of two stuffed turkeys, in the deafening context of the Pastelero bar on 'English night'. He is very good-hearted and did his best, but as there was no sign of life in us, he wisely meandered off to swap platitudes with more congenial company. Finally he returned and gave us a lift home, where another crisis occurred. I had mislaid the kitchen keys, which meant no glasses, toothbrushes or water. There was another barrage of, 'Well, where have you put them? You must know where they are, you had them last,' from Dan. We clambered crossly into bed, back to back, lying perilously along the edges with the widest possible gap between us.

The next morning I found the keys, along with some suntan lotion and a biro, neatly laid out on the holding tank. They must have fallen out of my bag, and the builders had kindly retrieved them. But our tribulations were not over. I lost my chequebook. I fretted about it and Dan went through the all-too-familiar spiel. I lost my temper and growled at him and he told me I was pathological about money. I said indignantly that if I was pathological about money it was because I had been solely responsible for supporting two boys for eighteen years, a task that had not come easily to me, and that my whole objective in buying the house in Spain was to be *freed* of responsibility, yet since we had arrived it had become my unwelcome lot to memorize the whereabouts of every single object in the house. '*And* you diss me when you roll your eyes to the heavens.'

There. I'd said it. The truth was out. Dan was mortified and apologetic, and scurried about trying to make amends by shifting rocks from outside the bedroom door where they constituted a life hazard. Suddenly he groaned and went pale. He had put his back out, and could not sit down, stand up, bend over or walk. It was all too grimly familiar.

I managed to find my back notes, Xeroxed from a book Leo had lent me. They suggested ice packs, exercise, pain-relievers and muscle-relaxants which I happened to have. I had been given Valium for this purpose, and its effect on Dan was startling. He lay in bed, motionless, and wept all afternoon, silent tears trickling down his tanned and manly cheeks. I rang my chiropractor in Bath, who found the name and number of a colleague in Málaga. The next day, after my solitary departure for London, he sorted Dan out and restored his self-esteem. The tears had sprung from Dan's vision of himself as a chronic, hopeless old invalid.

But this episode was unusual. The unfair truth was that we were having cake and pigging on it. I was being paid generously to spend just a quarter of my time at work, and fretting in the gloomy confines of the office was just a fraction of what I had to do. The rest was all pleasure: driving out to picture-postcard villages in Gloucestershire, Suffolk, Oxfordshire, talking to kind, friendly people about their passion for plants, returning home at sunset and maybe stopping for supper in some riverside pub. Even I, spoiled brat that I may be, could not complain.

Then, having done my stint, I could escape back to Paradise. The builders were always effusively welcoming and Dan was transparently overjoyed to have me back. The place was always heart-thumpingly gorgeous. In mid-winter, carpets of brilliant blue irises flowered at the base of El Torcal, and at the top, hellebores and coppery euphorbia. Powerfully fragrant white narcissi grew wild among the limestone rubble, along with acid yellow broom, and pale spikes of asphodel. Milky blue periwinkle twined itself about hot pink cistus, and lavender flowered on the roadside. There was a magical field of poplars densely carpeted with *Oxalis pes-caprae*, canary yellow until lunchtime, then demurely furling their petals like tightly rolled umbrellas and turning – presto! – green. A million *Calendula arvensis* performed the same trick outside the village, and old men waded through the shag pile of orange flowers carrying bundles of delicious bitter wild asparagus. This is an early spring treat and, in one of his philanthropic smash-and-grab raids, our deaf neighbour Señor Arrabal burst unannounced through the new front door one morning, clutched Dan with his sandpaper hands and dragged him from his roost by the fire. They returned with sheaves of asparagus picked from our hill – Señor Arrabal showed Dan where the best clumps were, beyond the range of grazing goats.

The weather was unpredictable: there would be violent rain and 100-kilometre-per-hour winds, dramatic and unheralded explosions of hailstones as big as marrowfat peas, fragile mists obscuring the valleys, and sun. Day would dawn dreary grey, as a reminder that this was winter, then the clouds would peel back to flood us with windless, perfect sun. Short sleeves, lunch outside, heat that warmed our bones and compelled us to potter about, weeding a bit, sweeping a few clods of mud off the brick paving, tying the jasmine and passion-flower to their supports. On blustery days, we had multiple power cuts, which meant no light, no water, no oven and no computer. At night – usually cold and clear with a scintillating splatter of stars – we burned chunks of olive wood and played cards by candlelight.

Perfect happiness was just the two of us, reading,

talking, cooking, playing backgammon or Scrabble. Very simple. Dan strummed his guitar and I couldn't help but sing, though people usually asked me quite quickly to stop. From time to time we would take our glasses of *tinto* and sit out swaddled in fleeces under the bigger, brighter Spanish stars. And that, as the long cold winter of 1998 played itself out, was the pattern that slowly established itself.

Almond Turrón

One of the compensations for dark days and leaking roofs is the cornucopia of extra-fattening Christmas treats that appears in every food shop. A yuletide diet of candied orange peel and almond turrón guarantees that every new year begins with zips that won't fasten.

1 egg white
50g lump sugar
50g honey, as pale as possible
60g almonds, lightly toasted, peeled and roughly crushed
greaseproof paper and rice paper

Line a standard size rectangular tin or mould, first with greaseproof paper and then with rice paper.

Beat the egg whites until they form stiff peaks – so that you can invert the bowl without their falling out. Heat the sugar and honey together in a saucepan. When the sugar has started to melt and combine with the honey, fold in the beaten egg whites. Stir constantly to mix but do not let it brown, as it must stay as white as possible. Remove from the heat. Add the almonds and continue to stir. Return for a moment to a high heat. Just before it begins to caramelize, remove it from the heat and pour into the prepared tin or mould.

1929

11

VAN ORDINAIRE

Ted and Doris had made the pilgrimage to see us for New Year's Eve, and the rain was relentless. There was a strong possibility that we would be unable to escape from the house, since the roads had become mud-slides. I was sorry for the children, cooped up indoors without friends or diversions, but they were generous about it, and did not even bicker.

However, on New Year's Eve we put on our auspicious red knickers and sallied forth in some trepidation. Getting to Almogia was all downhill, and this was scary in the old Citroën with nil visibility and extra slither. We called in at Barbara and Chris's to borrow a jacket for Ted – apparently smart formal was essential for his *Vieja Noche* at Taco's bar. He was seriously embarrassed by the Ted Heath navy blazer with gold buttons, but he looked terrific – tall, green-eyed, black-haired and handsome, the perfect candidate to play a saturnine defrocked priest – with a navy shirt and Chris's appalling paisley tie. Gorgeous.

Almogia at nine thirty was a ghost town. La Loma, the habitual haunt of the English and a sort of staging-post from which to clock everyone coming or going, was dark and shuttered. Las Molinas, the night-club, was locked. The main street was empty, apart from a small flurry of activity as an old lady crept from her front door and returned with a huge feline muff draped round her shoulders. It watched us with disinterested yellow eyes. We skittered down the slippery streets to the main square, thankful with every cautious step that we had not attempted stiletto heels or naked glamour. Doris, Dan and I were bundled up like mattresses. Ted Heath kept clearing his throat and tugging uncomfortably at his tie.

We threaded our way down to the square, and as we approached we heard a tinny Spanish rendition of 'Jingle Bells'. We turned the corner, and witnessed – well, not much really. The town-hall façade was tricked out with a gappy *Feliz Navidad* in red, green and missing lightbulbs. In front of it stood the most etiolated Christmas tree for which money has ever changed hands – entirely bare of needles, its skeletal branches were fetchingly arrayed with lights and red bows. The English bar on the square was icy but had attracted the habitual English crew.

As midnight approached, Doris managed to procure some fake snow canisters, and the town hall dispensed little red and green Cellophane bags to us all, each containing a dozen grapes; the more experienced hastily depipped them. The village children, giggling with panicky excitement, made rushes at us and sprayed us generously with snow, until we were speckled, deluged and blinded.

Midnight was announced, not by church bells as I had been expecting but by a businesslike factory hooter. It had almost finished its toll before I realized what it was, and had to gobble down twelve grapes at once – presaging a joyless year with an orgy of good luck in December. (Each grape swallowed on the twelve strokes of midnight gave a month's good luck.) The town hall dispensed bottles of cheap champagne, which the Spanish used as sparkling spray guns, and the British consumed with greedy pleasure.

For ten glorious minutes everyone was kissing each other, sworn enemies were chatting amicably, people who'd never noticed each other before were suddenly finding intimate common denominators and, for a brief but convincing flurry, fun broke loose upon the world. Then we found that the Spaniards had trickled off, and the doughty, desperate thrill-seeking Brits were alone with their booze and each other. Ted and his friends, looking a mite apprehensive, set out for their night of festive frolics at Taco's bar, and we left the serious drinkers to their serious business.

New resolutions came with the new year. In order to continue to masquerade as an efficient journalist while I commuted to London, I needed a telephone answering-machine and fax – and, of course, a telephone. Michael Stallwood had talked to Telefonica, and they were going to install one . . . maybe.

Michael was endearing and maddening in equal measure. Like his father, he was endlessly obliging but, unlike Chris, he was incapable of listening, so his generosity sometimes backfired. He was working as dogsbody in Barbara and Juan's estate agency, bored to desperation. When we dropped in to say that we were going to Málaga to buy an answering-machine and fax for our, as yet, non-existent phone, he was in the back of the car before we could say, 'Well, boy, how about it?'

We were captive for the drive down, as Michael regaled us with information about the mouth parts and digestive systems of bees, the distance of Jupiter from Earth, the workings of satellite radio and the different kinds of mammal to be found in Alaska, and were a little tetchy when we finally arrived at Carrefour.

Michael sped off to the telephone department, and bustled back with a boxed Samsung, which he plonked at the checkout. 'Right, let's go and have something to eat. I'm starving,' he announced.

OK, I thought, as I paid for the Samsung. Lunch had not been part of the deal as I remembered, but it had been kind of Michael to come with us. Aloud, I said, 'Where shall we go?'

'Well, there's a rather good Mexican place nearby,' he told us. 'Something a bit exotic.'

On this occasion his choice was cheap, if disgusting. A pseudo-Mexican establishment, with all the decorative charm of McDonald's and awash with pulpy, mushy, tasteless refried beans. Why fry them in the first place? Why, oh, why, fry them again? Why not just throw them away? We ate our tasteless pap, and drank our overpriced drinks, and went home.

'At least we got the answering-machine,' we muttered to each other, as Michael told us about the formula for bombs, the constituents of Saturn's rings, the diet of wolves.

Three weeks later, when Telefonica connected us, I spent a mind-stretching afternoon learning the workings of the answering-machine – whose instruction book had segued from Japanese into Spanish, collecting misprints and complications *en route*. It became obvious quite quickly that it did not have a fax element.

We trundled back to the office and told Michael, who was back in the car before we could say, 'Go easy on the jokes.' We had not intended to take him with us this time, since it had not been a success before, but Michael is unstoppable. Before long we'd learnt about the diet of athletes, the composition of limestone, the communication systems of aquatic mammals and the working of a jet engine.

But when we got to Carrefour we were grateful for his presence. We stood at the returns queue for half an hour until finally a woman whose lips were outlined in brown turned to us. We explained our problem, said that we had not used the thing, had not even unpacked it because we needed a fax. Could we change it and pay the difference?

'No. It is too late,' she said. 'For this you must bring the machine back within fourteen days. Next.'

I was speechless and Dan was growling about consumer-protection laws, but Michael, who had lived in Spain for ten years and gone to school there, took on Mud-crust Lips. The endless stream of talk that had driven us mad in the car was put to effective use, and wore her down faster than a Kango hammer. Michael was still talking when she propelled us out of the shop, carrying the complete package this time. When he asked brightly where we would eat, I said, 'You choose, Michael, as a reward for your success.'

'Well, the best place, the one I've been wanting to go to for ages, is the restaurant in the bullring. They have a traditional menu with local specialities, and a good wine list.' The Refried Bean boy as Bon Viveur. Dutifully we followed him.

Michael swept into the restaurant, and asked for a table. Dan and I looked on aghast: this was all napery and silverware, the sort of place you bring your girlfriend when you want to ask her to marry you – soft lights, pink tablecloths, a single rose on each table. It seemed a bit excessive for Michael, who had merely changed an answering-machine.

We had never met a menu like it for variety, and there were no prices on it – always a bad sign. With a sense of foreboding Dan asked for rabbit, I wanted a salad and fish, and Michael ordered steak. The waiter kept telling me that I did not want salad and fish. And I kept telling him that I did. I won. He shrugged, and strode off muttering. I had in mind a sliver of roast salmon on an elegant rocket and mixed-leaf salad.

To start with, he brought tiny, delicious aubergine fritters, which were served with light molasses, crisp, melting, unexpected. We all relaxed, with a glow of false security, until our main courses arrived.

My salad was the size of a small suitcase: eggs and cheese, tinned asparagus and palm hearts, apricots, tuna, sweetcorn, beans, carrot, lettuce, onion, sultanas, anchovies and unidentifiable things from the back of the fridge. The salmon was whale-like. A few minutes later the waiter returned with a silver salver from which protruded what looked like cricket bats. These turned out to be the athletic legs of Dan's rabbit, which I would have guessed to be a kangaroo judging by its heft and muscularity. This great solid boomerang of meat made us all feel rather depressed. Michael's steak was as big as Africa in the Oxford atlas. We ate doggedly, enjoying the uncharacteristic lack of talk.

Dan was defeated by his rabbit and had to leave quite a bit. I hardly made a dent in my whale and suitcase, but Michael, who is shorter than me and slight, ploughed through the steak and chips, then asked for the pudding menu from which he chose something called fried milk.

'You'll love it. You'll wish you'd ordered it when it comes. Mmm, yummy.' Dan and I both groaned.

The Spanish are lousy at puddings, and fried milk was no exception. Michael enthused but I thought it was like nothing so much as a rectangular slab of cold, damp, sweetened wood glue. But now I was preoccupied by the thought of the bill. I was frightened by trying to guess how much all this cutlery and napery would cost, not to mention the Rioja.

'You've got to have good wine with this sort of food,' Michael told us. 'It would be criminal to wash it down with *vin ordinaire*.' Perish the thought.

In the end, it was amazingly reasonable – £28 for the three of us. Dan and I decided to return, preferably without Michael, and choose carefully from the menu next time. Perhaps starve the previous week. But our wild spending spree that day was not over. Not by thousands.

As we drove up in my old Citroën ZX through the suburbs of Málaga towards our hill, Dan spotted a beautiful red Citroën van, with the message 'Cristobal, 952 031 444' in its window. He gasped, smitten with passion. Never had he seen van so fair. Michael, naturally, had his mobile phone about his person, and rang Cristobal immediately while Dan chirruped and stroked his love object. As it happened, that particular van was already sold, but Cristobal had a stable of similar, just back down the road. My old Citroën had performed valiantly during its stay in Spain, but we were going to have to take it back to England because I needed it for work. Without it we would be stuck in Spain, where there are only two buses a day from Pastelero to Málaga, neither at a convenient time. It is true that in a moment of astonishing self-ignorance Dan had bought a mountain bike, a top-of-the-range Cannondale, which he had customized expensively on Spigs's advice with extra spokes front and rear. Having spent a small mortgage on this acquisition – only made because the bike was a fetching shade of yellow – he used it just once, to go to the bakery five minutes' walk down the track. He set off bright and perky and in the prime of life and returned an old and crabby man.

'Well,' said Michael, after his conversation with Cristobal, 'sounds like *karma* – get it? Come on. Let's go and have a look. Can't do any harm.' We knew otherwise but, weedily, we capitulated.

Cristobal was pallid and overweight, shiny white face buffed and polished with sweat, and a puckered scar like a cat's arse where someone appeared to have rammed a girder through his cheek. Dan took to him immediately, and they left me fretting in the old Citroën while they assessed and test-drove other vans. I would see them whizzing past the end of the road in something white and covered with mud, then returning in something grey and fastened with string. Back and forth they went in different clapped-out old vans, until Dan had made his choice, assisted by Cristobal's sales patter. 'He is not the youngest car, but he is secure for you. I want you to be safety. This car will walk.'

The message may have been puzzling, but the mature silver van won Dan's heart: 'It's eleven years old, but cars don't deteriorate here, and it's diesel. Incredibly economical. He's only asking fifteen hundred pounds!' Plus another thousand or so to put things right at the garage. Yep. He bought it.

Michael helped with the acquisition and the paperwork, and drove the van to a petrol station, where we met him, to fill it with diesel. Dan had to prise his fingers off the (upside-down) steering-wheel, and we arranged to convene at the garage on the outskirts of Almogia, an hour's drive away. With unexpected cunning, Michael suggested that we put my old Citroën through a car wash – as a delaying tactic, I now realize.

'It's looking a bit tatty, frankly. You won't know it when it's clean.' Dan set off up the road, and Michael and I got to work with brushes and sprays. When I went to pay I admired its as-new gleaming navy. While I was at the till, Michael sprang cat-like into the driver's seat.

'Oh, Michael, I'll drive,' I said, as casually as I could. He is notorious for being one of the worst drivers on the Costa, and had recently written off the fifth car that we knew of. He stayed put.

'I'll do the driving, Michael,' I said, with what I hoped was nannyish authority. He did not move. I had the choice of wrestling him out of the car, keeping the keys and just sitting on the forecourt for the rest of the day, or letting him drive.

I gave him the keys, climbed into the passenger seat, still protesting feebly, and we shot out of the garage. Michael just *had* to drive, even if it was only me in my boring old ZX. 'But,' I reasoned with myself, 'he does know the road. He's been driving up and down it for five years, and I'm sitting next to him. He's going to be on his best behaviour, and a successful trip will boost his confidence. I'm sure that's all he needs. A bit of support.' As we sped through the intricacies of uptown Málaga I had a misplaced conviction that he wanted to be my champion.

Queen was our undoing. We had reached a tricky new road layout, when Michael instructed me to get his Discman from the back seat. With a sinking heart, feeling that he should concentrate on one thing at a time, I scrabbled over my shoulder and grabbed it by its earphone tentacles. He reached across for it, and drove smack into an oncoming car.

Of all the feelings I had in the ensuring minutes, stunned incredulity came top. How could he have done it? What critical brain synapse had misfired? What lapse in his circuitry had made him forget he was driving? We were not injured, but my poor car was. And we were stranded in the middle of a busy major road, my shiny blue and the skinhead victim's eau-de-Nil cars *in flagrante delicto*. Huge lorries trundled round us, adding an extra bass beat to the shock vibrations. A small crowd collected, as the skinhead pushed his vehicle off the road and we did likewise.

Michael steamed with embarrassment, dismissed the damage as minimal, and changed the front passenger wheel, getting rather dusty in the process. The door, the bonnet, the wing and the mirror were not susceptible to instant cure. We waited for the police by the roadside as the wind whistled in from the snow-capped Sierra Nevada. Michael looked very bothered, and when I asked him, he said: 'Yes, I am a bit uptight. Mum will never forgive me for this shirt.'

This *shirt*? What about my *car*?

Now I had to decide how we would get back to Almogia. Let Michael drive the bruised and battered

Citroën? Or forbid it utterly and for ever? Call me a fool, but best for his confidence, I reasoned, if he gets right back into that driver's seat. He can't possibly crash this time. And, tremulous reader, he did not. He drove so slowly that old crones with rickets skittered past like crisp packets on a breeze, and he beeped assiduously at every one of the forty-two hairpins. For the duration of the drive – an hour exactly – he held a conversation with himself on how to keep the episode from his mother and Dan. He decided that we should say we had had a slight bump on leaving the garage forecourt, though why fudging the location was going to exonerate the perpetrator was a mystery. However, since he was at the wheel when we drew up to the garage where Dan was waiting, his lengthy rehearsal of the acceptable evasion went for nothing. And Dan refused point-blank to lie to Barbara.

I had imagined Dan would be beside himself with worry – we had taken three hours to reach him – and expiring with thirst because we had all the money. I was right on both counts, he was hot and bothered, and not overpleased to see us. 'You shouldn't have let him drive,' was his short, cross response.

That afternoon we had to return to Málaga to sort the matter out with the police. It took ages, but to my surprise and relief we escaped unfined. I said that I could use a coffee. With his usual sensitivity to the prevailing mood, Michael directed us to a gigantic shopping mall on the other side of town. We sat in the middle of a giant bemuzaked dishwasher, and drank expensive pretentious coffee, while the clatter of cutlery and the soupy background music vied with live piano and violin.

Michael got chirpier. 'Well, I'm glad that's over. No

harm done, eh? Just a bit of a prang, nothing serious, luckily. Mmm, this cake is moreish. I think I'll have another.'

Dan, meanwhile, was lugubriously cataloguing my idiocies, and their likely cost. He pointed out the error of my ways, and predicted correctly that my insurance company would not pay. Michael by this time was singing. My car was wrecked and barely driveable, the other guy was demanding quite a bit of money to fix his, and *Michael was singing.*

I huffed off to the ladies', and stayed there for ages, cursing. Then I swept into the café, paid up, marched down to the car and commanded silence from both of them. Dan drove back as slowly as he could to keep me from panicking, and as fast as he could to deposit Michael. He tried to catch my hand and make peace, but I would cheerfully have pulled his arm off. Michael kept up a relentless storm of small-talk for as long as he could sustain it, then finally ebbed into silence.

Eventually Barbara and Chris very kindly paid for everything. God knows how much it came to. One thing *you* need to know is that while in England the driver is insured, in Spain it is the vehicle.

Apart from Michael, sleeping dogs, herds of goats and posses of wide women taking their constitutional, there are two kinds of road hazard in Spain. One is fast and scarlet and whizzes by at 200 k.p.h., fuelled on high-octane teenage testosterone. The other is the old grey Citroën van, meandering along in the middle of the road at a slow walking pace, stopping without warning, turning right or left as whim dictates, drifting slowly from one side of the road to the other, apparently driverless. When finally, exasperated beyond sense, you race past on a blind corner skimming the ditch, you will see a pocket Methuselah at the wheel, wrinkled and fissured, gazing at the world in innocent wonderment.

My most poignant memory from this time concerns an ancient white Renault van, creeping along the middle of the road into Villanueva. It had two flat tyres, the exhaust was dragging along the Tarmac apparently held on only with rust, and the back doors were open, leaving on the road a trail of miscellaneous household effects – dented kettles, chipped enamel pans, tin cups. When it finally puttered to a halt, I saw that an ancient man was at the wheel. I was troubled by this – had he ever driven before? Why was he driving now? Had he been thrown out by his wife and seized a dumped car before he remembered that he didn't know how to drive? I'll never know.

Michael's Sangría

This was Michael's lethal contribution to our party – it was brilliantly liberating at the time. Carpe diem, *we thought as we whizzed gracefully through the air. There was very little whizzing the following morning.*

fresh fruit: oranges, peaches, apricots, apples, mangoes
fruit juice to taste: orange, apple
2 bottles red wine
sugar to taste
1 bottle lemonade
1 small glass each of vodka, gin and Cointreau
2 small glasses red Martini
ice

Mix together in quantities that taste good and leave to blend for as long as you can bear. Drink.

12

DOG DAYS

By the time serious winter came, our new north-facing sitting room and kitchen had been more or less completed and the renovation of the old central core of the house, which would eventually be our bedroom and the bedrooms for the south house, had begun.

Drenched and sodden winter drifted eventually into chilly spring, and we continued to live, a day at a time, on our archaeological dig. One day a white car ploughed up through the mud and a neat, diminutive, glossy-haired woman stepped out, with an enormous man in police uniform sporting a fistful of guns. We wondered nervously what law we had broken. She announced herself and, after much blank incomprehension on our part, the penny dropped that she was not a senior magistrate but the local building inspector. Delicately in her kitten heels she picked her way over the puddles, buckets and cables, and inspected the sitting room, bathroom and kitchen, scribbling remarks in a folder as she did. We followed, awed by her gun-toting companion, and apprehensive lest she take against the whole thing and command us to demolish and start again. However, she nodded briskly, and simply pointed out that the roof was too high to be absolutely in the vernacular. She did not seem unduly bothered. I was impressed that in this land of mongrel buildings any reference to vernacular architecture featured at all. By some stroke of inadvertent foresight, I had bought land in an area designated to be of outstanding natural beauty, which precluded not only my stately pleasure domes, but those of all my visible neighbours – a fact for which I am continually grateful, when I see what residents of the Almogia administrative region can get away with just a hundred yards to the south.

The house was gradually taking shape. We had three civilized waterproof rooms in which to live, plus running water, and it was beginning to feel like home. Over the winter we had also made a handful of friends, one of the most congenial being Chris, Michael's father and husband of Barbara, who'd helped with the buying of the Casa Miranda.

Chris has a piquant sense of the ridiculous, and particularly enjoys having Dan as his fall-guy. He was delighted when Dan backed the car into his gatepost, and had a great time threatening solicitors' letters and exploring the full potential for embarrassment in his nasal Brummie accent. He also enjoyed it when Dan hurt his back and was unable to accompany me to London.

'Don't worry about him,' he said, winking at Dan. 'I know a lady "specialist" on the coast, who'll help him recover. He's in good hands with me, Miranda, don't you worry. I'll look after him.' And he did.

Several weeks later, during another of my London stints, I had rung Dan and left messages, getting increasingly worried when there was no reply. Finally, in desperation, I rang Chris and asked him to visit the house to make sure nothing had happened. He leaped into his car and drove across immediately. 'It's like the *Mary-Celeste* here,' he reported back. 'There's the remains of breakfast, but no sign of the man.' Breakfast a couple of days old, as it turned out. Dan had simply stayed an extra day with some friends near Gaucin, but it was a comfort to me that Chris was on the case, and worrying too.

He suffered from chronic asthma, but refused to make concessions to it: on a blazing hot summer day he would be out mowing his balding 'lawn', which simply raised a local dust-storm under his nose. Imaginative, humane, funny, he was a totally likeable man, and would do anything to be helpful.

There was, however, one glitch in our relationship with the Stallwoods: both Chris and Barbara suffered from Common British Beastophilia. They had five dogs and a pugnacious cat called Tom. Chris was unaccountably fond of Tom, and proud that he was an entire cat – which meant that he was permanently covered in bites and scratches and had a passion for spraying in innocent people's cars. We found this less than endearing, and the rich ammoniac smell in the van lasted for a week.

When a young man called Kiko found a sodden little kitten in the rain by the side of the road he naturally zipped it into his jacket and took it to Chris, knowing him to be a soft touch for any abandoned animal. Chris decided that a cat was what we needed and brought it to us. 'We can't keep it, because my Tom would tear it to bits. He's a beautiful little animal. Look.' He held the kitten aloft. 'He's taken a liking to you.'

He was a cute little black and white tom, suspiciously similar to Chris's own Tom, his charm somewhat diminished by the jade green snot he sneezed in copious strings all over anyone who picked him up. Unlike every other kitten since the beginning of time, he did not immediately streak to some inaccessible spot behind the fridge, shivering and mewling. On the contrary, he sat on everyone's knee, purring like a traction engine and gazing adoringly at his new family, insisting on the kind of intimacy that makes foul fishy breath and projectile sneezing unavoidable. He ate what he was given with gratitude, crapped delicately on Dan's magnificent rug and deposited crusty little strings of snot on clothes and furniture alike.

But he was *in*. Doris, who was staying at the time, had taken a liking to him, and so had Dan. Ted, who was also with us, limited his PDAs to trying to shut him into a shoebox. I realized, with very poor grace, that we now owned a cat.

We had not intended to have any animals at this

point – we thought we might have to go back to London at any moment to supervise the sale of the house, the final removal, my work, anything – but Chris was persuasive and promised to look after our kitten if we were away. We ended up keeping Kiko, named after his discoverer, and nursing him back to health – at which point he stopped being tiny and affectionate and became omnivorous, delinquent and vicious. Dan adored Kiko, but I was less enchanted: he paddled around on worktops, leaving muddy – or greasy, if his path happened to cross the frying-pan – pawprints and eating any food left out for more than a nanosecond. He also had a habit of unexpectedly biting any ankles or elbows within reach. He was especially fond of sitting on the chopping-board, which I couldn't help feeling was a bit insanitary. He was also the clumsiest animal I have ever come across: he knocked things in passing, or leaned against them if he suddenly needed to lick his toes, and had a penchant for walking across Dan's palette then leaving multicoloured pointillist paw-prints all over the kitchen, before licking the probably toxic paint off his pads. You could follow his progress aurally, as pans, bottles of wine, glasses and cameras crashed to the floor. He was the only cat I have met who would lie luxuriously on a windowsill, then roll over and plummet ten feet to the ground. The sound of him thudding off the kitchen worktops became normal background noise. He efficiently despatched the local cats and rodents, though.

Fine, we said. That's it, animal-wise. Not for Chris it wasn't. In early February we returned from a shopping expedition to find several increasingly desperate messages on our answering-machine, suggesting a proposition, but suspiciously vague as to what it was. We listened to all of the messages with interest, and imagined a party. Fun? Carlos Núñez at the Cervantes Theatre? At that moment, Chris knocked on the door. He came in, a little sheepishly, but was happy to have a glass of wine while he circumlocuted inventively. Finally: 'I've got a dog in the car. A boxer, pedigree probably. A beautiful thing. I'd keep her, but my dogs won't have it. They'd just make her life a misery. She was found wandering on the *campo*, been seen around for days getting thinner and thinner, but she's a lovely dog, well bred. Boxers are such good family dogs, and make very good guard dogs too. You really should have a guard dog here, way out in the *campo*.'

In unison, Dan and I both roared, '*No!*'

'Fine,' said Chris. 'I'll just finish this glass of wine, and then I'll take her to the top of El Torcal and leave her there. I feel terrible doing it, but if no-one wants her, I don't see any alternative. She'll probably last quite a while. She's strong, and she'll find food, scavenge round the bins, that kind of thing. She'll probably catch rabbits. She can run.' He stood up and looked out at the sheeting rain. 'On the other hand, she may not last in this weather. Perhaps it's best. She'll get pneumonia, and the end will come quickly. That's the best thing. Well, I'll be off. Thank you for the wine.' And he walked slowly towards the door.

Dan said nothing.

'Well,' I began, 'seeing as there's a monsoon, we'll keep her overnight until you find her a home. I don't want a dog, let alone one that looks as though she's just heard some *very* bad news. So just tonight, OK? You'll collect her tomorrow? Agreed?'

So into our lives came Minnie. Miserable little

Minnie, face like a doctor's waiting room, every rib and vertebra clearly defined, and covered with ticks. I was rather alarmed by her, and kept my distance. Dan got on with her from the moment they met, and spent her first evening with us sitting on the sofa happily picking off her ticks. I'd never kept a dog, although I'd often wanted to. Dogs don't go with London and an irregular life, but Dan had always had one. He knew what to do, and had an easy affection for them.

At this point we gave Chris a document requiring that in no circumstances, no matter how strong the provocation, would he bring us any animal ever again. We stood over him until he signed. But Chris was right; Minnie is a lovely dog, affectionate, dignified, playful and great company. A pure-bred boxer with a powerful sex-drive, she had probably got lost when out chasing rough trade. At first she used to run off, disappear for hours, in pursuit of the local *campo* dogs, but soon she was firmly wedged into our lives, sat by my side while I worked, and we took her everywhere with us. She was exemplary on outings, a proper little lady.

However, there came the day when, instructed to send my next article to the office via e-mail, I set off to Málaga with Dan and Minnie in tow. I had written my current feature on a laptop, put it onto a disk, and we were on a hunt for an Internet café. We found a likely place, shut Minnie into the van with a slit of open window, and negotiated the perils of the Net. We were going from the Stone Age to the microchip in one dizzying leap. To our stunned amazement we succeeded in sending the copy down the line. I bought some *cava* to celebrate while Dan went to collect the car.

When he drove up, he was whey-faced. 'Minnie's gone,' he said. Someone had let her out of the window, carefully shut it and gone off with her. A worse possibility that Dan suggested was that kids had let her out and she was running, freaked, around the city. I once saw a Great Dane, out for a walk with its owner, decide to dive into the rush-hour traffic on the M3 at Chiswick. Its face was a haunting image of pain, shock and incomprehension as it bounced from one car to another unable to get out of the maelstrom. It might have come through unharmed as the traffic slowed down to a standstill, but it was a heartbreaking sight. It is burned on my retina, and it was all too easy to picture Minnie suffering the same fate.

We went home utterly miserable. I was unprepared for the surge of grief that whacked me sideways. I spent two days in tears, picturing Minnie's intelligent quizzical face, hearing the timpani of her claws as she walked across the terracotta, missing the quite affectionate workmate who habitually sat by my side. She left an astonishingly huge hole in our lives.

David and Anne, who own the kennels where Minnie had once stayed, suggested that I go to the pound. 'Go soon,' they said. 'They don't keep the dogs long. And they'll probably use a strong dog like Minnie for fighting. It's not legal, but Spaniards love dog-fighting and the pound supplies the dogs.' This was a new and terrible image to try not to picture.

'She's so trusting,' I sobbed. Dan submitted to a trip to the pound, where there was a desperate collection of dogs, bitches with puppies, an abandoned boxer with lopped ears, but no Minnie. It's a heartless thing to say, but the departures of past boyfriends did not grieve me half as much as the loss of Minnie.

But I am terribly persistent. I never give up. I made a brave foray into the Spanish tongue, and wrote a notice to place in the Málaga newspaper, *Sur*. Dan thought I was insane. 'The chances of finding her are nil,' he assured me. 'She's gone. The sooner you accept that, the sooner you'll get over it.' Not me. I found a photo of Minnie, and offered a ridiculously huge reward. My notice was inflammatory, along the lines of 'Some bastard stole my beautiful dog. If you come across the miscreant, savage him. Bring my dog back and collect this reward.' The nice lady at *Sur* was very polite, and pointed out that if I left the notice as it was no dognapper was likely to come forward. She reworded it more politely, and it went into that week's edition on the Friday.

I now had a problem: if anyone answered the ad, my Spanish was way too hopeless for me to understand what they said. Or even to make myself understood. And if anyone left a message in Spanish on the answering-machine it would be incomprehensible to me. I sat by the phone braced for battle, with a dictionary at my side and pure adrenaline coursing in my veins. The phone rang. Twice. The first time it was a sweet girl who worked with a Málaga vet and spoke some English. 'I know he is not your dog, but I see your ad. We have this boxer dog. He is found in a car – he has been there for four days, locked in without food or water. He is a lovely dog, beautiful head and body, but the vet cannot keep him. If you do not want him, we have to take him to the pound.' I explained that we would rather find our own dog, to which we had become very attached, but if we did not track down Minnie, I would ring her the next day and come and have a look at the other boxer.

The phone rang again. It was the phone call I had prayed for and dreaded. A young man, Jesus, speaking very fast, bored and irritated by my inability to understand him, telling me, I thought, that a dog like Minnie had been found somewhere. I understood him to ask if she had any distinguishing characteristics. I tried to say that she had coin-sized freckles on her chest. There was a silence. Then he asked brusquely did I not know *anyone* who spoke Spanish? Of course, I thought, Chris. Chris can help us.

The young man rang Chris, they arranged a pick-up point and time, and Dan found himself with a wad of pesetas, driving to a lonely lay-by near the motorway. He was convinced he was going to be mugged and left for dead. I stayed at home to man the phone in case this was not our dog.

When Dan reached the lay-by, a dog was trying to jump out of the back of Jesus's car, and it was Minnie. She bounced up to Dan, who paid the ransom without violence taking place, and drove jubilantly back to me. It was a bit of a miracle. She was unharmed, and thrilled to be home. For a few days she displayed a curious method of eating, whereby she tried to turn over her food bowl, nosing it from underneath – a mystery we did not solve.

The following day we went shopping in Málaga, with Minnie in the back of the van. I knew that the aircraft hangar of a supermarket was next to the vet, and I had been so stricken by the story of the noble abandoned boxer that I persuaded Dan to come and have a look at it. We waited in the echoing marble vestibule while the vet fetched the dog. He returned with a Hammer Films hound – a *big* boxer, with a barrel chest and neck as thick as its head, standing on its hind legs as it pulled and choked on its lead, strings of drool and froth hanging from its mouth. It was skeletally thin, and in this position its eyes bulged so that the whites were visible, and beneath was a huge hippo mouth with flappy black dewlaps and many big teeth. If I ever saw a rabid infant-eater this was it. 'Aah,' said Dan. '*Cute*. We'll take him.'

The journey home, with two mutually suspicious dogs in the back of Dan's van, was interesting. As soon as our new acquisition entered the house he did two things that confirmed *my* suspicions: he peed on the leg of the table, and tried to mate with Kiko. He and Minnie did not get on *at all*. They were both jealous and needy, and perennially having tiffs. I had never intended to have animals in Spain, and now we had a fractious family of three warring beasts who were unpredictable and badly behaved. I felt as though I had unwittingly recreated the very situation I was trying to escape.

But eventually the dogs settled down and became inseparable, though Oscar always fancied Kiko more than Minnie. I'll never know how Dan perceived the noble dog behind the fangs, but Oscar *is* noble, and disarmingly good-natured. He seduces confirmed dog-haters in droves, and Dan's mother and aunt, who loathe dogs, always write to him. His only fault is a little problem in the wind department. Now, though, in the snuffling and occasionally pongy cosiness of our animal-rescue home, we were adamant that our family was complete.

13

YOU'VE GOT E-MAIL. NOT

Because I longed to communicate with my boys, who were unfamiliar with phone use and had no conception of how letters work, and because being a techno-klutz had become a hanging offence at work, I bought a pocket computer that pretended that it could e-mail anyone, anywhere. For ages I had slogged back and forth with my old Mac Powerbook, which was portable if you happen to be into weights but reactivated my back trauma every trip.

My new baby computer had a mind of its own and, as I discovered having spent hours trying to get it to agree to tackle e-mail, a glitch with its call-up. I did not realize then that e-mail would be beyond us anyway, glitch or no glitch, until Telefonica's solitary old installation man had dug hundreds of holes single-handed for the telephone posts, to enable us – maybe – to get a land-line instead of our moody and incompetent radio phone. For the time being I still had to ring my boys, paying megapesetas to listen to football on their respective televisions while they answered my questions in distracted grunts, interspersed with roars if a goal was scored.

Spigs was working for my sister Jocasta, so his life, if rackety, was at least solvent. Leo, as far as I could ascertain, was living on air, but he made it a matter of pride never to ask for money. Well, hardly ever.

The radio phone had a variety of maddening tricks. To dial anyone in England required eighteen digits, and even if you were concentrating very hard and there was no dog being sick on the carpet or trying to mate with the cat, there was a strong potential for getting one digit wrong. Sometimes you dialled it perfectly and, on a whim, Telefonica put you through to a bun shop in Peebles; or you got a recorded message delivered by a smug Spanish woman whom I didn't understand and whom I learned to hate; or on your third attempt you succeeded in dialling Mastercard and got the English torture where you keyed in choices over and over again with lashings of 'Greensleeves' while you were held in an endless queue, hoping to speak to a real, living person before you died. And if there was rain or wind, the phone simply expired along with everything else electrical. The combination of radio telephone and Baby Glitch entailed several days of exasperation, while I tried to get to grips with a technology centuries beyond me. Rather intelligently, I thought, I bought us a pair of mobile phones for emergencies, which rarely got a signal at the house and, if they did, it was because you happened to be standing on a ladder up by the swimming-pool at the time.

Then the deputy editor said that copy *had* to be e-mailed, so my computer and I spent about seven hours on the phone going through the procedure with a patient technician in France. I attempted to hook up with a leading Internet provider. For some reason if you live in Spain they operate from France, so this complicated discussion took place in Franglais. I can also tell you that if you have the misfortune to find yourself attached to their French company, there is no way that they'll let you go. The moral is: *never* allow them to get their hands on a direct-debit mandate, unless you know that you're going to be able to get the thing to function and use it constantly. When eventually, stumped and frustrated by my inability to get e-mail to work, I tried to disengage myself from this provider, I was given the telephone number of their accounts department by my credit-card company. I rang it, and was astonished to find myself on the receiving end of Sexy Sarah, doing a lot of breathily described auto-erotic gymnastics. The second number I was given connected me to the personnel department of a bank in Ohio. When I finally got through to the company, I found myself speaking to a Frenchman who refused me a refund on the grounds that I had not tried to sever the relationship earlier. A second Internet provider, to which I was paying a monthly fee, agreed to everything and did nothing, while a third could not be contacted other than by e-mail, so if your problem was an inability to get e-mail to work, you were screwed. None of them believed in giving refunds for services unrendered, I discovered. At the beginning, in desperation, I had attached myself to all three, hoping that just one might work. Because I am a complete fool I continued to pay them all for a year or so. Sensible people have no truck with direct debits.

However, with insane persistence, I tried to get e-mail to work and embarrassed myself terribly by attempting to apply for a job with the National Trust.

They wanted an editor for their magazine, and it sounded wonderful. I had pages of ideas, and was excited by the potential: the National Trust has access to such riches, such fascinating people and stories, such beautiful places and objects. It sounded like career heaven. And it had been rumoured that the job was mine, if I wanted it. I did, I did. I knew I would have a hard time persuading them that I could do it successfully part-time from Spain, but I was convinced that I could. And it would rescue me and my editor from our arranged marriage, which was becoming more unsatisfactory with every passing month.

There was one tiny problem. The National Trust wanted evidence of computer skills, and suggested that candidates send their CV by e-mail. I could probably have had it engraved on a gold ingot and carried by a team of Olympic sprinters for less than what the ill-fated experiment cost.

I wrote out my CV. This bit was fine, and I thought pretty impressive: sort of cool yet deeply enthusiastic, witty and yet serious, well educated about Spode and Palladio but wearing it lightly. Then I had my seven-hour confabulation with the helpful Monsieur ISP in France, the upshot being that he could not help me, and that my only hope was to take the computer to one of the Internet assistance companies on the coast and get them to e-mail my job application. My bijou computerette had no truck with floppy disks, so an Internet café would not suffice.

Poor Dan. Here I have to make an admission that will confirm my place in hell. The next day was the final day for applications. It was also his fiftieth birthday. Not only were there no festivities, no *This Is Your Life* surprise party, no cake, no romantic dinner for two and no present, but I blackmailed him into spending the entire day with me at Mercury Internet, in a poky little office on a thundering motorway, trying to send my sodding e-mail.

After countless hours, sitting next to Jens from Denmark and Yvette from Venezuela while their computers and my computer bleeped matily, Jens finally said that, yes, Warren at the National Trust would have received my CV, and everything was fine. He relieved me of £100, and Dan and I went home, exhausted and unfestive. His half-century had been easily the dullest day of his life, and we were too corroded by boredom to do anything more celebratory than watch *The Simpsons* and bicker. Well, I thought, at least I've sent in my application for the editorship of the National Trust mag.

To my surprise I heard nothing from the National Trust. A couple of weeks later, however, I got a phone call from a lady working at the Royal Horticultural Society at Wisley, saying that, yes, she was also very impressed by my CV, but what job was I applying for? As far as she knew, they didn't have any vacancies.

So the magazine was stuck with me and vice versa. The deputy editor stepped up her e-mail campaign, and I still had hopes that somewhere in the world there was a system that would enable me to pretend to be conversant with the technology that modern babies master before they are weaned.

But on the computer front there was worse to come. A few weeks later I went to England for my week of work, to do an interview for a feature about a garden in Devon full of strange Antipodean plants. My feature was taped and ready to transcribe on my return to Spain where I had the weekend to write it on my old

Mac Powerbook and get it to the office somehow. I was staying in Brighton, and I woke up on the Friday of my flight two and a half hours late. Good start. There was no time to pack, certainly no time to buy the expats' essentials – Earl Grey tea, Marmite, bayonet bulbs, fizzy vitamin C. I had to sprint, sweating, up the steep hill to the station dragging my bag. I had missed the train that would have got me to Gatwick two hours in advance of the flight, but I arrived, steaming, at the station with two minutes to spare before the next. Brilliant, I thought, I'll just have less time to hang about at Gatwick being sprayed by brown-lipped women with perfume distilled from tom-cat armpits.

This was before I encountered Miss Bureaucracy, Connex South Central. 'No,' she said. 'You certainly cannot buy a ticket on the train.'

'I'll take my chance,' I replied.

She interposed her tightly upholstered body between me and the platform. 'If you get on that train without a ticket, you will have to go to court.' She implied that a lengthy stint in a high-security prison would follow. She primped her navy blue hat, and pointed with her navy blue glove at a ticket office with a snaking queue of dim question-askers all wanting to know about daft connections, and counting out piles of pennies with which to pay.

'Bollocks,' I'm afraid I said. 'Buy a ticket and miss my plane? I'll go to court.' I sped from her grasp and onto the train with a couple of seconds to spare.

For the duration of the train ride – and, yes, it was perfectly OK to buy a ticket on the train – I felt triumphantly vindicated. But this was before I came up against one of the Witches of Gatwick, Miss Bureaucracy, Britannia Airways.

Sensibly, I thought, I had packed just a haversack with essentials – like my Powerbook and taped interview – intending to take it on board as hand luggage. As I approached the head of the check-in queue I realized – more sweating – that I did not have my passport. I could picture it in the back compartment of the bumbag I had jettisoned as too small for my needs, still sitting on a chest of drawers at Brighton. I was already late – there was no time to go back and collect it before my flight. The man in front moved on, and I found myself face to face with a younger version of Delia Smith, quite unmoved by my extreme pallor and clammy fingers. I made one final desperate search through my bag and there it was. I had found it! Feeling as though I were suddenly addressing a large audience and had forgotten to put my clothes on, I thought, Thank God, that crisis is over.

And on to the next. Delia's scrubbed face looked bored and impatient. 'Put your backpack on the weighing machine,' she directed, while her face said, 'You addle-headed old bag.' It was then that I noticed a small sign that read: 'Only 5 kilos of luggage per person allowed in the cabin.' I had never come across hand-luggage weight restrictions before.

'If I had known, I would have packed differently,' I told Ms Smith.

Bored, uninterested.

'No other airline has imposed weight restrictions on me for hand luggage.'

Bored, irritated.

'My backpack contains my laptop, which is fragile and essential for my work.'

Very bored indeed, Ms Smith slapped three 'Fragile' stickers on the bag. 'It's overweight,' she snapped.

'You have to put it in the hold.' And waited for me to dematerialize.

'I can't trust my laptop to the hold. I'm a journalist and can't work without it.'

Very, very bored, and just a little exasperated she spoke very slowly and quite loudly: 'The rules are that you have to put it in the hold. You can take it with you, and give it to Special Handling when you get on the plane.' Her face said, 'Now fuck off, you tiresome old fool.'

Like a tiresome old fool, I did as I was told and entrusted my doughty Mac Powerbook to Special Handling, expecting never to see it again.

The journey was an adventure. Joanna Lumley told us in a recorded message that Britannia were giving us a wonderful time, with delicious food and glorious entertainment. They wanted to make sure that the flight was a real fun part of our holiday. Well, what do you think? Not only did this wish fail to come true, but when Tim, our captain, circled for half an hour in a completely black sky 5,500 metres above Málaga, at 200 miles per hour and an outside temperature of –9 degrees, fun was a low priority. Survival was the thing.

'Perfectly normal,' Tim announced. 'There's nothing to worry about. We're just waiting for a storm to blow over. We've still got seven tons of fuel.' How long does that last? I wondered. Hours? Minutes? Oh, God, I thought, my will. Everything is still given over to the boys and *Edward*. Dan won't get a bean. Perhaps I should write out a last will and testament and pin it to my body. No sooner had I thought of this than I was foiled by the practicalities: I had no paper, no pen and no pin – they were all in my backpack in the hold.

We landed to a nervous ripple of applause, and I

raced through to Baggage Reclaim. To my relief and surprise, my bag was there and still contained all I had stuffed into it, with my Mac Powerbook looking unbashed. I rushed through to meet Dan, who was bound to be beside himself with worry at our delay, only to find that he was not there at all.

Oh, God, I thought, he's crashed in the storm. He's fallen into a ravine. I kept being hustled by men who wanted me to hire cars from them, and was getting just a little hysterical when Dan showed up, none the worse for the disasters I had envisaged, delayed by shopping and getting lost. Instead of a rapturous reunion, we were quite huffy, both having been to hell and back and requiring sympathy, not competitive complaint. We drove back silently along the hairpins in the tar-black night. Because the rain had dissolved our track, the van could not make it to the house and we had to plod the last hundred yards in pitch dark, icy trickles down the back of our necks, wading through ankle-deep mud, carrying my contentious possessions. The electricity was not working, and the house was freezing. Not for the first time I felt we had been abandoned by the twentieth century, and cast back on Stone Age resources.

However, I had no time for trivialities: I had the Antipodean feature to write for the following Monday. Electricity had been restored overnight so, bright and early the next day, Saturday, I sat down at my laptop and typed 'FgGhXPPqkshfsFDgh'. This didn't seem right, so I tried again. 'MDSdshErjr3ovxzIDN'. Hmm. A light sweat was followed by dry throat and waves of panic. At this parlous point in my career I could not even think of faxing hand-written copy to the office. I had a wild hope that my insurance would cover my

machine, and that I would be able to hire or buy another that very day. Am I mad or what? Clause 17 (writ *very* small) absolved my mandatory insurers from responsibility for fragile or valuable goods in transit. Moral: only travel with worthless crap.

I made desperate multiple phone calls as precious minutes ebbed fast. Someone advised lodging a complaint with Flight-Line International from whom the tickets had come, which entailed returning to Málaga airport. Flight-Line turned out to be Thomson's, who turned out to be Britannia, who turned out to be Iberia. All this took a while and was conducted in my toddler's Spanish. I left with a claim form in duplicate and the name of a real person to badger and nag. Much good it did me. By the time their letter of self-absolution arrived I was deep in some other crisis and did not have time to make and write the necessary 5,000 phone calls and letters to get their paltry compensation.

Slithering home that night, late and tired, through the rain and mud, I was very cast down. Saturday had gone. I had no word-processor, not even a typewriter, and I had to own up to Kitty on Monday. What was I going to do?

I rang Clive, of course. He *walked* the mile from his place to ours, through the rain with a hundredweight of clay on each foot, carrying a nominally portable laptop wrapped in plastic. My hero! I did the article, put it onto disk, sent it from an Internet café in Málaga, and the management of the magazine never knew how close they were to being able to give me my P45.

It was early February, my boys seemed to have disappeared from the planet, but Clive was staying at his *finca*. I was grumbling that – being perennially and desperately short of cash – the only solution to my computer crisis seemed to be a computer-buying trip to Gibraltar, which I recalled as a cheapo gadget Paradise. Ten years back I had been able to buy a typewriter – a lovely, simple little manual typewriter – for a laughably small sum when I had been there with my mother. Since technology had moved on since then, I imagined hordes of slick, highly qualified computers for the price of a Sony Walkman. To my relief Clive offered to come with us, since he knows all about computers. He had even taken his motherboard to pieces and put it together again. Thrilled that he was going to accompany us, able to ask sensible questions and understand the answers, I found details of a wonderful fish restaurant at La Linea, the nearest town to

Gibraltar on the Spanish mainland, and suggested that we take him to lunch there as a thank-you.

We set off early on a flawless winter day. Because it was out of season the roads were almost empty, and we stopped for breakfast at a café with a view of the silky Mediterranean framed by handsome palm trees, and the exotic gardens of villains' villas by the shore. Gibraltar is a long drive from Almogia, and our breakfast stop was the last good bit. Thereafter we traversed an endless wasteland of open-cast mining, landfill sites, oil refineries and cranes. And the nearer we got to our goal, the uglier the scenery and the stranger the weather became. A cold wind blew up, grey clouds scudded across the sun, and we wished that we'd worn more appropriate winter clothing.

La Linea turned out to be the most depressing place on earth. Under a grey sky it had all the charm of a rundown Moscow suburb combined with an industrial-estate specializing in broken road-mending equipment. Of the vaunted restaurant there was no sign. We queued to cross the border, which also entailed the adventure of crossing the airport runway. They are the same narrow stretch of Tarmac, and I made a mental note never to fly via Gibraltar. To add to the general bleakness we discovered that Gibraltar has its own little microclimate – a thick grey doughnut of cloud crowns the Rock, and drizzles reassuringly to remind you that this is, indeed, a little bit of England.

Gibraltar is a curious mixture. Quaint Georgian military buildings – the sort that Jane Austen might have visited for an officers' ball – nestle up against pylons, kitsch and town-planning of stunning ugliness. The whole place would fit into Harrods. Within about ten minutes we had established that there were two computers on Gibraltar: both were being repaired and already had owners. Clive bought about 2,000 packets of PG Tips and several bottles of the renowned Taj Mahal whisky. No? I hadn't either.

Well, we thought, at least we can find somewhere nice for lunch. Wrong. We trailed around those strange little Georgian streets where everything was resolutely closed, and finally shuffled back to the main square and a Watney's pub.

'Things can't get worse than this. We'll sit in this little bit of sun and have a good old steak and kidney pudding. That'll cheer us up,' I said gamely, finding us a table in a sheltered corner of the square with a view of the sea, feeling horribly responsible for the entire débâcle. It started to rain in earnest and the place began to look like Ramsgate on a summer afternoon. The steak and kidney pudding was finished, so we ate little leather pizzas and looked forward to getting home.

Spain and Gibraltar may be physically connected, but each pretends that the other does not exist. There are very few signposts to Gibraltar on the mainland, and the border police made us queue in the rain for a couple of hours before regretfully letting us through. We'd been lucky. The following day they closed the border altogether on account of a fishing dispute.

I did eventually get a computer – which works, consents to use floppy disks, and that I can carry without a team of muscled bearers – from a Fablon cathedral of a computer warehouse in the desert by the M4. They saw me coming before I was even a speck on the horizon. What happened was that as I drove I was listening to a tape of Isabella Rossellini reading Kuki Gallmann's *I Dreamed of Africa,* and as I drew up at the warehouse, her son had just died from snakebite. I sat in the car and wept for about ten minutes, until someone tapped on the window and asked if I was all right. Awash in mascara, I answered indignantly, 'Of course.' I put on my shades – it was still winter and dark at three – and strode into the warehouse where I looked at various laptops in a blurred kind of way, snivelling. Then I bought the most expensive and overtalented one that Darren, the salesman, wanted to shift. It's not often that a snuffling panda in Ray-Bans gets washed up in a computer warehouse on a wet winter's afternoon begging to be exploited. It was bad to spend twice my budget, but not insane. In retrospect what appalled me was that Darren had managed to sell me insurance that cost a further £500.

But my machine has behaved impeccably, to the extent that whenever I drop it, or pour tea into it, it grumbles a bit then proceeds to mend itself. It is always covered in dust and sometimes bird droppings. Kiko makes a point of using it as a stepping-stone, typing runic messages across the keyboard on the way to investigating any food about the place. I had a minor excitement when a small computer beetle wriggled in behind the screen. It was there for quite a while, but has since moved on.

When you buy a house in Spain, water, electricity and a phone may or may not be connected. If they are not, you will be in for a long wait and a huge bill, depending on how far the workmen have to travel. We had been fortunate with the first two. We also had a phone of sorts and I now had a working computer.

However, we still can't do e-mail, and have no idea why people rave about it. I'm quite happy living in the Stone Age, I have since decided, and am always amazed at how tetchy people get when I suggest writing a nice old-fashioned letter.

14

RESURRECTION BLUES

Under the fierce perfectionism of our best builder, Antonio, who entered our lives that spring, the house continued to grow patchily whenever any money came our way. As it slowly became something like a normal dwelling, mysterious bureaucratic imperatives reached us via Barbara.

During one such ordeal, I discovered that it was not entirely true that Oscar's only tumescent moments were aroused by Kiko: he got his lipstick out, just once, for Minnie. I had dropped Dan at the airport – he was off to visit his parents – called in at Barbara's office on my way home and was told to go and get some documents signed and witnessed in a lawyer's office back in Málaga. I've no idea what they were, but Barbara gave me specific instructions as to which office, at what time, with what papers. I went home for the papers, then piled Oscar and Minnie into the van. This was unusual in itself: I'm not sure why I thought they'd be a sparkling addition to this trip – moral support, I expect. I drove down to Málaga with my usual insane caution, rehearsing every kind of disaster as I crept along – van breakdown, getting lost, infringing some obscure traffic regulation and being publicly humiliated and fined, finding nowhere to park, van towed away and being unable to retrieve it because of my infant-school Spanish. I was like that then.

However, I found the street with suspicious ease, and a parking place. Looking back, I can't believe the weighty paranoia I felt. I remember being as gloomy and apprehensive that afternoon as if I had been told I had two months to live. I gathered up all the papers (meaning all that I owned – I had already discovered that the absolutely vital bit of paper is always the one that seemed too irrelevant to bother with), locked the van (as if anyone sane enough to drive would want it), and wound myself into a barley-sugar twist, trying to put leads on the dogs. I managed all that without resorting to anything too embarrassing in the way of sobbing or collapsing on the pavement. I suggested to the dogs that they might like to perform a bodily function, and hung about shiftily among the palm trees of the Alameda Principal for a while, hoping. They airily ignored me.

Too bad. The next thing was to find the office. Again, that was easy. But the entrance was unnervingly smart, in a tall, carefully restored old building right on the Alameda Principal, overlooking the port. Think Bond Street or Madison Avenue. I felt a sharp twinge of regret that I had chosen the Cruft's outfit in preference to something professional, but it was too late now to impersonate a normal adult. With an indigestible glob of apprehension in my throat I tightened the leads as we surged onto the parquet floor and started the long climb up the slithery marble stairs to the penthouse. The dogs refused the lift. Many old couples were tottering down those stairs, and every single one uttered a little shriek and pressed itself in terror against the wall as I passed with my slavering beasts. Six floors, maybe ten couples.

We arrived at the lawyer's reception area, and I tried to convey the reason for my visit to the manicured and coiffed girl, who could not take her eyes from my drooling charges. She motioned us to sit, which I obediently did. Oscar and Minnie, however, had aerobic sniffing in mind, and that ten-minute wait seemed to last about three years.

It was nothing compared to the ignominy that followed. Our time came, and we were called to the advocatory presence in the penthouse. Under other, less canine-rich circumstances, I would have been thrilled to find myself in this expensive eyrie, with its acres of slippery parquet, its vast potted palms, its grandly architected gallery spaces, its slick slabs of unsullied glass where your average worker would have a coffee-spotted and overflowing Ikea desk. That day, to be there was an excruciating penance for some long-forgotten crime. On spotting the palms, it occurred to Oscar that he did, after all, need a pee. Seven lawyers put down their pens, and watched the brief battle that ensued. The astounded hush that greeted our arrival amplified my desperate attempt to dissuade him from lifting his leg against the towering Kentia, and drew attention to the expensive scraping of reluctant claws on parquet. I dragged both dogs to one of the lawyers, who indicated that our man was up in the gallery. With a sense of unutterable depression I looked up at a flight of ten floating open boards, leading to a smooth young man sitting at another slab of glass in another palm glade.

I could not leave the dogs down, and they had no intention of going up. I had practically to carry them (Oscar weighed 32 kilos, Minnie 24), and we landed in a sweating heap on the proscenium. Seven pairs of eyes observed every detail of the ensuing drama. First, I wound the leads round my chair leg, as far away from the palms as I could manage. Before I could launch into the reason for our presence, Oscar decided to check out the view over the edge of the gallery, and my chair slid perilously stairwards. Minnie was more intrigued by the chrome trestles upon which rested the two-inch-thick glass slab, and wound herself in a loose knot round the nearest. Not good, but in a brief moment of stasis, I plunged into my tiny Spanish repertoire, and threw my papers onto the desk. Smooth lawyer began a thorough reading, following the text unspeakably slowly with his scrubbed finger. At this point a distant dog barked, or maybe someone scraped a chair or cleared their throat, whatever. Oscar and Minnie sprang to attention, and lunged for the stairs. As Minnie pulled, the trestle jerked beneath a

hundredweight of glass. I dared not rise from my seat because my heft on the chair was the only thing preventing complete disaster. Smooth lawyer took his time to stand, languidly, and untangle Minnie, set his desk straight, and continue with his reading. The icing on the cake was the panic-sweat that was now trickling down my back to make the usual fetching incontinence patch at the base of my spine.

He was on to page two, just another three to go. He asked me several questions, to which the reply was always the same, '*No comprendo*', at which he sighed with irritation, slowly tracing the next sentence with his finger.

Meanwhile I unhooked Minnie, untangled her lead, which she had wound round my chair leg, reattached her, reined in Oscar, and achieved a peaceful hiatus, with both dogs held very tight side by side under my feet. They relaxed momentarily with a fusillade of *pfffts*: boxers are notorious farters. Smooth lawyer pressed his soap-scented hand to his nose, until he was forced to remove it to gasp for a signature. I had to stand up for this, at which both dogs also stood and

pressed forward under his desk, sniffing his nethers with some curiosity. I asked if he had a dog, to which he replied, no, he did not like dogs. Whether it was in response to this provocative statement or as a result of nerves and confusion I do not know, but it was at this moment, clearly visible beneath the viewing panel upon which lay my papers, that Oscar suddenly realized what a sexy beast his companion was, and attempted to mount her with a long and fluorescently pink erection. There is nothing quite as rude as a dog's erection. Minnie was not up for a shag, and a short argument took place beneath the glass.

I signed those papers quickly, heedless as to whether I was signing over all my worldly goods to the smooth lawyer, threw money at him, and dragged my dogs out of that penthouse faster than a Blues Brothers' car chase.

Over the winter and spring, as the rain pounded the cracked red earth transforming it into sticky goo, Dan and I began to colonize the outdoors. In March, the rocks were still dotted with sky blue periwinkle and helianthemum in white and pale magenta, the palette enriched by purple and pink *Echium lycopsis*, elegant wild shocking-pink gladioli, mauve irises, violet sweet peas and pink phlomis. The verges couldn't have looked better if you'd planted them.

We planted cypresses on the west bank, interspersed with olive trees, in the hope of filtering the wind's force, along with ten palms, though opinion is divided as to whether these will grow up to become tall, stately trees, or just grow outwards into the spiky, tufty, ubiquitous bushes that grow among the rocks and are ignored by the browsing goats. I also wanted the bank to have bougainvillea clambering up it in the most vulgar shades of orange and magenta I could find, and oleanders curving along its contours to disguise the remains of occupation by the builders – a heavy mulch of plastic bottles and tuna tins.

Dan made planting terraces with dry-stone walls down the west slope. Among the trees I optimistically put little cuttings of the daisies that grow wild on the hills, purple tasselled iochroma donated to us by Barbara, lavender, and fragrant yellow-flowered *Coronilla glauca.* I don't like yellow flowers, but these smelt so good and, above all, they had such a determination to survive that their colour was forgiven. I was hoping that the plants would follow the general pattern: go into the ground as vulnerable tiny tufts, moot survival for a year, and then turn into billowing giants the following spring.

The really weird thing about the soil was that twigs, cuttings, sticks all rooted. When a dog sat on my dipladenia, or crashed through my jasmine, I just snarled a bit and poked the broken vestiges of plant back into the ground. Echium, oleander, pelargoniums, marguerites, roses and lavender rooted eagerly; pinks, rosemary and carnations got round to it eventually, while the *transparente,* which I had been misled into thinking that any child could propagate, turned into crisp brown twigs, incurring a flurry of Spanish jabbering from Antonio, our foreman, and a bout of vindictive slashing with his knife. Unfortunately that spring I stuck about a hundred *transparente* twigs into the ground in the hope of growing a dense dark evergreen forest, with the result that large tracts of the land looked like a sorry and eccentric plant graveyard. But I decided to leave them there – you never know, they may just be biding their time. It's all part of my policy to stuff every inch of soil with anything that comes to hand, hoping to depress and outnumber the weeds into submission.

That spring I felt like a New York chief of police when I donned my boots and clumpy gardening gloves. Because I was planning a life-or-death campaign to defeat the forces of evil. The weeds were unscrupulous crack-dealers, cunning, ruthless, terrorizing innocent seedlings, and equipped with state-of-the-art advantages. They moved fast in thuggish gangs, adapted with frightening success, seeded themselves, layered themselves and took over an area with horrific speed. They feigned dormancy for months then burst into invincible life like the Alien. They were especially adept at settling in tiny cracks in masonry or tiling, and sneakily growing a supersonic root that shifted concrete and was completely ineradicable. I did battle sporadically, using a scythe on the outer perimeter and a fork for more delicate skirmishes closer to the house, but the ground was baked so hard that Spigs broke the unbreakable Wilkinson Sword stainless-steel fork, which my sister Judy had given me, during a particularly hazardous raid on a psychopathic thistle.

The soil here was surprisingly fertile, having been nurtured by Señor Arrabal for ten years or so, but it was dense clay, unshiftably heavy and solid when rain-sodden in winter, and drifting powder in the summer drought. Here, we go from March to October without a spot of rain. At first it came as a real shock to me that the landscape I knew from summer photos and visits – the croissant-coloured baked earth with no vestige of green – was replaced in winter by lush thick grass, a metre high. This grass, and the cussedly vigorous weeds with roots like rope, grow high and solid in a week. I am not exaggerating. In April Dan and I took a week-long trip to Marrakech with our friend Maggie Perry while she bought a *riad*. Before we left it had rained and the sun had dried out the surface so the earth was not of its usual cement hardness. I thought I'd just clear the pathetic little pocket of planting we called 'Garden'. I pulled up all the weeds, scrabbled the soil about a bit in the hope that this would turn it into a rich, friable loam, and waved a fond goodbye to the little trees and shrubs I had liberated from their too amorous wild neighbours.

A week later, when we returned, there was no sign of my tenderly nurtured plants, just a high, solid island of grass, mallows, some unpleasant thing that smells like wet wellington boots, and armed and aggressive thistles. Finding the remains of my nepeta, philadelphus and delicate perennial toadflax, whose seeds I'd bought on the island of Jura, was not easy. The local weeds know they have only a short time to race to seedhood.

For almost three years we could not plant at all, because of the incursions of JCBs, wheelbarrows, cement and rubble. I had things in pots, tiny sweet seedlings and cuttings that I crooned over, but Dan invariably forgot to water them when I went back to England, and I would return to find my lovingly planted jasmine and *dama de noche* looking like whiskery knitting needles. Sometimes, on fluffing up and watering their baked soil in the hope of reviving them, I would find a snoozing toad buried in the compost.

Dan made a compost bin from offcuts of wood and

wire netting, and after some experimentation we put it in the shade behind the west terrace below the kitchen window. It sat beneath the plum tree, the site of Dan's forced entry, conveniently catching the excess plum harvest along with everything else vegetable and just got on with the business of composting. We had an unexpected success with it – compost has always turned into rank sludge before in my experience – but this was the proper fudge brownie, which we slathered in a generous mulch on all the trough beds. The plants loved it and grew enthusiastically. The only disadvantage was that quantities of unexpected tomatoes, avocados and cherimoyas also sprouted from it.

The soil here is quite different from any I have met before. When it rains it turns into mud so dense and sticky that you can only take five paces before your feet are too heavy to move and you keel over. In summer it cracks into fissures and chasms, and dissolves into cocoa. As any garden person will tell you, this is pure clay, could be made thriftily into pots, and needs lots of organic matter to be dug in. Dan collects horse manure from nice Paco in the village (extra nice, since he refers to me as Dan's young and beautiful wife – *yes*, he may be blind), and tends then to leave it strewn about the garden in its orange plastic sacks. I am in a quandary as to what constitutes 'well rotted', but eventually that, too, will add its bit to the clay.

I felt passionately about the bit of land immediately surrounding the house. These geometric white houses needed swags of green to soften their uncompromising angles, leafy tunnels and pergolas to shade them from the glaring sun. You couldn't have anything like an English garden, soft and blurry around a dominant heart of green lawn. You *could* grow grass, if you were prepared to spend money and time. It tended to be a coarse annual grass, feeling to the bare foot slightly like a shag rug that has become stiff with potato crisps and dog vomit. I was certainly not prepared to spend even the glimmer of a thought on anything so unlovely requiring such energy, and we designed the house surrounded with paved terraces, some of which are bordered by flower-beds. I wanted a garden to sit and be lazy in, not one that was an extension of housework.

Gazania and night-scented stock seeded themselves in a rather alarming way, making dense thickets in surprising places. I forgave them wholeheartedly: throughout that summer the gazanias flowered doggedly in such wonderful strange off-colours, and the scruffy clumps of stock scented the night air with a rich, spicy sweetness that was astonishing, coming from such a homely source.

It was a revelation to find that the simplest annuals looked thrilled with life in Spain. I suppose that constant dazzling sun is what they evolved for, and it takes them out of the humble into a much grander league. Marigolds flower with sunburst petals of silky orange satin, nasturtiums punctuate their mounds of cute round leaves with singing blotches of scarlet and flame all winter and onwards, refusing to die as annuals should. Gypsophila grows in exuberant white clouds, softening the more architectural planting like a drift of lace at a cavalier's wrist. Cosmos expands into great filigree bushes covered with pink and soft magenta flowers; California poppies look like jewels against their feathery grey foliage, and ivy-leafed geraniums spread wide and flower all winter.

All grey-foliaged plants did just as well as I expected, thriving joyfully in the pitiless light: rosemary and senecio, *santolina* and artemisia tumbling in great billows down hot walls, sage making neat little cushions, lavender becoming rugged heaps of silver topped in summer by a haze of purple spikes. They spread gratifyingly, filling their allotted spaces and more, cunning weapons in the anti-weed armoury.

Paeonies, euphorbias, hellebores and irises grew wild on El Torcal, and were happy to be tamed. Hibiscus burgeoned like bosomy Hawaiian dancing girls. I wanted to have magnolias and melianthus, which Beth Chatto said reminded her of a brontosaurus. We planned a dinosaur garden, with oversized spiky and serrated leaves, cardoons and artichokes, yuccas, aloes and palms jostling with melianthus for dominance. Gardening here was more fun and less serious than I had ever known it. Whatever did well did ridiculously well, and the rest just died. This suited me perfectly. It's those plants that hover guilt-inducingly between life and death for ages singing one final, ultimate, terminal aria that are the real pain.

Less successful was the sexy *Brugmansia suaveolens*, which used to be called datura, with night-fragrant white trumpet flowers and felty leaves, which I had seen at Modena and lusted after. It hated the wind – a knobbled arthritic stump was the best it had achieved thus far – but I lived in hope, and chatted to it encouragingly throughout the summer. So far I was unable to lie beneath mine and become intoxicated by its poisonous perfume, as the ancient Greeks were wont to do. I just get a face full of leaf litter. The truth is that we're just too high up for some plants.

It was one of many unwise and expensive horticultural acquisitions I made that spring. A garden nursery had opened, just close enough for me to undertake the scary journey alone – I was pathetic about driving for ages – and I would go there with a basil plant in mind, and return with the van crammed with apricot, gleditsia and false pepper trees, jasmines, pelargoniums, hideous hybrid teas because that was all they stocked and I had to have roses, dipladenia, passiflora, felicia, carissa, a cute little kumquat in a pot – a rampant jungle of the lush and unsuitable. I always forgot the basil. Dan still teases me for buying a huge banana plant, which towers reproachfully in its pot, permanently shredded by the wind.

But the apricot tree, which was planted on the pitiless west slope as a tiny sliver of twig – Antonio's preferred method – burgeoned, and after two years produced five of the most delicious apricots that tasted like they did when I was a girl and my tastebuds were still perky. And the fig trees that were dotted around the house produced fruit that would have done credit to the Garden of Eden. Dark purple skins, cracked by the sun's heat, exploding pinkly in one's mouth in a rude orgy of sweetness. Fresh figs are definitely a pornographic fruit, only distantly related to the cold, expensive, shrink-wrapped things you get in Waitrose.

Having recovered from the shock of being unable to nip down the road to a food emporium (Sainsbury, Waitrose or Tesco, all five minutes down the road in London) that sells everything you want and all sorts of things you never knew existed, there was something satisfying about being able to produce their fancy speciality foods free, and tasting so much better. Living in Spain was my initiation into the startling concept that homemade was better – hitherto it had always been much, much worse. An anxious or angry woman can never be a good cook, and in London I was frequently both and out of time to boot. My home-made-is-crap nadir was when my sons begged me, politely but firmly, not to make them birthday cakes, ever again. At the time I was obsessed with worthy, and wanted my tiny gorgeous boys to glow with health, so birthday cakes always induced a crisis. White sugar? Refined flour? Butter? *No. Never. Over my dead body.* They never developed a taste for wholemeal carrot cake.

To our surprise, the ancient and ailing lemon tree behind the house survived having a ton or so of rubble dumped on it, and produced a bowlful of misshapen fruit. On my previous visit to London, my friend Suzy had made a most delicious chicken casserole whose flavour came partly from the preserved lemons she cooked with it. They had come originally from Morocco and she had bought them in some deli where they did not cost pennies.

We could make those for nothing, I thought, surveying my beautiful new kitchen replete with brand-new Spanish cooker that worked fine as long as you realized that the knobs and dials were designed to come off in the hands of small children, and the temperature gauge bore no relation to the heat within. Wide worktops beckoned, whispering culinary seduction, the big double sink had a view through plum blossom of Señor Arrabal's pretty *finca* and the setting sun, and I was itching to get cooking. When Dan went down to the village to collect a vanload of horse manure, Paco gave him another bag of lemons – knobbly, speckled with bright green and certainly not sprayed with anything noxious. I considered my own chicken casserole to be just as delicious as Suzy's, and I even made lemon curd, using our own lemons. It took all of six minutes in the microwave. I was thrilled to have a microwave – this was novel to me, a fascinating combination of food and physics that was my new best friend until the great strawberry jam débâcle, in which a pound and a half of strawberries and an equal amount of sugar cascaded in a molten Vesuvius from around the door, providing an original distressed floor and worktop finish, and half a jar of very expensive jam.

Gardeners, as everyone knows, have hearts of gold, so there was an orgy of rallying round to help these poor overwhelmed beginners. Whenever Barbara visited she brought some choice cutting from her own garden – baby nispero trees, which in a more propitious setting would have produced their apricot-like fruit but turned up their toes for me; aloe and agave offshoots that I am glad to say have survived the arid site and hopeless gardener; magenta *Pelargonium domesticum*. Mabs, Barbara's saucy mother-in-law, an obsessive gardener with a magic touch, gave me the more exotic plants that have survived – glistening white dimorphotheca, handsome spiky dracaena, an obliging succulent *Aptenia cordifolia*, which spreads into thick mats of bright green ground-cover punctuated by tiny magenta stars. Mabs and I formulated an ideal system: seed companies keen to ingratiate themselves with garden editors would send me their latest F1 hybrid seeds, and I would give them to Mabs. She returned the favour by giving me the sturdy little plants she had grown, and under my sporadic care they either shrivelled immediately or, with native determination, thrived and became feathery cosmos, or kitschly brilliant zinnias.

I tried very hard, but gardening here was still a mystery. I just couldn't get the hang of when you did what. My vegetable garden was a case in point. One November day Señor Arrabal sauntered over and casually chucked a few broad-bean seeds onto the ground. They prospered. I braved the gales of February, chose an auspicious patch of earth, dug and wrestled with weeds, raked and sprinkled with goat manure – sweaty work in this solid clay – and tenderly planted lettuce, basil, cavolo nero, rocket, bean and mesclun seeds. What came up? Cardoons, which grow wild everywhere and for which I have yet to find a use.

Tomatoes seem to spring from uncultivated soil too, though they may just mark the site of the builders' preferred rubbish tip. Nothing in the vegetable world comes close to your own homegrown, sun-warmed cherry tomatoes. It is not often that I drool over low-calorie things, but those inadvertent tomatoes were miraculous.

However hard we tried to get it right, practically everything we did was a source of consternation to Antonio and the other builders. In summer they would worry about the quantity of desiccated grass that was strewn around, seeing it as a terrible fire risk; in winter they would fret about the imperfect drainage that might cause our cherry trees to drown. Juan took against a small and very sickly mango, which we planted in the courtyard against Dan's studio wall, rushing at it like an angry dog, demonstrating with convincing body language that this little tree was just biding its time, plotting against the moment when our backs were turned and it could heave the building down the hill. I have an inappropriate passion to grow mangoes. One builder after another would come and sigh mournfully and say, 'How many mangoes do you see growing around here? None. Because they will not grow here.' I fear they may be right.

Señor Arrabal was our most regular surprise visitor. He looked ancient but was probably about our age and incredibly spry. As a young man he'd been a bareback rider and stuntman, and his dapple-grey mare was still his favoured means of transport. Each day he would ride the five miles from his new gilt and plastic house in Villanueva to his farmhouse down the hill to feed his dogs, sometimes with his grandson Eugenio perched on the saddle in front of him. One day he happened to coincide with Dan skinny-dipping. There is a wall around the pool, just high enough to conceal private parts from someone standing on the other side,

Señor Arrabal and his new foal

but not high enough to conceal anything from a man on horseback. It made me laugh: Dan standing in the classic naked-man pose, both hands cupped around his particles, trying to conduct a polite conversation with Señor Arrabal, without having recourse to hand gestures or body language. Communicating thus hampered with a man who could not have heard a bomb explode, put a severe strain on Dan's ingenuity. I suspect that Señor Arrabal enjoyed the situation. He was certainly in no hurry to move on.

Throughout that year, his secret weapon was that he would turn up from any direction, at any time, and with no warning. We know about the approach of everyone else – except Paco White Pantaloons who walks everywhere – because we hear their cars, but Señor Arrabal took to popping up out of the *campo* from above, behind, below. He would do a spot check at nine in the morning, then drop in again at five in the evening. One sunny breakfast we were sitting out clothed in lungis and droopy dressing-gowns when he burst upon us from the general direction of the swimming-pool. This was a new one, and caught us unawares. For a while we took to getting fully dressed before we stumbled out to sit in the sun with our morning coffee.

Not only did Señor Arrabal always erupt unexpectedly, but he was always the bearer of bad tidings, unless he was bringing us mysterious gift bags of short lengths of knotted black twine, which he did several times a year.

Usually he would indicate that we had to do something very time-consuming and hard-workish with our trees, or that we should train our dogs in a different way, or that we should be picking wild asparagus, that we shouldn't be growing passion-flowers alongside our grape vines or, worst of all, that we should be gathering thistle ribs – a truly horrible local delicacy which is *certainly* not worth the considerable pain involved. He fetched up in his rakish straw hat one otherwise peaceful spring afternoon, when I was doing a spot of desultory weeding, and became very exercised about the thistles I had idly chucked on the discard pile. Snatching his trusty knife from his pocket, he stripped off the prickly bits and indicated that we should do the same while he sprang about like an agitated starfish collecting more of the damned things. Obediently Dan and I punctured our fingers stripping piles of ribs, whose savoury charms Señor Arrabal extolled in his unmistakable way, miming breaking eggs into a pan, adding the thistle bits, stirring the mixture around, and kissing his fingers in ecstasy at the delicious concoction. We were dubious, but anticipated something at least slightly gorgeous after our painful travail. It tasted like scrambled eggs cooked with Granny's special soggy Christmas Brussels sprouts.

It is just possible that thistle ribs are eaten for medicinal reasons. This was the explanation for Señora Arrabal's strange daily ritual. She would emerge from the *finca* every morning to plunge her hands in the nettle clump by her door. When, mystified and suspecting zealous mortification of the flesh, I asked why, she indicated – I think – that it helped her arthritis, and for every dabble in the nettle patch she got a whole day of mobility and no pain. However, since she is as deaf as her husband and communicates in incomprehensible shrieks and smiles, there might have been a problem in translation, so don't blame me if all that happens is you get urticaria.

Juan cured an English resident of a more intimate problem. They were having a building discussion, and he noticed that she was shifting about uncomfortably in her chair. Her piles, she reluctantly admitted, were giving her hell, and she could find no remedy. He sprinted off down the valley and returned with handfuls of wild watercress. He instructed her to carry them in her jacket pocket for the rest of the day, which she did. It was only when she put her hand into her pocket and found the soggy remains of the leaves as she was having dinner that she realized her piles were cured. They have not troubled her since.

The next invited guests to brave the assorted discomforts of Casa Miranda were Dan's parents, Pam and David, and his aunt Nellie, who stayed with us for a week that April 1999. None of them is steady on their feet, and the house was at its most adventure-playground. In casual Superman mode, Dan built them a flight of stone stairs from their end of the house to ours, using a few of the heavy roughly cubic boulders that surround the fields. There was one respectable guest bedroom with an adjoining bathroom, complete but for the absence of doors. Although you stepped out of this glamorous suite straight into a rubble pile, it was pretty civilized by our standards. I spent a happy afternoon drilling holes in walls, and putting up brilliant quilted patchwork *rillis* from Pakistan as curtains across the doorways. When Nellie arrived, she made herself a little haven in the erstwhile 'kitchen', the crumbling outhouse that had been our bedroom the previous April.

The trio were admirably self-sufficient, and unperturbed by the rubble. We would come across the three of them sitting out in the sunniest corners, Nellie reading aloud, while Pam and David listened, basking and nodding. They were endearing company, tentative with criticism, fulsome with praise. David found my cavolo nero a little daunting, and said, with great politeness, that although it was delicious, he found it a bit difficult to chew. He was absolutely right – my delicate Italian brassicas had grown into something very like jute without my noticing.

One morning Pam and David emerged from their bedroom rather pale. When pressed, they admitted that they had not slept a wink because something big had padded past the curtain into their room and breathed heavily next to their bed all night long. They had clung together, paralysed with terror. We concluded that it must have been Señor Arrabal's large white dog, gentle and ancient, but having survived the horrors of living with uninvited rodents the previous year, I could sympathize completely with their fears.

They had several days of good weather, but it is changeable in spring, and they spent their last day with us sitting on the sofa under a pile of blankets, with a blazing olive-wood fire toasting their toes.

At about this time Chris Stallwood chivvied Dan and me into going down to Málaga for Easter, which is *the* big event all over Spain. I was hoping that there might be some flouncy girls in spotty dresses, and did my best to persuade Dan that it was an essential event, and that he would enjoy it, really. My convent education meant that the combination of sensual overload, self-flagellating sincerity and kitsch did not come as quite such a shock to me as it did to him.

Every two-bit town has its own *trono* – a huge, heavy religious juggernaut belonging to one *cofradía* (brotherhood) or another – bearing statues of the Virgin Mary or Christ, surrounded by lilies, purple irises or bright pink gladioli and vast banks of candles. Sometimes there is a whole crowd of polychrome Christs and Virgins, plus Roman centurions jammed together. There is Judas Iscariot, suffering from high blood pressure, Pontius Pilate, looking frazzled, the good thief, worried, St John, trying to cheer up an inconsolable Virgin. Blood, tears and teeth are a major feature, as are sumptuous velvet gowns crustily embroidered in gold, acres of hand-made lace, hefty gold haloes, crowns studded with precious jewels, gold crosses set with emeralds. The Madonna tends to look like Madonna in her Material Girl phase, but very shiny about the face. Christ is usually clad in a cheeky loincloth or a simple velvet gown, with a fearsome crown of thorns, various ropes and chains, and a halo consisting of an unostentatious trio of gold plumes.

The *tronos* are carried through the streets on the shoulders of up to 280 men, some of whom have shaven heads, bare feet, or wear blindfolds. They shuffle very slowly along their route. Occasionally someone will break rank to race into a bar and get a drink, then sprint back to catch up with his compadres. Dan thinks they are downing 40 per cent proof, but I'm sure they aren't.

Málaga, as you would expect, has not just one *trono* but seventy-five (in hot competition with Seville), a Christ and a Virgin for each *cofradía*, and the route through the town has to be carefully choreographed to avoid collisions and bottlenecks. In front of the *tronos* walk senior *penitente* in tall, pointed and horribly sinister Ku Klux Klan-type hoods, purple, red, brown, green, blue or white, with slits for their eyes. They carry tall candles, which are an object of fascination for small boys who rush out to collect the wax drips to make into balls. Not all the wax drips, however, and the ensuing weeks are enlivened with crashes, as car brakes fail, and shrieks as people fall over on the polished wax streets. Almogia, which is built on a steep slope, is particularly lethal, and you can whiz from La Loma at the top to the swimming-pool at the bottom in one swift and painful slither.

Each *trono* comes with its own brass band, which plays in a lugubrious drone, and taking up the rear there is a token handful of women, sort of Mary Magdelenes dressed to the nines in short black lace dresses, or white lace on Resurrection Sunday, cleavages, mantillas and high heels. These are the people I feel really sorry for. Bare feet may be dodgy, but eleven hours of treading cobbles in party shoes is hell. And that is how long it takes to carry the Cena *trono* round Málaga.

Every day for the duration of Holy Week they set off at intervals from the Alameda Principal. On Palm Sunday thirteen *tronos* set off, starting at ten thirty in the morning, accompanied by hundreds of children, and they trudge along those narrow twisty streets, weaving along a carefully pre-planned route until the last finally staggers to its destination at two a.m.

We went on Good Friday, stationing ourselves at the Alameda Principal as the sun was getting a dusty penumbra ready for the sunset display. A portly middle-aged woman leaned out of her balcony window and sang beautifully in a clear, unaccompanied soprano to the passing *nazarenos*, and the gypsy *trono* was surrounded by foxy women, tightly clad, dancing and singing. The Andalucíans are afraid of gypsies, but are not immune to their sexy charm. So much of the flavour of Andalucía is piquant with all the things they fear – gypsies, Moors, Africans.

Apparently a prisoner is still released every year on Holy Wednesday, in a grateful memorial that goes back three centuries to when prisoners braved the plague to carry a religious statue through the streets.

We lasted about two hours, but Dan was suffering from religious persecution and eventually his groans got too much. It was time to make our heathen way home.

Paco's Preserved Lemons

Essential for Moroccan cookery, and wonderfully easy to make, exotic preserved lemons were the obvious solution to our unexpected lemon glut, and gave a piquant edge to Dan's chicken casserole.

8 large thin-skinned lemons
300g rock salt
300ml lemon juice (8–10 lemons)
½ teaspoon black peppercorns
1 bay leaf
1 tablespoon olive oil

Scrub the lemons and cut them into four from the pointed end, leaving the quarters joined at the stalk end. Open gently and remove any visible pips, and press 1 tablespoon salt against the cut edges of each wedge. Push the lemons back into shape and pack tightly to fill a 2-litre clip-top jar. Add 1 cup lemon juice and the rest of the salt, the peppercorns, and the bay leaf. Fill the jar with the remaining lemon juice. Seal and shake the jar and put it in a cool dark place (use the fridge in hot weather) for six weeks, inverting it each week. After four weeks the cloudy liquid will clear. The lemons are ready when the pith is no longer white (open the jar to test, and if necessary reseal until ready).

Each time you use the lemons, cover the brine with a layer of olive oil before resealing the jar. Rinse off the salt before using.

15

A PROFESSIONAL ABROAD

One day, shortly after our phone had been installed, it rang. This was an event. I sped through an adventure playground of wheelbarrows, girders and buckets of cement and grabbed it. It was Francine Lawrence, my previous editor, now editing a magazine for Dulux. She wanted three features on painted houses in Spain, and was prepared to allow me one month to get it together. 'We need sunny pictures. Bright unusual colours that we can match from the Dulux range. Pink, green, yellow, and details of painted furniture, pots, just simple things glammed up a bit – you could do it yourself, just paint some old dresser or something. It just has to look colourful, sunny and good. Go for the right sort of people – you know, smart, sussed, stylish.'

The sensible response would have been to laugh and put the phone down, but we needed the money and I wanted to foster work possibilities just in case I had to freelance in the future. I also have a cringing Pavlovian need to simper and say, 'Yes,' to any work offers.

'Of course,' I said, 'it'll be a pleasure. A great opportunity to do a bit of exploring.' Too late it occurred to me that I knew no-one in the entirety of Spain who had a painted house. Let alone anyone who fitted Francine's personality requirements. Four weeks is not a lot of time to find people, recce houses, send Francine snapshots, get the OK, set up a photographer, do three shoots and three interviews, write them up and get the completed packages to London. Thus began another endurance test for Dan and me. He was relegated to chauffeur and butt for my anxiety. What we explored most over the next few days was how depressed it is possible to become without killing yourself. Even the weather, which had been sparkling and radiant, turned to sludge.

Our new phone was thoroughly tested as I rang everyone I had spoken to, every nebulous contact, every painter and fancy decorator who advertised in the glossy freebies that estate agents give away down on the coast. They sounded positive, invited us to call in and see their portfolios, and were thrilled that Jocasta, originator of a trillion paint effects, was my sister.

With high hopes Dan and I set off for the fleshpots of Marbella, getting horribly lost with the new road, arriving late, hot, sweaty and feeling like shambling impostors. I got overexcited as we leafed through impressive decorating portfolios full of bold yet simple paint effects, which I could just discern over the oil slick that was my nose. This was it, exactly what Francine wanted. I had a moment of relief thinking that my grail was in sight, but it was not to be. We were free to photograph anything boring or white, but as for setting foot inside Rod Stewart's entirely leopardskin apartment (they were stencilling the lavatory seats at the time), Antonio Banderas' or Bruce

Willis's place, No Way. To be honest, I knew they were not entirely what Francine wanted, but I was longing to snoop. From a promising beginning we drew a disappointing blank.

I next tried our lawyer's chic assistant who knew some people she thought might help. She was very patient, and gave me loads of contacts, among which one sounded a likely possibility, a Dutch painter, auspiciously called Art. On the map it looked like he lived a couple of hours' drive away so I made the phone calls, arranged an appointment, and heaved another sigh of something like relief.

It took us six hours to get to the Dutch painter's house, having wiggled our way through most of Andalucía. We recognized it by the massive palm trees. The house was beautiful, with cloistered courtyards, swathed with roses, and what he called a rosary tree in the middle, because its fruit were like ivory rosary beads. There were cool high rooms opening off it, with quirky antique brass beds and dressers. Everything he had done was superb and Francine would have loved it but for one thing: it was all white, from one end to the other. Even the garden consisted of flocks of white lilies and irises. Dispirited, we took the long drive home.

Two weeks had passed, we had come up with nothing, and I took up the abandoned habit of nail-biting. As usual, my friend Hester helped me out of the fix. She sent me faxes of a feature she had done with a painter living near Granada. I rang to discuss it with Francine, but soon realized it wouldn't work. The house was filled with broken paint finishes and we needed flat dolly-mixture colour. But Hester's contact, whose crime was uneven paint, knew someone else who, she thought, would be perfect.

The next morning the phone rang, and I streaked through cement-mixers, piles of gravel and heaps of tiles to snatch it up. I was assailed by an unintelligible stream of Spanish. My mind went blank, and the magic mantra – *mas despacio, por favor* – was nowhere to be found. I stood at the phone making goldfish noises, unable to formulate a sentence in English. The Spanish woman repeated her stream of gibberish, louder and more vehemently. Finally, because she is very bright, she tried in English: 'My name is Rosa. I have been given your name by an English painter, who says that you want painted houses to photograph for a magazine. I am at Salobrena, and my house is painted all over, inside and out. I think it is what you are looking for.'

Yes! Dan, who was getting a little pissed off with all the chauffeuring and this was another three-hour drive along the coast, and I shot over the next day. We had arranged to meet in a huge plastic hotel crammed with off-season geriatrics. 'I shall be in red and black,' Rosa had told me. She swept into the hotel, and there was no doubt about her identity. Abashed, and suddenly feeling fat and colour-uncoordinated, we owned up that we were the journalists she was meeting, and followed her meekly along the coast road and down to her house overlooking the sea.

It was perfect. Rosa is a quirky natural designer and loves to make and decorate things – she had painted every inch of the house inside and out, and there were pebble sculptures and strange kinetic objects strewn around confected by her in an idle moment, pots she had covered in mosaic, and curious wire arabesques holding photos and postcards. What fascinated me most was not relevant to our trip: she and Juan, her husband, had one of those walk-in wardrobes, a proper room devoted to clothes, all hung in order of colour, with neat shelves laden with a designer's subtle beige and grey palette of cashmere and silk. A temple dedicated to Sartorius, the god of sharp knife creases and shiny shoes.

Their house was perched on a ledge overlooking the sea. It was not big and had grown organically, with extra rooms added as necessary – an outdoor dining room roofed and walled with jasmine, a glazed south-facing studio in which Rosa worked, and there was a swimming-pool on the edge of the world, with just sea beyond. They had planted ancient olive trees – which do not mind suddenly finding themselves in a new location – and strung hammocks between them.

Dan and I sprinted around taking recce shots of the eclectic interior – Alessi this, and Paloma Picasso that, *verre eglomisé* urns and Moroccan *tadalekt* bathroom walls, and when we were through Juan suggested that we go and eat on the beach. We drove down through fields of sugar cane, avocados and mangoes to a *chiringuito* on the seafront with a view of the curving bay and the sun sparkling on the water. We ate grilled fish, wandering off from time to time to paddle in the sea whence it had come. Both Rosa and Juan spoke excellent English and we all loved talking about designers, architects, films, food, travel and music. One down, I thought, considerably cheered. Just two to go.

My friend and colleague Thérèse Lang came up with the second house. Her previous boyfriend Martin was an art-dealer, and had built a house near Gaucin that he shared with his partner Kate. We trekked across the three-hour distance (half an inch on the map) and found a perfectly wonderful house, combining the best of stately Spanish *cortijo* with Gloucestershire country seat, packed with desirable antiques, and radiant with colour. Good ol' Thérèse, I thought, beaming at the sumptuous terracotta, ochre and indigo walls. The difficulty here was editing: everything merited a feature – not just the house, but the garden, the view, the wooded setting with a Stonehenge-sized rock radiating the sun's collected heat back at the swimming-pool like a giant day storage heater. They did everything so well, and it was all so richly, resonantly put together that my own decorative efforts seemed naïve and crass by comparison.

Martin and Kate were generous hosts, and we dined like sultans. I kept wanting to make notes – how to put together a garden out of huge rocks and aloes, how to serve couscous, what to put in a salad, how to assemble a mantelpiece still-life or make casually draped curtains out of Indian saris, what to wear, what to drink in the morning, the afternoon and at sundown, how to treat peasant floor tiles to make them glossy and gorgeous, where to buy huge antique doors and the best carpets in Marrakech, which are the fashionable names to drop, how to be a civilized, sophisticated inhabitant of this hillbilly place. How to live. It suddenly seemed that what Dan and I did in the way of living was pitiably amateurish. No-one would ever feel daunted by my sense of style, or crushed by the professional ease with which I orchestrated my life, I thought.

I might have left feeling like a homunculus, but at least we had another house in the bag. Just one more to find. I sat in front of the telephone and racked my brains. Like an angelic answer to my plea, a local friend, Heulyn, rang me at that moment to invite us to join her for lunch at a family-run restaurant in a converted olive mill she had discovered. We arranged to meet her in a village called Comares.

After the standard three-hour wiggly drive we started climbing, and found Comares teetering at the pinnacle of a towering limestone cone. We wound up through the village and fetched up in a square with a stupendous view down across olive plantations to the sea. El Molino de los Abuelos was in the corner of the square, and Dan, Heulyn and I were ushered into the *cortijo* courtyard with the same stunning view, and a fine old rambling building enclosing it. We had a drink out in the sun and were then shown into the dining room. It was a plain, smooth unbroken hyacinth blue with massive windows overlooking the view, and a huge pink fireplace. The wide airy room was littered with magnificent bits of olive equipment to which I could not put any name or purpose. The two women who had inherited the mill from their redoubtable olive-farming grandmother were doing the cooking and serving. They were living examples of *duende* – charm, magic. They were youngish, good-looking, and doing an amazing job. And the hotel/restaurant looked as though it might be our third painted location. We were taken on a guided tour of pink, yellow and pistachio painted bedrooms, full of fine inherited furniture. Yes, I thought, this is good: handsome, simple rooms, brought alive by the dolly-mixture colours that Francine had specified. The only tiny problem was that they did not speak a word of English and my Spanish would not cover a bus ticket.

Still, I had three locations. Now for the photographer. In my career as a garden editor I had commissioned and worked with maybe twenty photographers, all of whom were excellent at what they did – which happened to be gardens. Houses are a different beast altogether, and Spanish houses different again, with their blinding shafts of contrasty light: everyone must have taken a photo of a gorgeous sun-filled room, only to get it back from Boots with a shaft of ghostly objects in white against a black background. The light in Spain is so intense that contrast between light and shade is a photographic disaster.

Kathy, in the art department, suggested I contact Peter Williams. 'He does all our best cookery shoots. He's a wonderful natural stylist, and fine with lighting, calm and unflappable – a favourite-uncle kind of person, sort of like Clint Eastwood with a camera. And he has a house near you in Spain.'

He sounded perfect. Naturally a photographer of such calibre was not going to be able to drop everything to attend to my proposal, but he was happy to take it on, and free to come over for five days right at the end of Francine's period of grace. There was no leeway for grey weather or problems with cameras or cars. The driving alone would take almost a day. I would have to organize the shoot like a military operation with a timetable covering every waking minute – I, who cannot organize my shoes into matching pairs.

Peter and I planned it all on the telephone. We had never met and neither of us knew what to expect of the other or the task we were about to undertake. I was particularly jittery as I tried to arrange photography at Los Abuelos over the phone, in my hopeless Spanish, not really understanding what arrangement I had made, if I had made one at all. I *hoped* that we had been offered beds for the Friday night, dinner and *carte blanche* to photograph on Saturday. We had a budget and were happy to pay for all this bounty, the problem being that the hotel was only open at the weekend, and I was unable to establish what kind of access we would have. I wasn't even confident that when we turned up on Friday evening anyone would be there at all. Discreetly, I kept this little potential glitch to myself. I arranged to photograph the hotel at Comares first, Rosa and Juan at Salobrena next, with Martin and Kate as the grand finale.

Peter was everything Kathy had rhapsodized about and better. He came with a businesslike assistant, who had as many capable arms as Durga and a way of predicting what lens Peter would want and when. We met for the first time in the little square in Comares, and were instantly taken with Peter's quiet, capable air, his gentleness, and the way – like many tall people – he leaned conspiratorially towards you in a sheltering arc when you spoke.

Summoning all my courage, and trying to look casually confident, I knocked at the heavy, imposing door of El Molino de los Abuelos. The place looked very shuttered and dead, and while we waited I tried to disguise my apprehension by chattering inanely. Finally I suggested lightly, although my knees were quaking, that we had coffee at the amusingly Fifties bar in the square. Within, I was running through a desperate incantation of all the things that might have gone wrong, and wondering how to sort them; outwardly I was faffing away about the window grilles, which were in the form of skiffling jivers and musical notation all in wrought-iron.

It was getting late, and the light was going. I had

hoped that we would be able to get one or two pictures by evening light, but that possibility was rapidly evaporating. I left the others drinking and returned anxiously to the massive door. It was open, and I could hear someone inside the building. I almost fell over, I was so relieved. We were welcomed effusively by the handsome husband of one of the sisters, given a fortifying glass of fino, and taken on a guided tour of the public and private rooms. We were told that we could photograph anywhere we wanted (I think).

Peter and I worked out a rough schedule of photography, trying to predict where the light would be good and when. I kept trying to get him to agree to do sunny rooms. He kept backing away nervously and suggesting that we avoid full sunlight. I pursed my lips and shelved the tussle. I had a bigger problem looming. The interview.

Dinner, which was delicious, was for me like the condemned man's last meal. They had opened specially for us, and we were the only diners. They had made a magnificent three-course dinner, but we might as well have been eating dog food for all the joy it brought me. During that endless mastication I discovered original places to sweat. Back of knees? That's a new one. Behind the ears? No-one's done that before. Inner elbows? I think it's a first. The kinder and more generous our hosts became, the more miserable I felt. I wanted to rush up and shout, 'I can't speak a word of Spanish. Can't you see I'm here under false pretences? Do your worst. I forgive you.'

Instead I chewed on, and fiddled surreptitiously with my tape-recorder. With the liqueurs came nemesis. Sisters plus husband sat smiling round a small table, and indicated that I should join them. I did not run screaming from the room, but with feet like lead I took my place, turned on my recorder, took out pad and pencil, and dragged myself dry-mouthed into the most impossible, ghastly humiliation of my life. Dan, Peter and Peter's assistant were sitting well within hearing distance, and punctuated the ordeal that followed with helpful remarks, like 'You just asked them that.' I struggled on with my five-word vocabulary, getting them to repeat everything very slowly, and trying to avoid the questions that unleashed an avalanche of enthusiastic explanation. It was not the worst interview I have ever done because they had a story to tell. Whether the story I wrote was the one they had intended to tell will always be a mystery.

What I do have to say is that it is a great hotel, and the owners should be in line for a papal benediction. They were incredibly intuitive, kind and ingenious. They showed me pictures, gave me more material to work on than I deserved, and threw in dinner and beds for nothing.

Dan and I were assigned a sumptuous four-poster, and I hoped secretly that the world would end overnight and we could just sleep for ever. But it was not to be. I set my alarm for pre-dawn, because we had to get hold of some flowers to soften the rather stark interiors. Not only was it dark when we were roused, it was also drizzling. We tiptoed out to the trusty Citroën and drove through soggy clouds to a place I recalled as being awash in wild flowers. Dan is never at his best in the morning, and on that morning he was regretting everything, particularly taking up with me. He sat in the car and groaned as I shimmied up cliffs with my secateurs, collecting unwieldy tufts of pink helianthemum, wild mignonette, and anything else that looked even slightly presentable. After a glance at Dan, hunched over the steering-wheel in the sepulchral gloom, I asked God to teleport me somewhere else, but He was in His pinny making cloud muffins and did not hear me.

I slithered back down the cliff, arms full of prickly things shedding petals as fast as they could, and tried to prise Dan from his gloom. He is a man who needs regular feeding, and we had set off hungry. This did not bode well. I had a feeling that it was going to be a long day.

We got back to Los Abuelos to discover that we were in the doghouse, having managed to wake everyone by our soundless exit. I can't remember whether we breakfasted, I think not. But, boy, did we work. We sped around that building, setting up details here, panoramas there, moving pictures and furniture, putting the pink bedspread in the yellow room, the white one in the green room. No-one who has not done this footling kind of work can know how utterly exhausting it is. There's a constant pulse of adrenaline, ridiculous decisions to make about whether the white flowers are best with the fluffy or the architectural foliage, a lot of tense hanging about, and frenetic bursts of heavy-duty weight-shifting. The grey sky relented at about midday, and sun brightened our travails. Peter consented to take two sunny pictures. Our hosts continued to be hospitality personified: helping, feeding, watering, moving, explaining, keeping out of our way, not objecting to the chaos we caused.

We stopped well after the sun slid out of sight, finalizing with a big kitsch gold cherub sitting on a pink mantelpiece. We had achieved a great set of pictures, and total disruption for the hotel-owners. As we were leaving for Salobrena I was very moved when one of the sisters put her hand on my arm, and said, '*Mi casa es tu casa.*' We had ponced about all day causing no end of problems to them and their real guests, yet they were still kind and noble.

There was no time for poignant bonding, however: we had to get to Salobrena in time for dinner. When we arrived at nightfall, Juan and Rosa treated us to an indigestible feast of fried fish in an amusingly downbeat restaurant, and a great deal of Rioja. They were sparky good company, but we were barely able to speak.

Unfortunately I had organized our sleeping accommodation. Rosa had offered, but I felt it was too much to ask, and had ploughed through the Lonely Planet guide in search of somewhere to stay. We ended up sleeping in two separate B-and-Bs in that circuitous town. Peter and his assistant in an operating theatre, so scrubbed and shiny that traversing the corridors was like walking across an ice rink; Dan and I in a strange hybrid between bordello and cathedral side-chapel with the Sacred Heart (ten watts behind red plastic) glowing above our bed.

Morning came too soon. We scoffed dry buns and coffee and zoomed off to Rosa and Juan's. If the problem at Los Abuelos had been large spaces with spartan furnishing, here we faced claustrophobic confinement in which every surface was barnacled with objects. Peter tried to back through walls in his efforts to get sufficient distance from the subject of the photo, while I sped about ruining Rosa's careful compositions, trying to focus attention on painted walls rather than a lifetime's mementoes. I think Rosa was rather offended, and as soon as we moved on from each room, she would recreate her busy still-life exactly as it had been. But the day was a success, and we came away with another set of brilliant pictures. Rosa and Juan were gracious about our pillaging and plundering, inviting us to come back for Juan's saint's-day celebrations in June.

Uncomplaining, Peter stashed all his heavy and unwieldy camera equipment back in his car, and we set off for Kate and Martin's, some five hours away. We arrived late, and catatonic. They plied us with drinks and food, coped gamely with our zeebish silence, and pushed us off to bed.

We had completed two-thirds of our photography, and the pressure was off. We also had the luxury of staying two nights, so that there was more time to get morning and evening shots when the light was best. The problem here was that everywhere you looked there was some lovely detail or perfectly harmonizing assemblage of fabric, paint and furniture. Even our lunch, which Kate laid out in the shady, plant-wreathed loggia, was an Italian Renaissance still-life. Peter and I sprang about like darting springboks, squeaking with enthusiasm about this vignette, that view. We ended up with enough material from this house alone for three features.

The next day Peter returned to London with the pictures. When we got home, I sat down in the donkey room with the Polaroids and three most peculiar taped interviews. I spent two days inventing, fabricating and lying while lumps of plaster and assorted beetles fell on my head. I drew huge conclusions from the merest shred of evidence. I generalized wildly, I assigned whole rafts of decorative techniques to the innocent Moors on the basis of a guess at what they had been trying to tell me at Los Abuelos. I finished on time, and sent Francine what she had asked for. For a brief moment I felt like a super-hero.

Francine used Kate and Martin's house, which looked sumptuous. But then she decided that she didn't want to edit the Dulux magazine any more, so the other two shoots never achieved the fame I had promised. My name is mud in Salobrena, and there is probably a contract out on me in Comares. Peter had produced three magnificent sets of pictures, two of which would never see the light of W. H. Smith. Cruel whimsy is an unfortunate fact of life in illustrated magazines, but it was worse than usual because everyone had been so kind, and they were so thrilled about being published. I felt that the disturbance fee I passed their way was almost an insult, given the general disappointment.

But however ill-fated, we had had an adventure, proved that we could work efficiently in difficult circumstances and discovered the meaning of *duende.*

16

A FAIR TO FORGET

As spring slipped into shimmering summer both sets of children and an assortment of friends came to stay. The northern half of the house, our half, was finished, and most things worked as they should apart from the mystery water-heater, which betrayed a manic instability, blowing scalding or freezing according to whim. Electricity was intermittent too, subject to the vagaries of weather and experimental wiring – a surprising number of the lamps I bought had a potentially lethal fault in plug or switch. Any lighting more subtle than the ubiquitous neon strip – lamps, lamp shades, uplighters – was elusive, requiring much research in Spain, and when found it was to be approached with caution: rubber gloves and wellington boots.

The visitors' house on the south side was less functional than ours, with ancient beds that had once been the boys', a cooker that was so in name only, and a shower that did not even try for hot. We discovered its ailment the embarrassing way. We complained to Paco the plumber, who made the journey out to the house and demonstrated that the water-heater was suffering from oxygen deprivation; he opened and shut the door to its cupboard thereby making the water run hot and cold, with all the drama of a circus ring-leader quelling a tetchy tiger. The solution was so simple that we stood in a row, dumbfounded, and could only stare incredulously as he repeated the experiment three times.

Leo and Spigs came for a shorter holiday than I would have liked, and were immediately put to good use as furniture-removal men, pool-house cleaners and general muscle. They are both brilliant cooks, so we dined well, if late, from a menu that featured Chinese and Thai food predominantly, interspersed with blackened barbecues under a star-spattered indigo sky, after which we would play cards until four in the morning.

With the shower in proper working order, Doris came for a fortnight with her friend Alice and they gossiped and read mags and worried about their tans. It was always a pleasure having Doris to stay because she would voluntarily do vile things like defrost the freezer, that I put off for months, and she was an inexhaustible and creative cook. Dan was always at his happiest when Doris was pottering around, fussing about his well-being and inventing exotic cocktails to derail his tedious preference for a nice cup of tea.

Ted stayed three months, during which his friends Fish, Will and Hugo each dropped in for a week or so. Apart from these brief periods of animation, Ted sat out in the sun, silent and motionless. I asked if he wasn't very bored. What had he done all day? There was a long pause, and then he said gravely, 'I watched a cloud.' During those three months he spoke maybe ten words, and managed to evade any of the footling household tasks that I put his way. Except one. One day, exasperated beyond sense, I demanded that he cook supper that evening. This entailed a serious shopping trip to Málaga, where he mooched up and down the aisles of Carrefour, prodding, poking and consulting his list.

When we got home, he donned his Hawaiian shirt and shades and started chopping and scrubbing, looking like a Florida gangster and working with the precision of a genetic engineer. He had chosen to make *moules marinière*, and he worked away at it for hours. I think of *moules* as something you throw together in minutes, but when Ted made it we finally sat down to eat at ten p.m. It was delicious and worth the wait. But Ted sniffed one undersized mussel suspiciously, then said, 'I don't like mussels,' pushed away his plate and ambled glumly to investigate the panoply of inedible past-their-sell-by-date things in the fridge.

Out of the blue, he produced a series of exceptional paintings while he was with us. Dan was painting for an exhibition due to take place that autumn, sitting outside on the west slope quaintly clad in a green sarong and one of my straw hats. Ted set up an easel beside him, and they stood side by side, producing paintings that could not have been more different. Dan's were lyrical sensual tributes to the Spanish landscape, showing the rounded hills, the cubic white houses, the fantastic rocks and sunsets. Ted's were bright, bold, abstract, and I was so impressed that I bought one immediately.

Fortunately I don't have to buy Dan's: he lets me borrow them. He painted a huge, radiant landscape for my birthday, for which we found the most pompously portentous frame that Málaga had to offer. But the portrait of me that he claimed to want to paint as a birthday present the following year is still stacked uncompleted and ghostlike – a pair of sinister glittering eyes staring from ectoplasmic swirls of grey.

I loved it when Dan painted. He settled into a state of serene contentment when he had a paintbrush in his hand and a big blank canvas to cover. He has a natural talent for painting and drawing – which survived a stint at art school unwarped – and there was a quiet confidence about the way he worked that was soothing and good to be near. This was Dan at his best: he emerged from a painting trance as calmly benign as a Buddhist who had just done a meditation all-nighter. He'd got his achievement fix and, if I was lucky, would cook dinner without realizing that it was my turn.

However, in all this Zen serenity there loomed a tiny cloud. His van – the one he'd bought with Michael at the beginning of the year – was due to go for its MOT. Dan always became restive and anxious when this time approached, especially as the van was our sole link with the outside world, and his Spanish was not equal to the instructions barked at him by the uniformed official giving it the once-over. Early one morning he set off to Antequera for this ceremony with a leaden heart.

I did not see him again until nine o'clock that evening. When he finally fetched up, it was not in his van, but in a rugged four-wheel-drive Toyota monster, with Juan Dobles as chauffeur. Señor Dobles, locally known as Albondigas – Meatball – was the spherical owner of the local garage.

To Dan's astonishment the van had passed its MOT, but as he cruised up to El Torcal from Antequera he made the grave mistake of punching the air in triumph. Precisely at that moment, midway between nowhere and nowhere, the gods got the hump and his van dribbled to a halt. Dan stood forlornly in the searing sun by the roadside until someone took pity on him and gave him a lift to Señor Dobles' garage. Albondigas was involved with a tractor suffering from a hernia and could not drop everything, so Dan spent the day learning more Spanish and more about car parts than he ever thought he'd need to know. He was held to ransom by his van and its ailments and had no option but to hang around all day with Meatball.

Luckily the two-week lack of transport, during which the van was dismantled and reassembled, coincided with Hugo's visit – one of the few of Ted's friends who can drive. We bullied him into hiring a Twingo, and were mobile during the time Dan's van required for its operation and convalescence. But I decided that we needed another functional car.

Juan Dobles is a kindly man, and while Dan's van languished unusably with its guts in a pile on the floor of the garage, he took me to meet his good friend Señor Pastrani at the Suzuki outlet in Antequera. There I fell in love with, and Señor Dobles test-drove, a snappy soft-top Suzuki Samurai. He pronounced it a little gem. Ignorantly I believed him, parted with loads of pesetas, and after the paperwork had been sorted drove it home in terror. It has a weakness for sashaying off the road at tight corners, of which there are about a million in any direction you care to take, and just about every other impracticality you could dream up, but I love it.

There was an influx of visitors at this time, and I was prey to the usual contrary bout of misanthropy. As soon as the people I long to see take up my invitation to stay, I turn into Greta Garbo and have to be alone. I thought that this was the moment to get more intimate with my new car, to test it a bit – plough off the Tarmac and into adventure. I decided to see what was beyond the familiar snake-and-terrapin-infested riverbed at Barranco del Sol.

I took off one afternoon, and frightened myself with a few hairpin bends. With gathering confidence I rumbled up and beyond the village we can see on our route to the airport. I was dismayed by a bunch of male juveniles who peered into the car and shouted, '*Fea*,' triumphantly as I passed. 'Ugly' is what this word means, and it is only funny when applied to other people. Undeterred I drove on, and was soon lost. The road became a track, and the track became more of a donkey path. I found myself drawing up beside a woman hanging up her washing. In my BBC Spanish, I politely asked her the way to Villanueva, which I reckoned to be the nearest village. She stared at me, and I know now how a Venusian might feel landing on Earth. With a torrent of unintelligible stuff in a language I have yet to meet, she indicated that I should continue through her courtyard – at least, I think that's what she said. Since there was no room to turn round, I did, and drove through several gardens, surprising an old man taking a nap outside his back door and probably shortening his life by a few decades.

I found myself on a tractor track, meandering through an olive plantation. It continued through the trees and precipitously down a hill, where it made an acute turn. If you have ever seen *Wages of Fear*, this was the point where Yves Montand has to do a sharp bend on a rotting wooden platform over an abyss. I was sweating profusely as I negotiated a twenty-point turn with three inches in which to do it and no power-steering. There was a cliff behind me and a sheer thirty-foot drop to a rocky riverbed immediately below. I learned where reverse gear was with lightning intuition, and how to use the four-wheel drive, which I had not mastered until that moment. I successfully managed the turn, and sat limply behind the wheel for quite a while until I realized that the sun had it in mind to flip behind the hill and plunge me into darkness. Shaking slightly, I ploughed on, without the vaguest idea of where I was headed. Down across the riverbed, I drove up the hill on the other side, through orange trees in a landscape devoid of human habitation. The sound of my heart thumping was suddenly drowned by a trail bike that shot past me, through the trees and over the top of the hill. Well, at least there was one other person in this silent twilit wasteland, I told myself.

I thought with momentary affection of East Anglia where you can see Ely cathedral twenty miles away and just head for it. Here, each hill, and each side of each hill, presents you with a different, unknown landscape. Even different times of day can change the familiar beyond all recognition. And as for getting out of there in the dark – forget it. As the sun got lower and the air got colder I resigned myself to spending the night in the car. The hill I was climbing was all in shadow, outlined at the top with gold. It would have been very beautiful, had I not been bracing myself for imminent disasters – the motorbike boy might have been a homicidal maniac and be waiting round the next corner with his psychopathic friends, I might misjudge a corner and plunge invisibly down into the oleander at the bottom of the ravine, I might run out of petrol, the track might peter out and leave me stranded unable to go forward or backward. All things considered, I would probably never find my way home. Curiously, I found these gloomy predictions rather bracing, and continued cautiously up the hill and round to the sunny side.

I was hoping that suddenly I would know where I was. I did not. There was just another range of mystery hills, bare of roads and houses. Two snaking hills further on, I came across a huddle of people standing on the track. They glared at me ferociously as I approached, and I decided not to engage them in conversation or even to make eye-contact. Instead I drove through them, unwilling though they were to make room, looking doggedly purposeful. I could feel their eyes on my big end as I found myself on a very visible up-and-down, round-and-round switchback. Fear of humiliation was stronger than fear of death, so I drove confidently, insouciantly, as though I had known every inch of the track from early infancy. Wiggling round two more little conical hills, I suddenly popped out from the ancient drover's track onto Tarmac. *Tarmac!* I could have kissed it. I still had no idea where I was, but civilization was near at hand, with people who spoke a recognizable language, phones maybe, even a signpost or two.

As complete darkness fell, I recognized the outskirts of Villanueva, with El Torcal towering behind. On a map, I had travelled possibly three miles. Let me tell you, the Zambezi holds no terrors for me after my trip into the Spanish hinterland. And I was *very* glad to get back to our visitors.

A few days later Barbara visited us, buzzing with excitement. A young man, an Italian, a restaurateur, wanted to buy Ken and Olive's house overlooking the ravine and the accident blackspot. Her eyes sparkled as she gave us the low-down: his name was Giorgio, and he was running a restaurant in Covent Garden; he had a wife and small children, and wanted to open a restaurant in Almogia. The thought of a Sicilian Giorgio and a Slovakian Martina got us all into a tizz, as did the promise of a more sophisticated cuisine. Nobody except Barbara had clapped eyes on the man, but the village talked of nothing else. From an airy launching-pad of complete ignorance we discussed his life, his works and his family, the sale of his house in Wapping, the turpitude of his business partner, the educational possibilities for his children.

When they finally arrived they were worth the speculation. Giorgio was slim, muscular, good-looking in a strangely elfin way, and apt to experiment disastrously with his facial hair. He had perceptive dark eyes, and a general air of febrile energy like some nineteenth-century consumptive. Being a man of impulsive action, he took one look and bought the house on the ravine, no matter that they had initially decided to buy an organic farm. He returned to Martina in Wapping with a *fait accompli*.

He came back to Almogia alone to begin work on the building, and soon the village was discussing his plans, scratching its collective head about the excavation at the back which was the size of a small aircraft landing-strip, and weighing up the pros and cons of siting the restaurant on the ground floor or on the first floor. For months, Almogia thudded to the deafening racket of Kango hammers digging through the solid rock floor of Giorgio's restaurant to increase the ceiling height and conform to building regulations. The new front door was more or less exactly where Olive's organ had been, but three feet lower.

During the long, frustrating months of demolition and restoration, Giorgio was a desperate man, and would go out in his silver Volvo and return with an enormous granite fountain simply because it bore the Italian legend 'Gelati', or a grove of fully grown palm trees in mammoth pots for which he had no site.

Giorgio suffered from a fetish with livestock, and a varied animal population came and went with unsettling rapidity. His fatal weakness was for horses. On his arrival he had never ridden a horse, but had visions of himself racing across the *campo* like a centaur from Central Casting, all sweat, adrenaline and virility. His first horse, the one that ate the palm trees, was Curro, a fine, good-natured half-Arab, whom I eventually learned to ride.

But there was a problem with stabling: Giorgio did not have anywhere to keep any kind of animal, but he persisted with his dream and soon bought another horse. Dan was driving past his house one day, and was surprised to see him standing by the roadside, wringing his hands and appealing to the heavens. Dan stopped the car and Giorgio leaped into it with a histrionic flurry. 'I've losta my 'orses. They'va gone, disappeared. They'va run away. They were tied up. My God!' (St Teresa of Avila pose.) 'They coulda be anywhere.' Undismayed, Dan drove his weeping passenger around for the next three hours – along the road to the place where he had bought them, to the home of their previous owners, to the bar outside which they had once been tied and, finally, back home empty-handed. Where the first things to meet their eyes were two horses, Giorgio's horses, which had simply wandered into the next field and been brought home by a Spanish neighbour.

That summer Giorgio's mysterious Slovakian wife Martina became a reality. We met for the first time at a party of Helen's. Helen, we discovered, sticks by Glaswegian rules of entertaining, counter to the Spanish custom: when she said we should come for a barbecue at six, we assumed, since it was midsummer and Spain, she meant ten, and arrived at eight – the perfect compromise, we thought.

'Oh, God, everything's been eaten. No, Tommy, get those chops out of the freezer, we can just put them on the embers, they'll be fine, and look,' she greeted us with embarrassment, hastily piling the dregs of veggies past into a single bowl, 'there's lots of salad. Help yourselves. What will you drink? We've got . . .' and she reeled off a list of alcoholic bevvies that would have done a Manhattan cocktail bar proud. It was not until we were laden with enough food and drink to keep a rugby team beaming that she introduced us to Martina.

Martina was tall, as slim as a credit card, but appeared even taller and slimmer because she was wearing six-inch platform soles and was thinly veneered with black silk. Her attractive dark-eyed Slovakian face was a picture of irritation and, sighing with annoyance, she managed the briefest, most weary greeting before saying, 'I am so *bored* by Almogia.' She had been resident all of twenty-four hours. We felt a little crushed. The thought also crossed our minds that Giorgio's decision to abandon Covent Garden in favour of the wastelands of the Spanish *campo* might have been unilateral.

Our next meeting was at the local *romería*, a little

fair that lands annually on a flat piece of land just outside Almogia. Summer nights resounded to the music of fairs, flamenco shows, impromptu discos, and every tiny hamlet invested in bunting, put up a stage and found a band. This *romería* was tiny but fun, as innocent as the fairs remembered from childhood. We went down late one Saturday night, Dan grumbling all the way. In a pitch-black setting of scrubland and trees there was a tiny island of twinkling lights: a few rides, a handful of blokes getting quietly drunk unperturbed by the deafening background blend of treacly organ music and the shooting range, and a toddlers' train and tunnel resplendent with paintings of well-endowed Rubensesque Venuses. Dan and I went on a ride that made me scream with laughter as shoes, money, keys and just about everything else flew out into the darkness. I longed to throw myself at the bouncy castle, but the grim moustachioed *señora* whose domain it was had spotted me for an impostor, and told me, crisply reproving, that I was not a child. The candyfloss man was less ageist, and it was with a fine pink sugar goatee that I greeted Martina and the children as they undulated past on the merry-go-round, hanging on to those scarlet and magenta cockerels. She seemed unimpressed by the fair, but her three little blond and doll-like children – twin boys, Federico and Filippo, and their younger sister, Paloma – were awed at this eruption of magic in the middle of a field, and solemnly tried everything in turn. Giorgio was manning the bar with Juan and Barbara when we appeared, until he caught sight of a neighbour's horse that had escaped and was frisking irresponsibly in the wasteland behind the bar miles from home. The last we saw of Giorgio was his back, like a scribbled zigzag of a drawing by Lowry, streaking through the undergrowth in the darkness, in a desperate bid to catch it.

If our little local *romería* is like something out of Enid Blyton, the Málaga *feria* was invented by Georg Grosz. When August is at its most stifling, and there is no way you're going to look like anything other than an oil slick, that is when the Málaga *feria* is held. This steamy heat lasts only a week or two, and coincides with the *feria*. It is the biggest in Europe, occupying thirty acres of prime building land on the outskirts of Málaga, a vast empty space that languishes completely vacant for all but those two weeks in summer. Overnight, the concrete wasteland is covered with ferris wheels, dance arenas, bandstands, a whole twinkling city of booths in which you can eat and watch flamenco dancing, drink and flirt the night away. I have to admit that I love the idea of the *feria*, I love the fact that there is no question about selling off the prime stretch of land for more lucrative purposes, no question that everything should stop for the entire duration of the fair. Apparently a million people go.

What I'm not so sure about is the thing itself. There is something about the harsh lighting, the itinerant cast of loiterers, the general sleaziness of fairs that always makes me want to go home as soon as I have arrived. But Dan loves them, the creepier the better, and has painted them many times.

It was so hot that August that we just managed to come alive around midnight, and played cards, sweating and moving very slowly, until four or five. After Hugo and his Twingo left, we retrieved the van from Señor Meatball and took Ted and Doris to the *feria* to make up for the geriatric quiet of their stay. We went on the last night, when there are fireworks on the beach as a grand finale. We dressed up in our finery, and set off, arriving at about ten, probably two hours earlier than we should. Most Spanish things start jumping at around midnight. The car park was an adventure in itself, miles and miles of it, in total darkness, with crunchy, sharp and squelchy things underfoot. Way over there we could see the glare of the *feria*, and someone being hanged – no, they were just doing a bungee jump from a giant crane.

We ambled apprehensively into the fairground, and wandered towards the rides. I wasn't sure what the deal was – whether you had to be a member of the fraternities whose logos emblazoned the myriad booths in order to drink and watch the flamenco within, or whether any strolling punter could wander in. Dan wasn't keen to be sucked into those steaming booths anyway, so we wandered around, deafened, until we found a place selling plates of barbecued something. This kept us occupied for quite a while, since we did not realize that the system depended on taking a ticket. Having finally eaten the barbecued thing, we wandered off among throngs of barely clad girls, sunglassed boys, moustachioed matrons and small energetic men in search of fun.

There was a cutely kitsch ghost train that looked sufficiently unfrightening for me to suggest it confidently. The other three looked at me in pity, and reluctantly agreed. We took our seats, ready to scream at skeletons, spider's webs, spooks and ghoulish things jumping out at us. We did scream, but it was mostly at the sight of a man with a spanner, trying to attach a crucial girder that had somehow come loose. The whole cardboard structure wobbled as we careened round bends, and the things that jumped out were iron rods at more or less decapitation height. We were very relieved when the tacky little train clattered past the last badly painted anatomically mutant skeleton and let us off.

Having survived that, we had a rush of courage, and looked round greedily for the next thrill. The fair was so big that it was difficult to grasp what the different areas consisted of. I suggested that we go on one of the high rides, so that we could get a bird's-eye view and orientate ourselves. I didn't grasp the full horror of the one we chose. I should have twigged when Ted said he didn't think he'd join us. Being inexperienced, I laughed and joined the queue. Did I say orientate? I mean, of course, kill ourselves. And the way I had chosen to do this was called the 'Viking Swingboat'. I remember saying, 'Look, it's just a huge swing, and when it goes up you get a view of the whole *feria*. It looks like fun.' At each end of the Viking Swingboat there were strong metal cages, and I wondered briefly why everyone else wanted to cram in there rather than sitting out in the airy unencumbered rows of seats where we were.

The following eternity was the most terrifying nightmare of my life, worse than getting claustrophobia in the stuck lift, worse than losing 500 feet in the plane coming back from my honeymoon, worse than any four-in-the-morning bouts of terminal hypochondria. Gradually the momentum built up. At first it was the vicarage-tea-party ride I had expected, and I seem to remember chatting about what we could see below. Quite soon it got too serious for screams. With each pendulum swing of that endless ride we tipped higher, until we were suspended upside-down over the concrete, unfettered, unharnessed and very unhappy.

My hands were so sweaty with fear that they slid off the chrome bar of the seat behind, and I just grabbed Doris. I will be grateful to her for ever. Far, far below I could see Ted. If anything kept me from toppling out, it was his supercilious smirk. A lifetime later the thing swung itself out. We tottered back onto solid ground, Doris covered in bruises and staying well to the far side of Dan, lest panic overtake me again.

Still shaking, we braved the big wheel, which was very big indeed, and by a brilliant coup of serendipity we were becalmed right up at the top when the fireworks went off miles away on the beach. We had the most thrilling private view. I love fireworks and those were wonderful.

Slightly less impressive was the firework finale to the Pastelero *feria*. That summer, twenty streetlights had been installed, going up the hill to nowhere, and the village held its own first *fiesta*. This consisted of eating outside at Paco's and Antonio's under a blitz of lightbulbs, while watching the normally lumpish girls of the village saunter past magically transformed into absolute stunners in their spotty meringue dresses and hair slicked back with combs and roses. The village boys countered this display of glamour with an array of hideous nylon football gear, impenetrable shades and novelty haircuts. The music was provided by seven old men, who stood in a circle, mostly with their backs to the audience, playing various quaint instruments – Verdiales they are called. According to the *Eyewitness* guide, these are *'pandas'*, bands, performing 'wild primitive music from Moorish times, played on medieval instruments' by men with beaded multicoloured fluffy tortoises on their heads.

It wasn't wild and primitive when we saw it, more like a 78 r.p.m. record performed at 33 r.p.m., and effortlessly conjured up the thrill of watching morris dancers in some rain-sodden field in Sussex. The Verdiales have since become a serious tourist attraction and have multiplied, smartening up their act no end, hampered only slightly in that there appears to be only one authentic tune that they repeat for the requisite eight hours of the celebration. On this occasion to augment their arthritic syncopations they had brought along a hirsute transsexual, who was a great singer. The entire village turned out, baby girls with ribbons and gold earrings, baby boys in miniature suits, their downy hair Brylcreemed into a side parting, grandparents who must have witnessed enormous changes since the death of Franco in 1975. Everyone ate, drank and shouted, arguments were forgotten, innocence and amiability prevailed. This is the gift of a benign climate.

Every two-peseta town has a summer festival – the Almogia *fiesta* coincided with one of my trips back to England so I missed the bevy of Brazilian beauties clad only in fishnets and a feather or two. But Dan made one of his rare forays out from his frowzy lair to see them and still talks about the feathered dancers and those fireworks.

In the main, however, Dan was too busy for *fiestas*. His exhibition in Chelsea was approaching fast, and he applied himself to his easel with quiet determination. I felt very proud of him, and enjoyed watching as he stood, sometimes clad in nothing but a palette, putting the finishing touches to Señor Arrabal's *finca* or his favourite rocks. It was a challenge to organize the exhibition from Spain, but we managed to find a perfect venue, had invitations printed and sent, and arranged wine and food while Dan worked away at views of Málaga's handsome town hall, and El Torcal.

We invited both our families to the private view, children, ex-wife and ex-husband, all our friends, journalists, Francine, and Rosa and Juan on the off-chance that they might be in London. Dan had painted a romantic version of their house with the Mediterranean in the background. He managed to put together an impressive collection, but as we were packing them up, I remarked that there was not a single painting of our own house.

Dan agreed, and wandered out to find a good view. He came back later, disappointed. The house was in a scruffy transitional stage, surrounded by bare earth and cement-mixers, and did not look good from any angle. But he agreed that it was a serious omission, and ruminated over the photograph albums searching for inspiration. He found it in one of the photos I had taken when Spigs and I first saw the house: a view from Señor Arrabal's of the bright green diagonal of the sloping field, with the house looking like a tiny white village, caressed by the low branch of the *transparente*. It was very simple, bright green and white, with a flawless blue sky. He muttered disapproval at doing a painting from a photograph, opining that nothing good would come of it, but did the small landscape. I loved it, its simplicity, the sense of heat and light, and the crude old building Spigs and I had first seen and fallen in love with.

We packed them all up, set off for London, and spent Sunday hanging them before the beano the following day. Dan put the painting of our house rather dismissively in a dimly lit corner.

The party was a terrific success. Just one person did not come – Dan's aunt Nellie. Apart from this important absence everyone was there, and it was wonderful to see them, and to be able to introduce Elly, Dan's ex-wife, to Brendan, my ex-husband, Jocasta to Rosa and Juan, my sister Judy to Dan's parents, Doris to my niece Polly and her daughter Martha, Leo to Doris's beautiful cousin Rachel, Spigs to his old friend Marg from the magazine, Joyce and Nick to Hester and Chris, and Francine to Peter Williams.

We were too busy having a good time to attend to the serious business of selling pictures, though, and as a result sold fewer than we might have wished. My gain: I love those paintings, and have them all over Casa Miranda. I wondered why Rosa and Juan did not buy the lyrical painting of their house. Rosa, who has to speak the whole truth on all occasions, replied that she thought Dan needed to decide whether he was a strictly figurative or sentimental romantic painter. I thought she was mad. But Suzy bought a great portrait of the Pastelero bar flanked by its two huge palm trees, while various views of Señor Arrabal's house, plus a few rocks, El Torcal and some watercolours all sold.

There was a painting that *everyone* wanted to buy: the one of our house that Dan had dashed off so reluctantly. When we peered closely we saw that it had a red spot. Aunt Nellie had cunningly come by before the show began, and had bought it. We ended the evening in a crowd at the Chelsea Arts Club, at a big table, drinking too much.

In contrast to landscape painting, Dan had a lucrative line in dirty drawing – he was commissioned to illustrate a book, a very very rude book of insults by its author, the lexicographer Jonathon Green, husband of my friend Suzy. Dan spent the summer drawing unspeakably scatological and obscene subjects with delicate wit, and it came as no surprise when he was invited to illustrate the following volume, devoted to bodily functions. He was justly proud of these books, but however much he would have liked to show off to his mother, he just couldn't subject her to them. She was able to experience a waft of maternal pride, however, on seeing his *Sunday Times* illustrations for Joanna Simons's wine column.

He has since discovered a passion for computer graphics, did the illustrations for his latest book using a mouse, and taught himself how to make animated films on his moody Mac. In my experience, no-one over the age of ten can get to grips with complex computer programs. Dan was well over ten, had never used anything more complicated than a dip pen and Indian ink, and came straight from the quill age to advanced information technology in one easy bound, self-taught. Personally I see this as close to genius.

Ted's mussels: Cuisine Reservoir Dogs

Serves 4

2kg mussels
2 tbsps olive oil
1 onion, finely chopped
4 cloves garlic, peeled and chopped
3 sprigs fresh thyme
2 small tomatoes, skinned and diced
150ml white wine
pepper
large pinch saffron
cream (optional)
handful chopped parsley

Scrub the mussels, chucking away any damaged ones, or those that fail to shut when tapped. Heat the oil in an enormous pan, and sauté the onion for a minute, then add the garlic and thyme. Stir for a little while, then add the tomatoes and cook for a couple of minutes. Add the wine, pepper and saffron, let it bubble for a couple of minutes, then add the mussels. Put on a lid, turn up the heat, and cook briskly for 5 minutes, shaking the pan violently from time to time, until the mussels have opened. Take them out and keep them warm in a bowl in a moderate oven, discarding any that are still closed. Let any grit sink to the bottom of the remaining liquid and either strain it over the mussels as it is or reduce it and add a dollop of cream. Sprinkle with the parsley and eat immediately with good bread to mop up the juice.

17

A BOOT IN THE ARSENAL

In autumn 1999, Arsenal seemed to have accepted that expanding the stadium in Highbury was going to cause more problems than it would solve, and issued a press release that suggested they were looking at other options. I sprang into action, and put my house on the market immediately. There was no way I was going to let them foil me a second time, should they change their minds. I should feel grateful to them: since I had first put up the house for sale, an astonishing revolution had taken place in the housing market, and it was now worth well over 50 per cent more than it had been two years before.

Buying that house had been a panicky and impoverishing experience when I did it seventeen years previously. It was the fifth house for which I had made an offer that had been accepted: I had been gazumped on the point of exchanging contracts with the other four. It was a practical house, big enough to accommodate throngs of galumphing boys, handsome though crumbly, in one of my favourite wide and leafy streets, and I never stopped worrying about money from the moment I moved in.

When I put the house back on the market I was travelling back and forth between Spain and England, and had to leave the selling to the boys and the agent. Understandably, Leo, Spigs and their friends were reluctant to move out, since their rental contribution somehow never added up to what we had agreed. I suspect that they did not welcome prospective buyers with the obligatory roasting coffee beans, baking bread and flowers, so I am impressed that we sold it at all. But we did. At last there was enough money to pay off my debts, resume building in Spain, and even a bit to invest. Goodbye, Highbury, hello, Freedom.

Emptying the house, finally, was as vile as such things generally are. More stuff had accumulated, and somehow it was grimmer and sadder for being winter, cold, rainy and dark at three. On the day our buyer was due to move in, we were exhausted, drifting in grey, dream-like slow motion through the messy misery of empty rooms, and still finding things that needed packing. But finally we locked that familiar door, handed over the keys and left that bit of life behind.

At the time of being ejected from the family home, Spigs was remarkably well organized. He was still working for my sister Jocasta at Paint Magic, and had found himself a house to rent near Alexandra Palace with a bunch of mates. Leo was invited to house-sit for our friends Clay and Maggie for a month, so that he had a bit of time to find himself something more permanent. He and Winston, his paranoid ginger cat, stayed there for rather longer than anyone had intended.

The final transactions for leaving Highbury turned out to be much more complicated than I expected.

There seemed to be an astonishing amount of paperwork, people to inform, bills to pay and all sorts of unpredictable crises. Dan washed his hands of the whole procedure, as he tends to do with anything involving meetings, business or money. UK Removals delivered everything safely to Spain, where we dumped the two pantechnicon loads of boxes in the newly completed kitchen and just left them there; there was nowhere to put their contents until the builders finished the four remaining rooms in the south house. It is such hard *work* moving.

To my relief I have never felt a second of regret for the Highbury house. The years of living there were the ones that had reduced me to a crippled wreck. It does have good memories, of course, but mostly I associate it with being out of my depth, always overdrawn, perennially squirming from the latest onslaught by tax inspector, bank or electricity company, working eighteen hours a day when I was in mid-book, a prey to carnivorous editing, wanly persevering with subsistence relationships, and at the forefront a permanent knot of grief – the heavy feeling that I was failing in the struggle to bring up my sons.

The old millennium had ended for me with the sudden severance of historic ties, and that was how the next one began. In January 2000 a new broom swept me into history, as far as the office was concerned.

On the 10th, the editor called me into her very tidy office, flung her beige pashmina defiantly over her beige shoulder and said, 'If you resign now, you can leave on April the tenth, which is a Monday.' I was a bit taken aback: in my book, resigning is something you do voluntarily.

'What's the matter?' she asked. 'You look shocked.'

'Well, yes,' I replied. 'It's hard to make being sacked look pink and fluffy.'

'I'm not sacking you. Well, I am. But you wanted to leave anyway.' To be fair, this was true, but I had in mind to go when it suited me.

The next day she called me in once more. 'If you want to, you can clear your desk now. Just send in the copy for the next three months.'

It was not the fact but the suddenness of my dismissal after thirteen years as garden editor that I found shockingly brutal. There was no farewell speech, no party, no Liberty vase. For maybe all of eight seconds it was a sickening blow to my pride. Primarily, though, it was a glorious liberation. No more meetings, no more deadlines, no pressure to do bungled radio interviews with Geoff in Croydon or wear a deadly green polo shirt and sell subscriptions to the magazine. The moment had come when I could *really* live in Spain and put down the roots whose absence was making me feel so wobbly.

Working where I did, in the job that I did, there was just too much of everything – too many new faces, too many events, too much paper, too many deadlines. I'm used to being solitary, and was suffering from people-fatigue. I had got so that I couldn't distinguish between the precious and the rest. I hated the telephone and would growl and lock myself in the loo when it rang. There just never seemed to be enough time to be a person, no moment of still and quiet in which to attend to the inner woman, to formulate a wish, a need, a sense of wanting anything other than to be left alone.

For over a year, life had consisted of three weeks in

Spain, interspersed with one week of chaos in London, sleeping in a different place every night, trying to do everything – interminable bank business, meeting maybe fifty different people, interviewing and writing, dealing with office politics, trying to hang on to friendships and beloved family when almost catatonic with exhaustion. I had plodded on one day at a time, and could not afford the luxury of missing Dan. I should not have afforded the luxury of retail therapy either, but schlepping into shops and buying more stuff, compulsively and shamefaced, was what I did. Books, music, clothes, more suitcases, makeup, any old schmutter, I just had to have it.

In fact, I was longing to settle, put down roots, feel at home somewhere. And while the house in Highbury lay in the shadow of Arsenal's vacillations my life had been on hold. Now that the house had been sold and I was no longer employed by the magazine, I could reacquaint myself with myself. I was quite apprehensive as to who I would turn out to be.

I feared that leaving the magazine, with its familiar habits and patterns, would make me feel like an amputee. It did not. Instead I was alternately youthfully frisky and very tired, as though I had to catch up on twenty years of sleep. In between bouts of hibernation I was transformed from a voyeur of life into someone actually, triumphantly, living it. I was suddenly the woman who planted the roses and made the cakes; the lucky creature whom I had been interviewing and observing enviously for the past decade.

While I was in the throes of office politics I used to try to picture how life would be without it, whether I would feel lonely, what and who I would miss, whether I would ever write again or just stare vacantly into space.

Would I have an identity without work? Would I get bored – so bored that I would be forced to write the novel that has stalked me from O level English and Miss White? Would I know how to write anything longer than a thousand words with 'compost' in the first paragraph?

The answer to the latter is that I did. I wrote about ten million letters – to banks, insurance companies, water, gas and electricity services, Internet service providers, British Airways, the post office, British Telecom, credit-card companies, accountants, financial advisers and, it seemed, enough petty functionaries to fill the Isle of Wight. I had never realized quite how complicated it is to segue from one life to another. Until I discovered that nothing but a letter would get a result, I listened to enough Enya on the telephone, while punching in my next selection, to last many lifetimes, running up phone bills that turned my knees to water. I have since been told that you just punch the hache key when they start on the selection spiel, and you are put through immediately to a real person.

I was expecting the transition from one life to another to throw up some surprises. People function on automatic pilot most of the time, carried onward by habit. In Spain we had to create a new life from scratch, with no familiar patterns to guide us, no tried-and-tested solutions to the problems of depression, isolation, hypochondria and boredom. With lakes of cheap booze and many examples before us, I wondered if we'd become slumped alcoholics. I expected the worst, and pictured us like Sickert's *Ennui*, gasping with boredom and mutual antipathy. I also believe in self-fulfilling prophecies and felt like a wicked fairy, bringing my bad dream with me and depositing it on whatever luckless bloke I was with. At the beginning, I was taken aback to find that Dan outdid me. He regularly worked his way through a handful of terminal illnesses before breakfast. And whatever dark thoughts came to plague me, he had already been there, done that.

Gradually we shed our heavy baggage, going through occasional crises and painfully scrabbling out of them. The secret is that, apart from all the tumultuous love business, we really like each other, enjoy the same things, and love this place. He might pout and pack his spotted handkerchief, and I might climb to the top of the hill and mutter imprecations, but we both know that there is nowhere else we'd rather be, and no-one we'd rather be with.

A luxurious, lazy, time-wasting spree took care of several months. I can't say that my enjoyment of it was unalloyed, but it was a bloody-minded necessity, a two-fingers for twenty years of deadlines and living to other people's timetables. I had decided to award myself a year's sabbatical, and I splurged time on just staring into space, and later, when I got my functioning laptop, on playing endless games of Free Cell. My theory was that while the simple-minded game occupied the frontal lobes, the creative subconscious would be busy coming up with the novel. Several thousand games later, I was still playing Free Cell, stuck at 63 per cent success, and look! no novel.

Our other masterplan – to speak Spanish like natives through unassisted osmosis – also failed to happen. We ran aground after the first three words of any halfway interesting conversation. With exasperating slowness we struggled to get the words to stick, and they remained cussedly unavailable when we needed them. Apparently you can learn twenty languages with no difficulty at all if you are two, a generous handful if you are ten, and have trouble hanging on to your own if you are fifty. This is a scientific fact, and we are living, mumbling proof. So I was thrilled when Spigs brought home a translation program for my computer. At last, I thought, I shall be able to understand those official-looking letters with things underlined in red. I typed in a moderately red letter from Telefonica and, quick as a flash, my computer came back with:

> Dear Client,
> We wanted to indicate him that, until today's day, we don't have perseverance that the payment of the reference invoice has been made.
>
> Of existing some reason for which has not been possible effective the amount of the same one, him *agredeceriamos* contacted our Service of Attention to the Client, 1004 (gratuitous call).
>
> Otherwise we would be forced, very to our grief, to interrupt the phone service that we come him *suministrando*, a to leave of the day.
>
> The unpaid of the invoice, starting from the suitable date, doesn't exempt him of the payment of the corresponding fixed quotas as well as of the quota of the rehabilitation of the service.
>
> Of taking place the mentioned not wanted circumstance, lapsed FOUR MONTHS from the date of the present communication, he/she would take place the definitive interruption of the borrowed service.

So there you are.

Eventually we had a bit of a breakthrough, thanks to the innovative teaching methods of Michael

Thomas, whose Spanish course I thoroughly recommend.

I also started to get to grips with corners of the outdoors reclaimed from the builders. Adjoining the house on the south and west, there were what I suppose should be called troughs. I filled them single-handed with what felt like several tons of earth, and planted them with lavender and starry blue felicia, the delicious jasmine sambac, whose little suede-like white flowers smell the sweetest and strongest and

from which jasmine tea is made, wisteria, honeysuckle, and a scented white-flowered evergreen bush called carissa. For some reason this acquired spots and sulked; it was probably too cold for it up here.

My most spectacular success was with the deep troughs that border our circular swimming-pool. We painted the wall above and below a vibrant strawberry pink, and the steps to the pool are tangerine. Against this lush kitsch background – I had the bold bright Mexican buildings of Luis Barragan in mind – I planted saxe blue echium, nasturtiums, lavender and climbers. I was dubious about the white solanum, dismissing it as common as muck. It might have been, but it was a damned good tryer, and foamed with white flowers all summer. The fancy passion-flower, *Passiflora allardii*, on the other hand, managed to produce a solitary – if gorgeous – fringed and exotic pink flower before it became a tangled mess of naked twigs. Grape-vines were planted where they were supposed to shimmy up pillars and make a cool leafy awning above our heads. They showed no sign of doing anything so life-enhancing, preferring to wander off sideways absentmindedly without bothering to come up with much in the way of leaves. The dipladenia, a.k.a. *Mandevilla splendens*, was delicious when unpillaged by dogs, with its perfect pink trumpet flowers set fastidiously against rounded, shiny evergreen leaves. Worth persevering with, though it may be too refined for its hillbilly location, it is the Rudolf Nureyev of the plant world, surrounded by a rude crowd of West Ham supporters.

My general scheme when planting the garden was that anything went as long as it was truly vulgar. I really don't like bougainvillea, having a pettish prejudice against bracts, but I could not resist the idea of a tide of loud colour crashing up the bank. My marguerite, which I took from a sprig growing wild up the hill, reacted to its new environment by becoming as big as a bubble car, and was covered in white flowers almost all year, with just a brief pause at Christmas to recharge its batteries.

During that millennial winter we did one really positive thing. We have five acres of land, more than we know what to do with, and I decided that olive trees would be a great labour-saving way to fill the lower field attractively. I love olive trees, their shape, their colour, the undemanding way – as I thought – they colonize rocks and dust. I envisaged a sea of shifting green and silver spreading out charmingly below us. It seemed to me that olive trees and Andalucía grew up together. I didn't want a vast olive harvest – God forbid, we'd have had to gather it and do something with it – just a shimmering carpet of verdigris leaves, changing colour slightly as the wind shifted, where we could sit in summer, shaded and hidden, to read.

This was pure insanity. For a start, 200 olive trees take a lot of wrestling just to get them into the earth in cold, wet December. We realized within seconds of their arrival that we were far too lazy to do anything so active and recruited help.

The first couple to pit themselves at the task took an entire day to plant eight. To be fair, their perfectly planted trees do look much sturdier than any of the others, but at that rate we would have been bankrupted by the time half were in the ground. Barbara's daughter Emma and her boyfriend Jose David planted twice as fast for half the money, but we were still fighting a losing battle. And it was such sodden, cold, dispiriting and exhausting work. Then someone suggested that we get Bobcat Bob to dig the holes in the unyielding clay with his mini JCB. He agreed and suggested that his wife, Jackie, might help with the planting. I was dubious about this, picturing some tiny grey-haired lady having a fit of the vapours because of the work, the cold and the general awfulness of the job. But, as usual, I was wrong. Jackie did have grey hair, but she was a Trojan. She got down to planting and two days later 200 little olive trees were happily getting used to their new home, just in time for the millennium.

We breathed a sigh of relief. Wrong again. The usually empty landscape was suddenly abuzz with Spaniards, who'd come to tell us that we had planted the trees too close together. Not only that, but Paco White Pantaloons made a point of calling in on us on the way back from the bar one dark and cheerless midnight to harangue us drunkenly about how very hopeless our tree-planting exercise had been. He enumerated the reasons, over and over again, until Dan frogmarched him to the door. Paco described the pests, the diseases, the poverty of the soil, the lack of good husbandry, the inattention to pruning, the overcrowded planting, the general sloppy and slapdash failure of our enterprise with such relish that we felt a slow and painful death would be too good for us. It all boiled down to us being a pair of rank and feckless beginners.

In response to an urgent directive from Antonio, our builder, and in the teeth of all my organic principles, I did sprinkle blue fertilizer round the trees once, and later I sprayed them with something toxic once to kill the pests. As soon as Antonio moved off site, I left the trees to fend for themselves, which they appeared to do quite happily despite being overshadowed by weeds.

We pickled our own olives, from the five mature trees that came with the house. It was not a success. We had been given directions by a knowledgeable friend, who kindly spent a day picking and sorting them, splitting them with a stone, and putting them in brine in a plastic bucket. She instructed us to change the brine daily for the next ten days, and not to touch the contents of the bucket with our hands or anything metal. Punctiliously, we did as we were told, and at the end were dismayed to find we had a bucket full of scum. Well, it is just possible that we obeyed her directives until the ten days were up, then forgot about the olives for a while. By way of a daring experiment I put about a third into jars with pepper, chilli, garlic, lemon and herbs, but the more I bottled, the less appetizing they looked. I am ashamed to admit that I crept out at dead of night and chucked the rest into the compost bin.

Having landed in Spain, one of the unpredictable things to happen to me was a serial falling in love. Not with people – though Pedro the horse man, with his penetrating, interested brown-eyed gaze and calm yet passionate dignity, might in other circumstances have inflamed one to throw down one's saddle and rip off one's helmet – but throughout 2000 with places, activities, flowers and food. 'Gorgeous' was the *mot du jour*. Rapture became a normal state of mind, interspersed with becalmed doldrums. They were, I decided, two sides of the same coin, the common denominator being time. From being a time pauper I was suddenly a time millionaire, free to do anything I wanted, when I wanted. I could sleep until midday, I could stay up until four in the morning, I could spend six hours shopping. I could abandon phone and fax and just take off to the top of the hill. Or I could just plob around, enjoying an unprecedented excess of time in a sybaritic orgy of being bored and fidgety. If you want to get something done, ask a busy woman. How true. And how true its opposite. Days passed, and sometimes the afternoon found me still mooning around in a shapeless dressing-gown, wondering what to have for breakfast.

Sometimes I would occupy this freedom by snipping hundreds of blue and white cotton squares from men's shirts assembled over the years from Oxfam shops for the purpose of making delicious light patchwork quilts. That was the theory. Alas, as with Toad of Toad Hall and his brief obsessions, this one never lasted long enough with me to make a finished tea-cosy, let alone a voluptuous throw. But I have a trunkful of fine cotton four-inch squares, should the patchwork obsession revive.

My most enduring passion from this period was for cooking. I had always hated cooking because it was associated with stumbling home exhausted from work and having to think of something to feed two ravening adolescents whose idea of foodie paradise was Burger King Flamers. In London, I didn't really need to cook, because I could buy anything I wanted cooked better by someone else, so that is what I did as often as I could afford and organize it. My own cooking was a short list of *very* simple staples, and mad flurries of ingenuity when there was nothing to eat and I didn't have the energy or cash to schlep down to Sainsbury's.

But in Spain you can't buy certain essentials. Amazingly, you can't get hold of marmalade. So that was my first serious experiment as I stockpiled sugar and our entire kumquat crop plucked from the abused bonsai by the front door, and panicked about soft balls and burnt pans.

I was rather pleased with the result – a single priceless jar, attar of kumquat – and bucked by this success, bought quantities of Seville oranges, sold at the roadside for pennies a crate. Definitely this was attempting to run before I could walk, and there was a knife-edge drama involving a blackened pan and seething, overflowing marmalade in catering-size amounts. To my mind that bittersweet edge of blackened caramel was the perfect touch, and I was proud of it, despite its thunderous darkness, and undaunted by Dan's remark: 'How strange it is,' he said, leaning back in his chair and looking mournfully at his toast, 'that when you've got loads of homemade stuff it just doesn't taste as good as bought.'

I've since learned that the secret lies in pacing. My initial mistake was to frighten Dan with a glut. You have to hide preserves from yourself and your loved one, so that finding the odd jar of plum jam or pickled cucumbers comes as a wonderful surprise.

My dietary undoing was Dan's birthday present to me. He bought me Nigella Lawson's *How To Be a Domestic Goddess* because I love her writing, and had said that her books were the best female company in my woman-starved environment. When I am overwhelmed by blokes discussing football and the virtues of Photoshop, I read her cookery books, and watch Julia Roberts and Nora Ephron films. I even bought two CDs called *Woman 1* and *2*, and sang along with the tragic crew, brimming with sentimental recognition. But, in a curious, perverse way, I was glad to be sad. Constructing friendships with women is a far more delicate business than taking up with a man, probably because men come from Uranus anyway. Missing sisters, nieces and girlfriends, enjoying their company retrospectively, and having time to look forward to our next meeting was and is a luxury; there was never time to do this in London.

I didn't really mean to cook, just to enjoy Nigella's breezy wit, and have a tiny drool about virtual cheesecake. But somehow, insidiously, her insistence that it was all so easy made me think I could just try cooking something very simple from the book. After three key lime pies, four party-size batches of fudge brownies, a tin of coffee walnut biscuits, a sticky lemon sponge, a strawberry shortcake, a plum-crumble cake using our own plums, and some cynically produced and greedily eaten Snickers and peanut-butter muffins down the line, I had to admit that it had become an obsession.

'Mum, you're being just like a proper mother,' Spigs said in awe, after yet another serious tea. Fat, is what he meant.

Dan has always been good at bread. Once, just once, when we were staying in a huge, rather creepy house on Jura to do a feature about a garden, I awoke to the smell of new bread, which he had tiptoed downstairs and made while I was still asleep. It wasn't bread, it was manna, and we ate an entire large loaf, still hot, with half a pound of butter in a greedy frenzy. In Spain we can get *barras* of white bread from the baker and they are delicious for barely an hour before they turn into old roof beams. Anyway from time to time you want a change. So Dan made ciabatta, and did it again with black olives. Then worked with Spigs to make pizza. Generally I can't see the point of pizza, but these were amazing, rich, toothsome and savoury with a delicious thick sludge of topping. Next he turned his hand to pesto, which became his speciality: he used different cheeses, wild rocket instead of basil when it was in season and growing exuberantly along the track, and almonds and pistachios instead of pine nuts. They were all delicious. It was such a treat, too, to be able to throw generous handfuls of fresh basil at whatever we cooked – basil and cherry tomatoes grew with no help from us, and I shivered with pleasure every time I used them.

Spigs has always been a great cook, and his stay with us towards the end of 1999 coincided with the sparkling new kitchen in which everything worked. His new, improved, mild Thai curries – in which your tastebuds were not fatally cauterized by chillies in the first mouthful – were fabulous, particularly eaten to a background chorus of cicadas on the west terrace as the sun sank scarlet behind the distant strips of misty lavender hills.

Along with intrepid cuisine, Spigs always brought a welcome gale of feisty argument and energy, propelling us, squeaking indignantly, from our slothful torpor. Whatever he does, he does emphatically. On wandering into the sitting room one would come across him, brown and hirsute, doing press-ups from a chair to give them extra oomph, hundreds of them. Or standing in the kitchen, beating hell out of star anise, lemon grass and galangal. Or you'd see him *running* round the hill with the dogs in the blazing summer sun – they'd spend the rest of the day flattened on the floor, while he'd just wipe the sweat from his blue eyes and cycle off to Mrs Paco's in search of Serrano ham. The fact that he'd just given himself an almost bald number-one haircut may have given her a moment's terror.

We discovered Barbara Kafka's microwave book, and experimented with making our own coconut milk, intending it to give Spigs's Thai pork its velvety slightly sweet sauce. It was fiddly, took quite a while, then Kiko sneaked up and drank it. We found an Indian emporium, from which we bought naan bread and amazing chutneys, thinking the while, We could make these ourselves, with the mangoes and papayas that grow on the coast. There is a huge variety of exotic Spanish fruit and vegetables, parsnips being among the few things I miss, and Cox's Orange Pippins, although locally grown cherimoyas, mangoes and nisperos more than made up for them.

This kind of frivolous, unnecessary cookery – jams, chutneys and fattening things – was fun. In fact, we got so carried away that for a short while we pondered opening our own restaurant. Fortunately good sense prevailed, but to me it was like being four years old and let loose in the playdough and finger-paint cupboard.

Dan, too, enjoyed a trip back to the busy, mindless and, above all, timeless occupations of childhood. Rocks have always been his fetish, and multiple dry-stone walls were the result: he enclosed vegetable plots, infant trees and hidden stone seats in their own little walled microclimates. Thanks to his labours we now have a variety of secret places in which to sit, alone or not, with gin and tonic on a handy flat rock, watching the sun go down.

He also made a big spiky sculpture out of gesso on a wire armature, like a mad yucca, and has plans to turn our recalcitrant clay into glazed tiles and pots. Mud pies, playing, that's what we began to do as 1999 turned into 2000. We both felt we were satisfying a need we had ignored for far too long.

Spigs's Very Complicated Lasagne

Serves 8

Coriander leaves, dry-fried and added to home-made pasta dough made with 225g flour
5 tbsps olive oil
4 aubergines, cut into strips
6 courgettes, cut into strips
6 bird's-eye chillis, left whole
2 red peppers, chopped
2 onions, chopped
head of garlic, peeled and chopped
2 tsps cumin seed
8 tomatoes, chopped
tomato purée
salt and pepper
1 tbsp butter
1 tsp garam masala
1 tsp coriander seeds, crushed
1 tbsp sifted flour
1½ pints milk
225g cheese: grated Parmesan and Cheddar, plus lumps of blue cheese
chopped fresh herbs – thyme, parsley, coriander

Make pasta dough incorporating coriander, roll into sheets and hang over a dog-free chair to dry for a bit.

Fry the aubergine and courgette strips in the oil with the whole chillis until lightly browned and cooked. Set aside and discard the chillis.

To make the tomato sauce, fry the chopped pepper until the oil colours, then add the chopped onions and garlic and cook until they are clear and golden. Add the cumin seed and fry until fragrant. Add the chopped tomatoes and a good squirt of purée, season with salt and pepper and cook until it has an even sauce-like consistency.

To make the béchamel, melt the butter and fry the garam masala and crushed coriander seeds until fragrant. Add the flour, stirring continuously, and then the milk, drop by drop. Season. When it is thick and cooked, add the cheeses (saving some for the top) and stir for a minute or so.

In a deep baking dish layer the aubergine/courgette mixture, tomato sauce, pasta and béchamel, sprinkling fresh herbs between the layers and finishing off with a layer of béchamel. Sprinkle the remaining mixed cheese on top.

Cook in a hot oven, gas 6/200°C, for 30–45 minutes until brown, and let it stand for 10 minutes before serving.

2000

18

LITTLE SAUSAGES OF LOVE

All this peaceful pottering was way in the future. I was back in Spain after the dramas of the New Year but the experience had left me benumbed and shaky. Despite my brave resolutions about my New Life, I think I succumbed to a brief, lonely depression, and the weather didn't help. Dan and I had our north wing, albeit stuffed with a treacherous superfluity of furniture and boxes, but the rest was mud and rubble. Set foot outside any door, and we were ankle deep in squelching ooze. The icy wind from the Sierra Nevada filtered through doors and windows, and when it rained – which it did, often and violently – water bounced into the house through cracks in doors and windows in a wide hemisphere, soaking cushions, curtains, shelves and books. The dogs completed this picture of discomfort by bringing the muddy outdoors in and depositing it on the sofas, with a penetrating aroma of wet canine. Our days began in darkness, with the arrival of the unfortunate builders, who were sloshing around laying the foundations of the kitchen, sitting room and two bedrooms in the slurry at the southern end of the house.

One of my ex-colleagues, shocked by my sudden depature, had passed a commission my way. It was ironic in the circumstances. I worked at my desk in our newly plastered and damp bedroom – the only place where there was space – bundled up like a Dickensian beggar in scarves, fingerless gloves, woolly hats, thick knitted socks and depressingly saggy thermal long johns filched from Dan, and wrote a book about fireplaces. The pornography of fireplaces, in fact. Frozen, and writing, with torrid passion, about fire, flame, heat, logs and coal, I spent January and February in a state of unsatisfied lust about my subject matter. The bedroom had no source of warmth except a malevolent fan-heater that would gasp out a tiny tepid breath then trip the electricity, losing whatever work I had not saved on my computer.

There were occasions when England seemed so well sorted. As my deadline approached and the builders completed a usable suite of rooms in the south house, we decided to move up there to take advantage of the intermittent sunlight and extra heat. I earmarked an uninterrupted day to write closeted in one of the new bedrooms. First, I thought, I'll quickly go and collect the post from Villanueva, and the cement to seal the wood-stove. Then I'll just shut myself into my room and work. I did my shopping, then Dan suggested we should dump the rubbish and empty bottles, and fetch a couple of gas canisters from Mrs Paco. It's astonishing how long a few piffling essential tasks can take. However, all that done, we came home feeling virtuous. I collected a mug of coffee, retired with a heater to my temporary workroom, shut the door and, with a paragraph bursting to get out of my head, plugged in my computer. At which moment everything fused.

This was the second day on which the electricity had given up on us. Yesterday we had lived by candle-light and paraffin lamps for about eight hours – there was rain, wind and hail, so we were not surprised. But Paco *eléctrico*, who called in the morning, could not see any cause for our present darkness and ascribed our trouble to problems in Almogia.

Dan suggested that we move back into the abandoned north house, where the electricity still seemed to be fine. Spigs and I spent two hours or so hoovering and clearing, while Dan rigged up emergency electricity for the south-house fridge by trailing cables out from one to the other, a process that denuded the north house of all its extension leads and thereby most of its lights. The process of moving involved lighting fires, cleaning out the wood-burner, sealing its chimney, shifting furniture and rewiring two three-gang sockets, one of which Dan then chucked because he thought it was dangerous. Now we had cables draped across the hillside working Dan's computer and the fridge next door, a gloomy absence of lights but two sources of heat in the north house, and I made a final foray next door, collected my laptop and my surge-breaker, my Sony Walkman and some tapes. Finally I was ready to get to work, irritated because it was four o'clock and I hadn't yet been able to sit in front of my screen for a second. I couldn't remember what I had so desperately wanted to write, and I became so frustrated that I ate a whole packet of peanuts in chocolate and felt fat and *sick*. Eagerly, I plugged in the lead and . . . *bang*. A foul, acrid smell and plumes of sinister smoke came out of the extension plug. Was it possible? Could the £15.99 surge-breaker – the computer store had insisted it was essential – have been the source of our tribulations? Who knows? I took it apart to find what looked like a row of dried beans burnt black. And we were one multi-socket extension lead less.

Normally Dan built huge blazes in the sitting-room fireplace each evening, and when my daily writing stint was over it was heaven to shut the bedroom door – having switched on our ancient and dangerous electric blanket – and thaw out, draped with heavy-breathing, face-licking dogs while he cooked supper. I have to admit that the animal smell did not come solely from the dogs. The worst thing about that winter was the bathroom: facing north, perennially damp and musty, plagued with woodlice, it had no heat and no bath. I can't believe that I thought we did not need a bath, when I know perfectly well that there is nothing that can't be healed by immersion in hot water and bubbles. I showered minimally, with extreme reluctance.

After a little initial hostility during which they tried to rip out each other's throats, Minnie and Oscar had fallen head over heels in love. Now they bounced and gambolled around our tiny olive trees by the hour, him growling in a manly way, her biting his cheeks like a saucy tease. Oscar's cheeks became quite crusty with little scabs but, delirious with passion, he didn't mind, and we thought we'd make their happiness complete by letting Minnie have just one litter of puppies. We had been warned that boxers produce large litters, but ignorantly assumed this to be an old wives' tale. I can tell you now that, in the matter of litters, old wives are the people to listen to. But one problem – Oscar's penchant for boys, feline boys in particular – remained. He adored Minnie, but when it came to sex, cats were the thing. When Minnie came on heat, Oscar got wildly randy, and tried to shag Kiko with passion and persistence. Minnie's love of rough trade reasserted itself, and she went on the razzle with anything that had four legs and a bark.

There are two main kinds of dog in Spain. The dark brown Flokati and the caramel Anubis. The Flokati's dreadlocks were matted with various kinds of dung and the odd dead toad. It looked at you benignly, beseechingly almost, from its dim, thicketed brown eyes, but when you approached it with bacon rinds it inflicted on you a gratuitous bite. The Flokati was chained in every yard under piles of wood, and it never learned the length of its chain. Being human and much cleverer, you could judge the precise length, and saunter just an inch out of reach. The dog would launch itself into a hundred-yard dash, only to be throttled after ten. If you had once been nipped, it never failed to bring a vindictive smile to the lips.

Anubis was altogether sharper. Ears pricked, bright eyes perennially scanning the horizon for deals, this was a wide-boy dog, with better things to do than bite you. Constantly on the move, checking out the canine equivalent of a white BMW here, a camel coat there, it hung out with abandoned huskies (surprisingly common), short snappy mongrels and the streetwise of the dog world. Anubis made Minnie's heart beat faster.

Both Oscar and Minnie were miserable and confused. Disappointed by the incompetence and perversity of his love, Minnie snapped at Oscar. He was affronted, and howled when he was not trying to catch Kiko. She went off after the local dirty dogs, but a good shag did not have the magical effect that inebriated football supporters hold as axiomatic; instead, Minnie became fractious, worried and a sneaky stopout.

I had a theory that bitches could produce pups from several different fathers in the same litter, and as the queue of rough trade formed daily outside the door, none of which needed coaching, I had a secret hope that Oscar might have got it together just once. According to the builders, who had a keen interest in manly matters, pure-bred dogs needed a helping hand. Had we discovered canine pornography, I would have happily provided Oscar with it, but as for doing anything physical to further his suit, forget it. And, anyway, it would have been a gross and undignified intrusion.

As soon as Minnie became pregnant, she and Oscar settled back into their previous affectionate pattern, though I suspect that Minnie was just a bit sneery about him thereafter.

I had told Spigs and Leo that they were welcome to come and stay any time at all, and I was very pleased when Spigs announced several weeks later that he had a few days off in April and he had booked a flight to Spain. There were just two tiny problems.

'Mum, I've booked to come to Spain,' he told me. 'The cheapest flight is to Alicante. I get there at midnight on Friday, and the return flight is midnight on Sunday. I'll see you at the airport.'

This was an opportunity for Dan to renew his acquaintance with the man on the ceiling. Rather than tell Spigs to get lost – Alicante is a twelve-hour drive away – I bought an astronomically pricy British Airways ticket to Málaga for him, grumbling very quietly lest I unleash another splutter of indignation from Dan.

The other problem was that Spigs had elected to visit during the same week that Jocasta and her architect husband Richard were coming to recuperate from overwork. Spigs was managing one of Jocasta's Paint Magic shops at the time, and they did not see eye to eye on anything. In fact, Spigs was always straining at the leash to tell Jocasta exactly what he thought of her business shortcomings, and she thought he was a maddening cussed *boy*. They were always having rows, and I fully expected a smattering of nuclear tiffs, with me heavily involved in the fallout.

In fact, what happened was a touching reconciliation. Although they are both opinionated and bull-headed, they are also believers in blood being thicker than water, and it soon became obvious that Spigs's warrior stance was a disguise. Jocasta was taken with his paintings, which are original and energetic to the point of violence, and she had some good advice for getting them exhibited when Spigs bravely showed them to her.

'This one is about sex as you can tell from the two entwined figures. This one is about the women I loved who died during 1997, when I nearly went mad.' The latter is huge, larger than a door, and it shows the three figures of Spigs's stepmother Jessie, who died much too young of cancer and who was his mentor and support, my mother Eileen, and a girlfriend who committed suicide. In fact his strength and courage had been tested to its limit in 1997, as suicide, accidents and sickness took their unending toll. It was unbelievable: no sooner had he regained his balance after one death than he was assailed by another.

During Spigs's *annus horribilis*, Dan had been a terrific *mensch*, strong enough to parry Spigs's anger and aggression, wise enough not to take it personally, generous enough to let him rant. 'I'm an *angry man*,' was Spigs's frequent refrain as he squared up. He fought with everyone, and came to blows with Leo at one stage. I think that the promise of our place in Spain helped him, but painting had been the most important part of the healing process. Now Jocasta responded enthusiastically to the power and focused intensity of these big canvases in their strange strong colours. Altogether Spigs's eruption into our lives during Jocasta and Richard's visit was the best thing that could have happened.

Their visit came four months after UK Removals had efficiently delivered the last of the furniture from Highbury, and we had inefficiently filled the kitchen with the boxes. There was a narrow pathway to the door, and standing room only round the table and work surfaces. Jocasta loves a challenge, so our four months' lassitude was sorted in a day. She found places for everything and gingered us up into creating a semblance of order.

Actually, it was like Christmas: after waiting so long, it was thrilling to unwrap all my clutter. I felt a surge of fondness for it all, as the house was filled with reminders of friends and family – a little and very pleasing chorus of voices around me. It was the plates I noticed first, the bright hand-painted plates that Hester had given me over the years and which now, piled up in a jazzy tower, proclaimed that this was home.

Other presents had other voices. Leo's little cloisonné box with a fish on the lid instigated a morning's reverie, as did the green wooden box that Spigs had given me. Jocasta's magnificent Victorian washstand bowl, with its decoration of yellow roses round the edge, was perfectly at home, looking gorgeous with its cargo of cherimoyas and mangoes, papayas and kiwi fruit, until the fateful day when it slithered off a chair and smashed. It was mendable, but it will never be its perfect extrovert self again. On the other hand, the Eric Ravilious plates didn't look happy at all. They depict a Bloomsbury sort of woman – Virginia Woolf, say – sitting under a tree in a deckchair, reading a book, with what looks like a shopping trolley to hand, all in yellow and grey. Very English.

Having achieved an array of cute objects on every horizontal surface, we decided to have a party and invited Chris and Barbara to lunch. The sun was brilliant, the sky was clear, the air was warm. Although the Sierra Nevada still glittered with snow on the horizon, it was a sleeveless summer day in April. Bullied by Jocasta, to whom it comes naturally, we decided to eat outside. Minnie waddled about listlessly under our feet, as round and hard as a brown watermelon on stumpy legs, unable to breathe or eat because of her imminent puppies and the heat, keeling over when the effort of being upright was too much. Oscar lolloped around, getting in the way.

Jocasta and I manhandled the round blue table out onto the west terrace and found a mixture of chairs. Dan, needled by Jocasta, had reluctantly unpacked the pasta machine from its virgin box, and was glooping around with eggs and flour, asking where things were every two seconds. He was hampered by the semi-darkness consequent on a culinary flurry on the part of Richard, who had decided that this was the moment to experiment with fried aubergines, and had filled the house with a dense, choking, industrial smog. He had also covered the table and both worktops with a messy spatter of knives, chopping-boards, bowls of water, saucers of salt, flour, stalks and stumps.

Jocasta took a tray of glasses, crockery and cutlery outside, and I toyed with the dangerous but, I thought, festive notion of trying out a recipe for a version of Pimm's that sprang from the pages of the *Week*, saying, 'Drink me.' Hell, why not? It's a lovely day. Chris and Barbara will be here in a minute, we have no plans for the afternoon and there's a blue haze of borage growing wild down the track. I took the curvaceously sexy glass jug Hester had given me and sloshed in two measures each of gin and red vermouth, one of orange Curaçao. I filled the jug with half fizzy water and half lemonade and threw in some orange and lemon quarters, a few cucumber slices and two sprigs of bristly borage. I dragged a clatter of ice cubes from their reluctant roost, stuck to the freezer, gave the whole thing a stir and poured us a good half-pint each.

Spigs bustled in from the garden with an armful of basil and some wild rocket he'd discovered. Then, like the good boy he sometimes is, he started to grate the Parmesan and peel the garlic for pesto.

Dan, meanwhile, had succeeded in dominating the eggs and flour and needed a hand with the folding and rolling of the pasta. The lumps of dough were given a calendered shine by the smooth steel rollers, stretching longer and longer, finer and finer until you could see the grain of the table through them. As a grand finale, we pinked them into saw-toothed strips, which we draped over the GNU rise-and-fall airer to dry. For a while we did not observe that Oscar was springing with all the grace of a beer-barrel to pinch the pasta ribbons from their lines.

The aromatic peppery smell of the basil, the molten gold of the olive oil on the windowsill, the cool marble smoothness of the pasta combined in a sensuous feast before we had eaten a thing. In response to a tickle of nagging hunger, Dan opened a jar of the olives I had pickled the previous Christmas and glared at with suspicion ever since. I was certainly not about to eat them, despite the chilli and garlic, peppercorns, thyme and fennel. I murmured, 'Botulism,' under my breath, the memory of the unbecoming scum in the brine bucket being all too vivid. But, strangely, as the level of Pimm's went down, my confidence soared. Those olives looked like some arty still-life from the Conran catalogue, and they were delicious. Green, plum, maroon, the colours of faded tapestry, flecked with herbs and speckled with garlic, they were a perfect mixture of sweet and bitter, sharp and mellow – there was a lot going on in that olive jar.

The Pimm's finished, Chris and Barbara arrived, laden with good Rioja in a hairnet, and manchego *curado* – in fact, the seriously expensive *viejo.* I made another batch of Pimm's and we unwrapped the cheese, absent-mindedly shaving off at least a quarter of it, enjoying those salty prickles that denote a properly matured one, before it made its way onto the table in the sun. From which we had to rescue it immediately as we were not too drunk to spot Kiko lying unobtrusively in Minnie's shadow waiting for his moment to raid the table. It wouldn't be so bad if he just ate the damned food, but what he liked to do was maul as large an area as possible while sitting unhygienically on a plate, a chopping-board or in a salad bowl.

We piled Richard's crisply blackened aubergines onto a bright yellow Moroccan dish, and took it out along with a small bowl of holy honey – Spanish molasses that comes with a fetchingly crowned and gowned virgin on the jar.

As this chaotic lunch proceeded, we became very sticky, with dribbles of cane honey down our chins, clumping our fingers together.

I remembered that I had made some hummus, which I fetched from the fridge and sprinkled with a green flicker of coriander, a dusting of paprika, and anointed with a golden pool of extra virgin.

Dan was clunking the pesto in the mortar with the pestle, a huge vat of water was boiling for the pasta, and we had finally reached the moment to sit down and enjoy life.

'She's started!' We all froze. Minnie's first puppy was emerging. She had ignored the blanketty nest we'd made for her in the cool of the sitting room, and was having them under the blue table where lunch was spread. Curiously, none of us was very hungry any more.

The next seven hours were thrilling and terrifying. Would she know what to do? Would they know what to do? Would she inadvertently sit on them? Would she need help? How would any of us know when she had finished? Did *we* have to do anything? As each puppy was born totally enclosed in its amniotic sac, Minnie licked it off carefully and did all the right things, guided by instinct. She'd never done it, probably never even seen it, but she knew exactly what to bite, what to lick, where to sit so that her tiny puppies had access to her milk, and how gentle she had to be. I'm ashamed to say that I found the whole puppy-birth thing quite disgusting and, having established that there were sufficient highly qualified observers, slunk off out of sight.

Eventually Minnie produced eleven, mostly brown and undistinguished, with a smattering of piebald white. The white ones were, from the moment they breathed, feistier, bigger and altogether finer than the little brown boys. The little brown girls followed closely, quicker to suss escape routes, the location of food, and manage jumping. So there had been at least two fathers, then. When the brown puppies were small, their faces were pushed in, so I persuaded myself that Oscar was responsible for one or two.

The west terrace was entirely devoted to puppy-birth, but round to the east that day a turkey had landed. A large silver Volvo drove up while I was gagging in the kitchen, and Giorgio, our Italian neighbour, leaped out, brandishing a scruffy

adolescent turkey. He pressed it into Dan's unwilling arms, leaped back into his car, and purred off.

'I geev it to you, but the price is that you have to invite me to come and eat it with you.' He claimed that it did not get on with his chickens, but said that by next Christmas it would be so heavy that it would not be able to support its own weight. The thought of this was repellent enough, but the creature appeared to have been put together out of the leftovers after normal animals had taken what they wanted. It sported a mixed bunch of mostly whitish feathers, growing sparsely and at random in pimpled pink skin. Its legs were made from plumbing fitments, and it had the meticulously shrunken head of Alec Douglas-Home, with the addition of gross tumescent pinky-mauve protuberances and appendages. Richard took to it immediately.

It spent the first five hours of its short stay with us making turkey noises and getting under our feet. Richard followed it, talking soothingly and gobbling occasionally, while rescuing it from Kiko, Oscar and me. Nobody else cared for the uninvited turkey, but Richard conceived a mysterious passion for it, fretting when it was not within sight, and set up search parties. It was just to humour him that I feigned interest and followed when he said, 'I've found the perfect home for the turkey; a place where he's happy and he's safe.'

It was Richard who was in danger when I discovered that he'd made a little nest for it in the basket containing my hand-knotted tie-dyed silk scarves from Ahmedabad. He was right, it looked very happy, as it scruffed up priceless patolas and embroidered pashminas. But not for long. Boy, did that turkey learn to fly – and fast. OK, OK, so I just put it politely outside the front door, apologized to it through gritted teeth and wondered if it had lice.

The turkey stayed just long enough to contribute a few splodgy droppings to the dustballs and dog biscuits on the kitchen floor, then made off. The night before its unlamented disappearance the phone rang. Dan was astonished when he answered and a little sonata of gobble noises greeted him – it was Richard wanting a word with his new friend.

On the puppy front, Minnie took on complete responsibility for feeding and clearing up. For about ten days she was exemplary. She had a motley collection of ten tits – some prunes and some currants, and the prunes were speedily commandeered by the smart puppies. One of the others, having realized that he was surplus to the available nourishment, passed away. We kept him warm, and did what we could, but he faded slowly. It was horribly poignant, and Spigs carved a little gravestone in his memory under which he lies, surrounded by flowers: '*Here lies Mini's Puppy. May he rest in Peace.*'

'Aah,' he said, looking tenderly at the remaining ten. 'Little Sausages of Love.'

Hummus

1 small bowl soaked and cooked chickpeas – 100–150g dried chickpeas (save the cooking liquid)
5 cloves garlic
100ml tahina
1 tsp ground cumin
pinch chilli powder, or a few drops Tabasco
juice of 2–3 lemons
3 tbsps olive oil
salt and pepper
olive oil, chopped coriander and paprika to garnish

Put the chickpeas, garlic, tahina, cumin, chilli, lemon juice and olive oil in blender, adding enough of the chickpea cooking water to make a thick cream. Season with salt and pepper. Turn out into pretty bowl, float a pool of olive oil on top, and sprinkle with paprika, and some chopped coriander if you have it. Scoop up with toasted pitta bread or crudités.

Guacamole

2 ripe avocados
1 red chilli, very finely chopped
1 tomato, skinned, seeded and finely chopped
1 handful of chopped coriander (save some to garnish)
juice of 1 or 2 lemons
4 cloves garlic, crushed
½ small onion, finely chopped
salt and pepper

Mash together all the ingredients in a bowl, or whiz in a processor for a smoother purée. Sprinkle chopped coriander on top. Scoop up with toasted pitta bread.

19

SOUP OPERA

Throughout the first half of 2000 Giorgio and Martina worked doggedly to get the restaurant finished. Martina was always complaining about some new iniquity of Spanish builders – their ambition to kiss her whenever possible, their inability to understand the waterfall she had designed for their eighteen-foot escarpment at the back, or their cussed refusal to lay free-draining flat tiles. Despite her tribulations with the house, within a few weeks she had achieved a little miracle outside, making an original garden with rounded river pebbles and rocks from the *campo* interspersed with palms, figs, lemons and bougainvillea set in paving. Her plants bloomed, they settled happily into whatever setting she devised for them, looked *designed*, and I have to admit to a twinge of jealousy, and a tiny touch of *Schadenfreude* because Giorgio's latest animals always ate the choicest and most exotic.

We observed the rise and fall of their garden and animal population with interest, and wondered if Giorgio's restaurant would ever really happen. He definitely had the energy and ideas; in fact his problem was too much of both, with the result that he changed his mind about everything from day to day. Some days he was just going to run a bar for the youth of Almogia, others he wanted only designer-clad wealthy and sophisticated clientele for cordon bleu candlelit dinners. Some days it was going to be a many-starred hotel, others a humble artistic retreat; occasionally he threatened to shut down altogether. He mooted opening an estate agency, invited me to participate in a small hamlet of self-catering wooden chalets, which fortunately never materialized, and persuaded Dan to be the resident artist and tutor in whatever the final version would prove to be. Dan regularly took the children out every Sunday, ostensibly to teach them painting and BBC English, since their admirably polyglot household resulted in a musical originality of expression, charming but not *correct*. The real reason was that Dan was very fond of Giorgio and Martina, and particularly of their children, who made him laugh. It gave him an excuse to amble down to Barranco el Sol and paddle among the snakes and terrapins that lived in the rocks among the oleander, always his idea of a good time.

Giorgio's riding school, however, run by patient Pedro, was attracting business, despite tales of saddle-sore and adrenalized customers being galloped up cliffs and down ravines with Giorgio. Some – especially adolescent boys and Spigs – secretly preferred Giorgio's in-at-the-deep-end philosophy to the endless sedate figures-of-eight upon which Pedro insisted.

My old friend Sophie came to visit us for a week or so. Small, trenchant, energetic, she didn't feel happy unless she was doing something physical. She is the perfect visitor: an enthusiast, one who can drive, who will participate and do the odd bit of cooking, clearing, and pay the occasional supermarket bill, regaling one with outrageous gossip the while. After our first year, when we ended up very poor indeed, we had eventually to suggest, pink with embarrassment, that friends and relatives might just contribute to their costs. Spain is cheaper than Islington, but it is not free. This is a problem much griped about by the English residents, some of whom have gone to the ludicrous extreme, I think, of moving to a smaller house. We always looked forward to having visitors, just not being paupers.

Sophie does love a real man, and when we dropped in for a drink, Giorgio did it for her. Several years previously she had learned to ride in order to do a romantic horseback trip in India, staying in crumbling palaces way off the beaten track. And when we told her that Giorgio had horses, at least we thought he still did, she had squeezed herself into a pair of black trousers and a white shirt, found a baseball hat in lieu of anything more seriously protective and was snorting eagerly at the door.

She, Dan and Giorgio took off together one evening, as the sun slanted across the summer fields, and they were gone for such a long time that Spigs and I began to worry just a bit. When they finally arrived home, Dan was like a bunch of tulips that have waited too long for their water, but Sophie was glowing and unstoppable. '*What* a ride. That was the best ride I've ever had. *Wonderful* horses – Giorgio took us at a real lick across country. We went for *miles*. *Such* wonderful riding country – so many beautiful hills and valleys and the *views* . . . We rode through almond orchards and among olive trees . . . I soon realized that Giorgio didn't know *where* we were, and I just *had* to be team leader. I mean, we were *completely* lost, and it's really quite dangerous when it gets dark. Shall I make a little salad for supper? I've brought you some of my own walnut oil, and it's *delicious* with *lollo rosso* and Roquefort. Anyway, I got us back, orientated by the moon. It was completely dark when we got back to the stables. Giorgio said he didn't know what he would have done without me.'

And so on and on and on. She was still going on about it the next day as she put together a tray of toasted bruschetta, crusty and rich with anchovies, tomatoes and garlic – how wonderful it was, what a wonderful horse Caporal was, how brilliant the scenery was, and Giorgio, Giorgio, Giorgio.

At the time Giorgio was having second thoughts about running a restaurant, having succumbed to a short-lived romantic fad for being a shepherd, thinking it would be a quiet, philosophical kind of life and possibly give better returns. For this change of career, he acquired fifty sheep from Pedro's uncle and prepared to be bucolic. He was bored after two days, and swapped the sheep for goats.

Some weeks later Giorgio invited Spigs to go riding with him, asking casually if he had ridden before, and while Spigs was formulating an answer that took into account all the nuances – where a simple 'no' might have sufficed – Giorgio was off. Spigs leaped onto Caporal and followed. No helmet, no experience, not a clue as to what you're supposed to do with reins, feet, horse, he sped after Giorgio across country, falling off at one particularly hairy bend, and being knocked off again by an inconveniently low branch, and scrambling back on undaunted each time. They looked magnificent, sweating, tanned and stripped to the waist as they galloped over the brow of the hill into our field in the dusky evening glow. Sophie would have fainted with excitement. Spigs was as bad as she was – he waddled into supper incandescent with excitement, and blathered on about it for days.

After this baptism by branch and bend, we all took proper riding lessons with Pedro. A model of saintly patience, he watched us and instructed us in an interesting blend of German, Spanish, one or two words of Essex argot and body language. I am afraid of horses, but Pedro's calm is contagious, although there was always a cold trickle of terror down the back of my neck, particularly when Curro exhibited a frisky disdain for the infinite figures-of-eight. I was gratified by Pedro's comment about the youthfulness of my seat, while not knowing exactly what he was referring to. Spigs had a natural aptitude for anything dangerous, and Dan, a friend to anything that walks on all fours, rode with insouciant ease remembered from the lessons of his youth. After a few weeks of going round and round the training-ground, trying to make sense of reins and stirrups, Pedro suggested that we do a cross-country trip.

So, one golden evening we ambled across uncharted country, taking narrow tracks through plantations, and getting views of beautiful derelict *fincas*, pink oleander-filled riverbeds, and uncultivated rockstrewn *maquis* where deer and wild boar live among the pine, broom and rosemary. We stopped at an abandoned *cortijo*, unreachable by any other transport, and explored its dignified, dangerous interior. Upstairs there was a huge room, the entire width of the building, with three windows from floor to ceiling, very like the crumbling Georgian manor houses in the south of Ireland, but sunny. Old glass-fronted dressers still contained an assortment of dusty broken china, iron beds stood skewed on rotten bedroom floors, massive olive jars lay buried in the bare earth of the pantry floor, *bergère* chairs with cane seats long gone clustered in the great hall exactly where the family had left them on that last dusty evening when they said a final farewell and padlocked the front door behind them. I had a brief dream of becoming a millionaire and restoring this haunting, shuttered mansion – it stood facing south, on a steep hill with a cobbled forecourt enclosed by pockmarked stone balustrades. Massive cypresses framed a distant view of shimmering sea. The building itself and its many intriguing outhouses were on a saddle of land with *big* trees – a sheltered, enclosed haven of eucalyptus, pine, carob, fig and cypress. We wandered under the whispering leaves of this secret, forgotten place until the sun splashed the hillside opposite with molten gold. Then, reluctantly, full of plans for instant wealth, we rode back through the deepening shadows.

To allay our definite hunger, Pedro grabbed almonds from the trees we passed, and cracked them open using two stones. Don't try this at home, it doesn't work, and all that happens is that you clunk your knuckles. Partridges exploded out of the brush, startling me but not my horse, and Pedro, unlike most other Spaniards, did not immediately want to shoot them. He has grown up familiar with every centimetre of this bit of countryside and knows his way home in the dark – just as well since it was, by the time we made it back to Giorgio's.

* * *

Autumn approached, and with it the opening date of La Famiglia. While Giorgio made an experimental foray into pigs, Martina was busy too. As well as doing all the predictable things like looking after the children, cooking, creating a garden from landfill and keeping the house spotless, she somehow found time to write, play the guitar and the piano and, as if all this did not suffice, she painted a nice line in female nudes. Then, a couple of days before the restaurant's inaugural fling, she turned her talents to the external walls. A new *denuncio* was posted before the paint was dry. She had gone for rust red on the front wall, buttercup yellow on the gate, mauve on the gate frame, inky midnight blue at the back, enlivened by lime-green guttering and an end wall of shocking pink. Overnight, the mayor decreed that Almogia houses and restaurants had to have a large percentage of white on the side that was visible from the road. Out came the paint and ladders again, and she settled for soft terracotta walls, with the deep-set windows outlined in cream. Very handsome it looked.

Giorgio was unperturbed, being preoccupied with rabbits at the time, and he was very gentlemanly when Oscar and Minnie tried to eat them. They did not succeed but they did sit on the cage, fatally bending the bars, a problem that the rabbits exploited by making for the hills while Giorgio's attention was deflected by a brief detour into partridges and quails.

This left Martina free to pursue her interior-design ideas, which skilfully combined urbane sophistication and eccentric anthropology. The furniture was heavy dark wood, the lighting unusually kind, and the walls were basically an inoffensive cinnabar red. Martina embellished them with expensively enlarged photos of Papuan tribesmen clad only in more or less magnificent nose tusks and Papuan tribeswomen whose pendulous breasts could have doubled as scarves during a cold snap. She commissioned Dan to paint a life-sized Papuan on the wall, complete with penis sheath, and we wondered whether this would double as a coat peg. But the whole decorative theme caused such a furore that the plan was shelved.

Meanwhile magnificent loos had been installed in the restaurant downstairs, and a steel and glass kitchen, and a bar. As the inaugural dinner approached, Giorgio offered Spigs a waiter's job. Everything was turning out brilliantly: the restaurant really was going to open, Spigs would be in paid employment, perhaps eventually honing his culinary skills, and Giorgio would have a bright, charismatic waiter. Word went round that Giorgio was opening with a gala evening in the nose-tusk room with a full menu. On this occasion Martina was going to cook.

Spigs ran backwards and forwards for days, designing and printing menus, tracking down black shoes, white shirts, black trousers, and generally being helpful. On the opening day of La Famiglia there was a loyal turnout of Brits who had booked tables to eat, and a rabble of curious Spaniards who clung to the bar, and were ticked off by Giorgio for being inappropriately dressed: 'Eet is the gala opening, eet is a very important occasion, and they 'ave come 'ere in their working clothes! I tell Manolo *metálico* to finish 'is drink and go.' An inflammatory move, since Manolo *metálico* is an important and influential man in Almogia with a professional interest in alcohol.

We had a drink, and were shown to our table,

relieved that we'd put on our Sunday best. Spigs had apparently been promoted, was wearing a double-breasted chef's jacket and appeared to be helping Martina in the kitchen. Giorgio was the waiter, and Martina's younger sister, Michaela, was manning the bar and ignoring the optics in response to pressure from Manolo *metálico*. There were black damask tablecloths on the tables, elegant low halogens spot-lighting white lilies, and a muttering of Sting in the background. The menu consisted of salad as *hors d'oeuvre* – a tricolour of cherry tomatoes with real buffalo mozzarella and handfuls of basil, dressed with olive oil and balsamic vinegar – followed by mush-room and pumpkin tortellini in cheese sauce, or grilled baby lamb, served with red peppers and potato. Puddings were the ubiquitous whisky tart beloved of all Spaniards and seemingly made of sweetened extruded polystyrene, or the infinitely preferable apple tart made by Martina herself. I watched Spigs fondly as he and Martina quick-stepped round the island work area, working together in perfect harmony, and enjoyed a waft of maternal pride.

On Saturday Spigs worked from eight a.m. until four in the morning, starting with printing the menu at dawn and helping to cook dinner for Giorgio, Michaela and Martina as a grand finale. Giorgio then fired Michaela, who fled from La Famiglia in tears. On Sunday, he fired Martina. Spigs suddenly found him-self head chef, sous-chef, bartender and plate-washer. He stumbled home very late, unable to speak for exhaustion. On Monday he went to work, to find that Giorgio had fired him too.

After a period of non-speaks, Dan negotiated a truce between Giorgio, me and Spigs, because in this small community it is ridiculous to be at war. I expected much nostril-flaring and pawing of the ground from Spigs, instead of which he agreed immediately that it was all just too petty. The truth was that, buoyed by mad optimism and fidgety with frustration, Giorgio had opened long before he or the restaurant were ready and he was under severe stress. The eventual opening, complete with professional chef, was a convincing success.

Several more cast changes inevitably ensued, including Giorgio's mother, and a pair of migratory Argentinians who were great chefs and lasted three months while they blazed an amatory trail among all the village girls after which, possibly under pressure, they went back to Argentina. Finally, Martina returned to the kitchen where everything went just fine and she attracted a grateful crowd of regulars. The food swiftly gained the reputation of being dependably delicious, generous and always more interesting than anything you could find outside Málaga. Expensive cars clustered outside the entrance every weekend. Despite persistent problems with the dress code, about which Giorgio had to address them extremely firmly, the place continued to be very popular with smart young Almogians escaping from the confines of family to the Bohemian glamour of La Famiglia, which was now confusingly known as Papa Giorgio's.

At last, the hyperactive proprietor had a sufficiently demanding job to do, which kept him out of trouble and which he did well, rapidly becoming a favourite local legend for his startling eccentricity and drop-dead charm.

Giorgio's current animal was a guinea pig, which Paloma kept in a bucket.

Martina's Sun-dried Tomatoes: late summer

Martina is a stylish and inspired cook – the food at Giorgio's is always well turned out, delicious and twice as much as a non manual labourer can eat. I have a passion for sun-dried tomatoes – attar of summer – and was greedily pleased when she gave us a jar of her own.

Cut ripe tomatoes in half, dip in coarse salt, and lay cut side up in the sun to dry for two weeks, protecting with a net if you worry about insects. Pack into sterilized jars full of good olive oil and let them macerate for 3–6 weeks, depending on their size.

20

THE LION AND THE SCORPION

The weeks following the birth of Minnie's puppies were total and insanitary chaos. As her babies grew and grew, Minnie shrank and shrank. She drank litres of milk addictively, then would plod back wearily to the heaving greedy basket, where ten little faces would button themselves to her front. We moved the basket to a small corral by the window, fenced in by old doors and a sofa, and covered the floor with newspaper. It did not suffice: the puppies would clamber over any amount of fence, to teeter off and pee wherever they had a mind. Minnie was soon ousted from the basket and rapidly became pissed off with the whole venture. She would wander off like the irresponsible hussy she is, 'forgetting' her children. Far from making her feel like a natural-born woman, her offspring evidently made her feel fenced in. So she indulged in good-time-girl misbehaviour, coming home at all hours, using the place like a hotel, even inviting in her *campo* friends.

Oscar was mystified by the whole puppy thing, and was always getting himself into trouble by straying too close. At the beginning Minnie was extremely protective, and gave him a bollocking if he came within snapping distance. He dealt with this crisis by acquiring a baby of his own – a hideous Day-Glo orange monkey that Spigs had given Dan for Christmas. When squeezed it played a tinny little tune, so until Oscar's excessive affection reduced it to tattered orange shred, the house resounded to a strangled version of the Taiwanese national anthem. He was a lousy mother, continually tossing his infant into the air, and shaking it by its feet. But if anyone else approached he growled convincingly. Minnie got blasé and bored with the exigencies of motherhood, and was unconcerned by the diminishing number of her puppies as one builder after another decided they were irresistible and took them home.

Our chaos was compounded by the variety of guests who came to stay that summer, including my niece Polly and her indomitable two-year-old daughter Martha May. Martha is divine, funny and invincible – perfect but for the forcefulness of her love. She loved the puppies so much that she had to hug each one very hard indeed round the throat, then hurl it to the ground to hug the next. They seemed happy with the arrangement, but it worried me, and I became Martha's shadow, catching flying puppies as she tired of them, trying delicately to prise her powerful arms from the neck of the latest chosen one.

However, Minnie's remaining puppies were determined survivors, clamping themselves on to her front the minute she walked through the door, and hanging on even when she ambled off, bored by the cares of motherhood. They explored alternative sources of food, from foraging under the table to embarrassing Oscar by having an experimental go at his vestigial tits, of which he has two humdingers. They took to cow's milk quickly, and the smaller puppies staked their claim to extra rations by standing in the bowl as they drank. They were perennially falling off balconies, and trying to get stepped upon. They would lurk invisibly under a chair, then hurtle out to meet an approaching foot. Meanwhile if Martha was not strangling puppies, she was sprinting suicidally for the pool, or chucking herself down flights of stairs. There would be a few moments of peace each day, when she had her bath in a plastic packing case, engulfed in bubbles, out on the west terrace. If we confined her indoors, however, she busied herself with thorough examinations of the dogs' orifices and putting unsuitable things like CDs into the fire.

To counteract the anxieties caused by an abundance of small death-defying creatures, Polly and I took up yoga seriously. Polly had brought a video, in which a sharp Australian and a goofy Californian demonstrated impossible poses with a solemn commentary on the benefit to your big intestines. Over-enthusiastic yoga can damage your back, and I am still suffering from my flashy showing off. I just *had* to bend further and balance longer, while Dan, ignored in the background, muttered, 'No, it's *fine*, I'll cook supper *again*. After all, nothing must get in the way of your *yoga*.' I tried to interest him in doing yoga too, and he showed great interest theoretically. But on the one occasion that I managed to drag him to the video, he lasted eleven seconds, then said, 'I'm not enjoying this. I don't see any point in it.'

Polly and I did it daily. It was hard work, but particularly necessary in the midst of that period of chaos; a perfect antidote to the perennial daft questions that visitors always seemed to ask: Where are your aerobic steps? Have you got a rubber drive for the Dyson? Where is the funnel? Have you washed my boxer shorts? I still do an hour of yoga most days. You'd think I'd look like Cindy Crawford by now, but sadly not. In fact I'm reminded of my first meeting with a great friend of mine, when I asked him what he intended to be when he grew up. He said his lifetime's ambition was to have the mind of Raquel Welch and the body of Evelyn Waugh. In my case, substitute Baby Spice and Golda Meir and you've got the picture. I am hampered, of course, in that Minnie's son Alfie ate my yoga mat.

Just after Minnie had had her puppies, a pair of house-martins decided that the apex of the sitting-room ceiling would be an ideal nesting place. They had checked out various other spots – the curtain rails, the telephone junction box, the glass cupboard – leaving splatters of shit on rejected sites, walls, sofas and my computer. But, having given the matter a deal of consideration, the apex beam had location, location, location. This was bad news. A little line of splatters on the floor attested to their choice, which was about eighteen feet overhead and unreachable. They would lurk up there, hidden by the beam, and as soon as you closed the glass front door, they would shoot down and bang their heads on it. Open the door for free access, and they would mope on their beam.

Three doors lead from the sitting room to the outside world. If you'd successfully ushered the martins out of one, they'd streak in at another. This tiresome pastime continued for weeks, and I was perennially waving brooms, tennis racquets or sticks at our uninvited residents. Oscar watched this performance with interest, and after several days he realized that his human was not performing a mating ritual but suffering from a bird phobia. Always obliging, he made it his mission to assist.

Oscar is a barrel-shaped dog, not built for speed, and for ages the hills were alive with the sound of heavy breathing, as he shot back and forth in pursuit of the flying grail. The passion was infectious, and soon Minnie joined the chase, while the swallows and swifts played tig, tittering into their feathers at their ungainly retinue. Minnie is a serious dog. When she decides to do something, she concentrates hard and all other preoccupations go hang. Dan was drawing peacefully on the terrace one evening at swallow-swooping time when he heard a loud splash. Minnie had been so carried away by the chase that she had careened into the swimming-pool. Oscar was standing at the edge frantically trying to pull her out by her ears. Dan fished her out and dried her off, whereupon she immediately resumed bird duties.

The puppies had survived Martha's love, and were then subjected to Leo's. He had come for a purpose. He had something to say, but he is the most laconic man with whom I have ever tried to hold a conversation of more than three words. In fact, he's almost on a par with Dan's Ted. We did not get his news, did not even realize he had any, until the awful events of his last evening with us.

He had spent the week mostly sleeping out in the sun, surrounded by a frieze of puppies. He had a special fondness for a large, very plain white one, with just the smallest brown blip on the back of its head. He was right: that puppy had an endearing way of gazing deep into your eyes with a steady, wise, unpuppylike gaze. But there was another with a speckled nose that had a passing likeness to Oscar, and the two got on well. That's Oscar's boy for sure, I thought, so we kept him and called him Alfie, after the object of Oscar Wilde's infatuation. Now, despite knowing that there is not the remotest possibility that he is Oscar's son and despite his passion for destruction, we have grown very fond of him.

When Leo wasn't outside in the sun puppy-minding, he was mending things, for which he turned out to have an unexpected genius. We had a sorry collection of partly functioning appliances: a Dyson vacuum-cleaner that coughed dust everywhere, two televisions and a video machine, none of which we could understand or get to work properly. I told Leo I intended to take them to an electrician in Málaga and ask him to try to fix them, and dump them if he couldn't.

'Don't say that, Mum,' he answered, in gentle reproof, 'they're good machines. If you say that he'll just sell them probably.' Sometimes I feel such a fool – that possibility had never occurred to me. I wondered how many perfectly mendable things I had consigned to this fate.

Calmly, patiently, Leo took apart the broken machines, inspected their workings and cleaned them with a paintbrush and a fine cardboard nozzle that he made and attached to the functioning vacuum. I thought, Well, they can't get any worse, I am ashamed to say, and I resigned myself to having wall-to-wall broken machine parts all over the sitting room. It had been known to happen in the past. However, not only did Leo achieve total success on this front, he also mended Dan's uncooperative computer, and did something about which I still feel ambiguous, but without which this book would never have been written. He took Free Cell off my laptop. 'It's for your own good, Mum. I know how easy it is to waste time with computer games, and you've got better things to do.'

On his last evening Leo disappeared into the bathroom and I expected him to be there for the usual four hours. But almost instantly a startling apparition bolted out – face bearded with shaving foam, barefoot and hopping. Assuming him to be doing a one-legged Father Christmas impersonation, I slapped my thighs and laughed. Wrong. He had been stung by a scorpion – he had trodden on it – and was expecting to die. I laughed again, in a 'What a fuss about a tiny little scorpion sting' sort of way, sure that it was nothing that a cup of hot sweet tea couldn't solve.

Just to be sure I rang Barbara. 'Get him to the doctor *now*!' she yelled. Smile wiped off face, I shoved the semi-bearded hopper into the van and Dan drove us at top speed down to Almogia. Leo brought the malefactor with us in a glass jar. It looked a bit dazed, but was remarkably frisky for a small scorpion that had just been trodden on by a well-fed six-foot-two man with enormous feet.

The doctor was not there when we arrived, but a pert, flirtatious nurse took charge. She examined the sting, shrieked on coming across the perpetrator in its jar on her desk, and gave Leo two injections, anti-tetanus and an anti-inflammatory. This was a situation in which we really could have used some elementary Spanish, but as usual we were gurning wordlessly, exploding with '*dolor*' or '*caliente*' every now and then when we finally remembered an elusive word. At least we were spared having to act a scorpion. When the doctor arrived, he rang the toxicologist in Málaga immediately, looking very grave. He had never seen a scorpion before, and kept peering into the jam jar with horrified excitement. For the first time, it occurred to me to worry. Oh, God, I thought, Leo might be paralysed. He'll spend the rest of his life eating puréed goo, unable to operate the remote control for the television. This was too awful to contemplate. Edgily we listened to the doctor's tone. At first he jabbered excitedly into the phone, then there was a long silence broken by the occasional grave '*Comprendo*.' Then a question. Finally he emerged to announce that there were no life-threatening poisonous creatures in Spain. He sounded disappointed.

Meanwhile the nurse had been busy with her dictionary. 'The scorpion he gives you only one prick, but I give you two.' She smiled winningly. Leo blushed and hobbled out to the car.

There are venomous creatures here, though. Apparently the droning toads whose *sotto voce* gives a bass boost to the night air can kill a small dog with their poison. And there are other beasts that can do the same. Dan had a run-in with one when I was in England. He had gone to bed in the donkey room, and was chatting and laughing to himself in his sleep as he usually does, when he became dimly aware of a tickly sensation by his feet. He scrabbled his legs a bit, eager to return to the cocktail party that his dream life consists of. A few more minutes of party chatter ensued. Then he felt something skitter across his face. Indignantly he brushed it off somewhere into the bed, and found the matches and the candle. He had been sharing his bed with one of the six-inch red millipedes with a vicious bite that lurk under stones, and whose home had probably been the donkey room for life and generations back.

'I've got something to tell you,' Leo announced as, our feathers settling after the drama, we drove home. This was a lot of words, all at once, from him, and demanded attention. 'I'm going to be a dad.'

Dan almost drove over the edge of the road – we were at the accident blackspot on Ken and Olive's ravine. We didn't even know Leo had a girlfriend. Suddenly all his devoted puppy-sitting made sense. He had been practising.

Advanced interrogation elicited a name, Saki, and that they'd known each other since just before Christmas. She lived in a flat near Finsbury Park, worked in the same job centre that I'd worked at twenty years previously, and she and Leo were not exactly an item. Leo was vague and evasive. This is not the sort of news a mother wants to hear, and it gave me a whole new repertoire of things to worry about, particularly since Leo did not have an income at the time.

I did not meet Saki until their daughter was a week old, so it was many anxious months before I discovered she was the best thing that could have happened to Leo.

The scorpion has had an exciting life. Leo smuggled it back to England, as a birthday present for Spigs who loves anything lethal. He christened it Kanu, after an Arsenal football player, who apparently does a scorpion-like victory dance. Spigs kept it in a heated tank with a collection of little toys including a tiny Veterano Osborne bull, and fed it grasshoppers bought from a pet shop, and spiders that he caught himself.

When he visited us in Spain, Leo took over the programme of scorpion care, and nurtured his uncuddly charge for several months. After a while, he decided that Kanu was looking a bit peaky, pining for home and the sun. So the globe-trotting scorpion was brought back to Spain, and ceremoniously given his freedom by Spigs and Leo in the ruin along our track. Doubtless he's poncing about, regaling his mates with tales of world travel.

Polly's Spanish stew

Polly did aerobic cuisine, scattering celery over a wide arc of kitchen floor, but whatever she cooked – especially Martha's food – was simple and delicious. Top marks. She makes this to remind herself of Spain, and we make it to remind ourselves of her.

onions, peeled and chopped
celery, chopped
carrots, chopped
***chorizo picante* for cooking, sliced**
garlic, peeled and chopped
potatoes, peeled and chopped
vegetable stock cube
bay leaves
1 large tin of white beans

Fry the onions, celery, carrots and sliced *chorizo* gently, then add the garlic and potatoes. Cover with vegetable stock and poke in bay leaves. Cook over a very low heat for about an hour, and add the beans at the end for long enough to heat them.

Leo's Very Simple Chicken

Serves 2

Come winter laziness, Dan and I live on Leo's chicken with vegetable variations. Real food does not get much easier than this.

4 peppers, red, orange or yellow, cut into quarters
olive oil
garlic cloves, peeled
4 chicken thighs, with skin
salt and pepper

Lay the quartered peppers on a baking tray brushed with olive oil, and roast at gas 5–6/190°–200°C for 10–15 minutes, until you can smell them cooking. Sprinkle with whole garlic cloves, add the chicken thighs, drizzle with oil, and bake for an hour and a bit until brown and crisp. Serve with linguine or broccoli.

21

A ROMANTIC INTERLUDE

The summer of 2000 was thronged with our nearest and dearest. Apart from final cosmetic tweaking and making sense of the garden, our house was as finished as it would ever be and everyone came to stay. Dan and I celebrated the end of six months of constant chaperonage by having a small and bitter argument, during which he uttered the hackneyed classic of every Sixties B-movie, 'Well, it's been fun, but I'm leaving now.'

Whenever I have been party to a fight to the death – a really momentous heave in a relationship when the earth has moved, raking great fissures in something precious – it has always been characterized by stunning cliché. I would have been devastated, were it not for the fact that the previous autumn had been marked by Dan's 'What relationship?' and the one before that with 'I need some space.' This time I was prepared, and came back with a tsunami. '*Fun?*' I shrieked. 'You call it *fun*?'

The problem was that while the house was a work in progress, we had no privacy when visitors came. From the first arrival in April to the last departure in September, we couldn't have a conversation without an audience, and by the end of the summer both of us were frazzled, tired, poor, each convinced that the other was not doing enough. We were endlessly cooking, washing sheets and clearing up. It is perhaps ungracious to say this, but their holiday was our labour. One or both of us would trek off to Antequera, fill the van with a scary amount of shopping, and have to do it all over again two days later. None of our dependants seemed to drive, and because they never participated in the slog round Carrefour, they felt that absolved them from paying for anything. This always led to our annual, terminal row.

So we were feeling quite shaky when we arranged separate trips back to England, through gritted teeth, ensuring as much time apart as we could. Dan had to go for work reasons, and I had to have my old Citroën MOT'd and insured. We planned to bring it back to Spain together. Of course, ten minutes' absence made our hearts grow fonder, and very soon we were fattening our phone bill and whispering expensive sweet-nothings. Well, I was. I've never yet met a man who approached the telephone as though it were any friendlier than a hand grenade.

Dan is an action man, so it was he who arranged for our little honeymoon-type cruise from Portsmouth to Bilbao, paying £120 over the odds for a cabin with a window. This was to be our treat, our holiday alone together during which we could patch and nurture our tattered affection for each other. And we were going to take our time, and see a bit of the country we had chosen to live in. We gloated as we planned the itinerary: Bilbao and the Guggenheim, Burgos, two days in Toledo, possibly even a detour to see the Picos de Europa. We packed up the car with more than was sensible, as always, and set off on a night of thrashing wind and sleet. Guy Fawkes Night it was, and when the boat eased out of Portsmouth our departure was marked by a lull in the storm and the glittering scintillations of a scarlet, silver, blue and green firework salute, which splashed across the black sky and echoed in the inky water for us personally. As we slid away from England, we stood on the deck and Dan said appreciatively, 'Well, this is one huge boat. Nothing will rock this baby.'

I know it's foolish, but for me this was the most thrilling journey ever: a loving hiatus organized by my man. I had even jettisoned my grizzled old Marks & Spencer's underwear in favour of something that was not aversion therapy for my favourite heterosexual.

It started well, with champagne and smoked almonds in our cabin, enjoying the view of a calm, starlit sea from our costly window. We had a surprisingly good dinner in 'Le Bistro', and listened for a while to a surprisingly good band playing raunchy folk music. We giggled back to our cabin, and I slept well, lulled by the soothing *sotto-voce* hum of the engine. The next day I gave myself a treat in the Steiner salon, had a full aromatherapy massage and a haircut, and felt pretty stupendous. The captain of the ship chatted to us from time to time over the Tannoy, and as we were going for dinner somewhere in the middle of the Bay of Biscay he advised us that we might not be able to avoid the hurricane that had lashed the British Isles. The night, he said, 'might be a little roly-poly'.

'Ha ha,' we smirked. 'You bet.'

Dinner was fine, if strangely protracted. The reason why became clear when we withdrew to the comfortable armchairs in the smoking room, and watched our coffee slide off the table and smash against the panelling. Then we noticed that the gritty, sticky texture underfoot was not the swirly Braille carpet, but the cream and sugar of previous coffee-takers.

But our hearts were high, our spirits were strong, and we laughed. We dawdled over our *petits fours*, listened to the band which was playing gamely through the entire Hank Wangford repertoire as it slithered from one end of the bar to the other, before we careened merrily back to our room. We scoffed as we bounced past the Met map, which predicted severe force-nine gales.

Thus began the longest night of my life. The advantage of having a window became quickly obvious: you can see imminent death as it whacks the glass; you can hear the popping rivets, and observe the boiling wrath of the black ocean that will shortly be your grave; you can ponder whether it will be the chill of the freezing water that gets you, or whether it will be its frightening power as it flips you casually with a hundred-foot wave against the wreckage of the ship. One minute our window was filled with inky sky, the next with churning sea. In between everything went opaque as frenzied spume smacked the glass. I did not flirt with being sick or any of that nonsense. This was clearly The End: there was no time for frivolities. I debated whether there was anything to hand with which to break the glass, should the ship founder, or whether we would be better staying put and breathing the last pocket of air as it went down. I have a bit of a phobia about confined spaces, do not like taking lifts or using the Underground, but I thought that running out of oxygen in good company might not be the worst way to die. Dan slept peacefully through the night.

He awoke, fresh as lemon sorbet, to find himself lying next to a hundred-year-old woman. 'Breakfast!' he shouted. 'But first I'm going on deck.' I groaned, and was grateful to the captain, who chose that moment to announce that no-one was even to think of going on deck as it was 'still a bit bouncy'. In fact, he came clean, and admitted that he'd never known it as bad. There had been winds of 120 m.p.h., and he had hove-to for four hours when the route became unnavigable at around midnight. The storm was still raging, and we would be well over four hours' late docking at Bilbao.

Lemon Sorbet and Ashen Centenarian went to investigate breakfast to find the floor awash with smashed crockery, people cautiously planning routes of no further than three yards, a pile of mixed geriatrics in a heap by the reception desk, while the erstwhile civilized calm of the Steiner salon looked like some of the more fire and brimstone detail in a Hieronymus Bosch hell. Mirrors, lotions, rollers, hair-dryers, dyes and shampoo were all blended in a wall-to-wall electrochemical soup.

I was incredulously glad to be alive, and by daylight I felt that I could swim to Bilbao if need be. We were lucky. Half the poor sods on that boat were halfway through a rollicking 'minicruise', which had been designed to give them thirty-six hours' drinking on board ship, an adventurous day exploring Bilbao, then a further thirty-six hours' drinking on the way home. They just had time to teeter queasily around the docks, and did not appear to look forward to the return drinking stint.

Bilbao was characterized for me by strangely undulating pavements and a quality of shutness. The ground continued to shimmy around for three days after our voyage. The promised pinnacle of this trip, the Guggenheim, was closed on Mondays and so, we discovered, was almost everything else. While we were making this discovery someone tried to break into the car, smashed the locks, then petulantly slashed a tyre out of frustration. Dan sashayed into Superman overdrive, calmly unpicked the tightly packed puzzle that was the boot, did not scream when he realized belatedly that spreading out all our possessions in the car park had not been necessary, and changed the tyre. No problem.

The sun was still shining, and we headed through some beautiful country for Burgos. We arrived at twilight, having avoided Avila. That, I'm afraid, is all I can remember. By the time we reached Burgos there were some tiny blips on the flat encephalogram, since Dan, having driven all day, was not about to try out his crummy Spanish in the quest for a hotel. We happened by chance upon the tourist office, and I asked for the oldest hotel in the town. We booked into a medieval palace overlooking the cathedral. A bottle of champagne was waiting for us in our room, and we quaffed it too greedily to notice the invitation to exchange it for a chilled one. We didn't mind – we had a sumptuous suite at the top of the rambling old building for not much more than a youth-hostel bunk, and there was a bath with unlimited hot water, my formula for luxury and total happiness.

There is a joke about Burgos, which is that summer

starts on St Santiago's Day, 25 July, and ends on St Ana's Day, 26 July. When we emerged that evening to find somewhere to eat, we discovered how true this is. Most of Spain is on a high plateau, and the wind rips into you like a flying glacier. We bobbled about with drips on the end of our noses until we found a suitable restaurant, and shivered in anticipation of returning to the hotel. I was too cold and too tired to remember what or where we ate.

The next day was sunny, and we did a bit of shopping – including a thick woolly scarf for Dan who had elected to wear a T-shirt and goosepimples – and continued with our journey. We had decided that Toledo would be our next night's treat, and settled in for a long drive. It was, and we arrived in darkness. Toledo gets accolades in every tourist guide, so we were excited and ready to give it two whole days. I wanted to see the old town, the crooked streets, and the legendary locally made steel – I have an inexplicable passion for penknives and dinky folding tools.

We were tired when we got there, and the walled town has an incomprehensible one-way system. We fell into the first hotel we came across, moderately grand, on the outer perimeter. The first room to which we were given keys had a voluptuously rumpled bed, lately vacated by a pair of aerobic bonkers. Having swapped it for one less pheromonal we stepped out into the night. Toledo seemed to be in the grip of a plague. We walked for miles in bitterly cold streets devoid of life, and the only food we found was McDonald's. No way. We went back to the hotel and ordered dinner in their restaurant. This was a big mistake, and Dan spent that night in the loo. When he wasn't exploding he was groaning. I lay counting the minutes through what was to be yet another sleepless night.

Dan thought he was probably going to die, so I drove him home the next day through slashing gales, taking a fatal detour at one point that led us meandering through back waters and tracks that had never seen transport so sophisticated. We looped and curved and teetered, while Dan snored.

'I just hope we don't meet anything coming the other way,' he said, in intervals of lucidity, when his head wasn't lolling and drool stringing from his open mouth.

We got home that night to my wonderful Spigs who had cooked us something delicious, and our very own freezing cold, gorgeously friendly bed. Romance might not have been dead, but we very nearly were, and I settled with gratitude into our safe and familiar routine.

Winter stir-fry

Serves 2

This stir-fry provides central heating on cold, grey winter days. According to the Chinese, ginger is an anti-depressant, so we spring perkily back to work, undaunted by four inches of rain and the leaking roof.

2 tbsps sunflower or peanut oil
1 tbsp sesame oil
2 carrots, scraped and cut into fat matchsticks
1 handful fine green beans, topped and tailed and cut into 1cm lengths
1 red pepper, cut into 1cm scraps
2 sticks celery, cut lengthwise into 3 and then across into tiny cubes
4 Brussels sprouts, finely sliced, or a shredded wedge of cabbage, or broccoli cut into small pieces
1 walnut-sized piece of ginger, peeled and finely shredded
1 hot chilli, red or green, very finely sliced
4 cloves garlic, sliced
1 onion, finely chopped
1 leek or 2 spring onions, cut into thin rounds
1 courgette, cut into fat matchsticks
½ carton beansprouts

1 tbsp miso
2 tbsps teriyaki marinade
3 tbsps soya sauce
½ tin coconut milk

Pour the sunflower or peanut oil and the sesame oil into your wok, heat, and add some or all of the vegetables, in the order presented, cooking over a high heat, and stirring whenever you get a break from chopping.

Add the miso, teriyaki marinade, soya sauce and coconut milk, and keep stirring until the courgette is cooked and everything has had a minute or so to braise in the coconut milk. The result is a rich spiky mixture of vegetables in a delicious sauce, to which you can add pre-fried chicken, pork or salmon at the last minute plus a sprinkling of toasted sesame seeds. Or you can use blameless but boring tofu, whose lack of flavour is not a problem amid such a tastebud riot.

22

A BAD DAY AT CASA MIRANDA

At the end of 2000, almost a year since the umbilical connection with London and work had been severed, I went through a brief dark tunnel. The day dawned bleak, cloudy and cold. A gale had blown all my washing into the pool, and when I fished it out, I also rescued a young frog that had been swimming gamely round and round in circles. Antonio, young Antonio and Manolo were wearing mufflers and thick jackets as they put the roof tiles over our magnificent antique Mongolian gates, acquired from a *brocante* in Torremolinos. I took them bowls of hot lentil soup as they huddled in the shell of my workroom having their lunch – whether they ate it for central heating or consigned it to the dogs as suspicious foreign muck I shall never know. Spaniards are conservative about food.

We were again awash with furniture, a Manhattan skyline of boxes and dismantled wardrobes, the last remnants of what had been in my Brighton flat, which I had let. I no longer had a home in England, Spain was where I lived. I had been in permanent residence

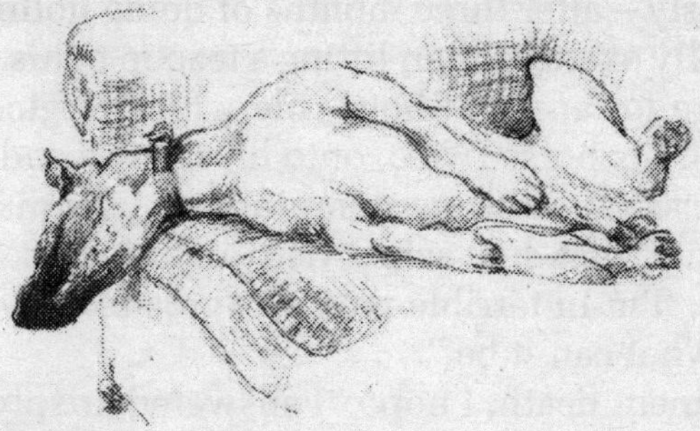

here for almost exactly a year. My sabbatical. The year of vegetating I promised myself.

This day, one of the worst I can remember, started with an orgy of human abuse by dogs. They were rapturous to see me when I got up to make coffee for the builders, scampered outside and disappeared over the hill as soon as I opened the door. The sitting room looked as though a posse of angry gorillas had been at work – the hi-fi was on the floor, surrounded by a litter of chewed CDs, there were papers wall to wall, some semi-eaten. My huge coffee-table book on Spanish cuisine – *Culinaria* – had a tattered, soggy scar where its spine used to be, as did Dan's precious *Times Atlas*. My gorgeous leopard-pattern specs were minus their lenses and earpieces. The contents of the dustbin were strewn over the papers, and Alfie, Minnie's teenage son, had had an experimental nibble of the insecticide I'd bought to paint our wooden beams and decided that he preferred my favourite Martina-style black platform-heeled mules, which he had comprehensively destroyed. He had also eaten one of my hideous Ecco sandals. Oh, and there were *four* piles of dog-shit on my Moroccan flat-weave rug.

Dan was at his most exasperating: a couple of days

previously – after three months of doing nothing more physically exerting than lifting a teacup to his lips – he had gone for an eight-hour ride with Giorgio. He had fallen off his horse twice, onto his elbows and back on one occasion, but contemptuously dismissed the possibility that his aches had anything to do with the ride. 'I'm in terrible pain,' he groaned, 'everything hurts. What can it be?'

'Imminent death, I hope,' I answered crisply, as I set off alone for our weekly Spanish class.

I had the misfortune to pass Paco White Pantaloons hanging about outside Paco's bar, hoping for a lift into Almogia. Like a sucker I stopped, and he had not been in the car more than five minutes before he started down a familiar route. '*Big* house, you've got.'

I nodded, lips pursed, knowing how this monologue continued.

'*Mucho dineros*,' he added with a carnivorous smirk. '*Tu es capitalista rica*.'

There is something sharply irritating about the unmerited accusation of being a great, greasy, loaded capitalist, particularly from an unwished-for passenger. It would have been sensible to throw him out of the car at that point, but I gave him my best scowl instead, and pointed out that I had worked my butt off for twenty years and earned every breeze-block.

For the rest of the journey he contented himself by burbling on about how dismal, wet and expensive England is, and how dramatic his relationship with his English girlfriend Elspeth. The most recent development had been the Burning of the Clothes: she had incinerated his entire wardrobe during one of their scuffles. I had a tiny joyous moment of *Schadenfreude*, dropped him from less of a height than I would have wished, and sped on to Juan's office where the Spanish lessons are held.

In the office it was building-bill time. Beverley across the mountain, who had had seven workmen busy on her house since the beginning of the year, got a bill from Juan for 2,400 pesetas. Elvia down the valley got a bill for 2,350 pesetas; her house was finished within a year. I got a bill for 285,000 pesetas. This *capitalista rica* appeared to be subsidizing the entire valley. After three years of money haemorrhage, I still didn't have a workroom and Dan's studio was amusingly airy with no doors or windows. I dared not calculate quite how much we had spent, or how much was still to be paid. And I could not think where the last chunk of money needed to complete the house was going to come from.

The Spanish lesson that followed was a brilliant opportunity to exercise my paranoia. Everyone else had done their homework, had memorized their vocabulary, and knew all the answers. If there had been a back of the class, I would have been there, sticking my chewing-gum to the hair of the girl in front, carving 'Pauline is a show-off' into my desk. Unfortunately we were all seated round the conference table, and our teacher expected us to behave like adults. I had to be content with flicking my biro nib up and down. I crept out of the lesson, feeling like the thirteenth fairy, and drove down the greasy (after Easter) switchback road to the bank to get some money for Juan. But since my last visit someone had put the Spanish equivalent of double yellow lines all over the village, and inaugurated a one-way system (long overdue, but did they have to do it *now*?) so that I was unable to stop until I had made the complete circuit back to Juan's office.

Bugger that, I thought, and sloped off home.

Hoping for a sympathetic ear, I told Dan about my tribulations. 'Don't worry about money,' he said. 'That's the last thing you should worry about. It always turns up. I've never known anyone worry about money as much as you do.' What is he like? In his world money turns up. In mine you slog for twenty years, and then some government official fines you. I wanted to grab him by the ears, and shout, '*Get real!*' very loudly from uncomfortable proximity. Instead I stomped off feeling martyred.

A new and exciting source of worry had appeared on the horizon while I had been out struggling to learn Spanish. In my absence, Tomas had arrived with his JCB and appeared to be gouging a hole out of the olive plantation on the skyline above Señor Arrabal's *finca*. I jabbered in frantic apprehension at Spigs and Dan who were lounging about in the sun like a pair of obese possums.

'Don't *worry*. They're not building a house up *there*,' they both said, with one drawl. 'They *couldn't* build up there, they've got no access. You're so *paranoid*,' Dan added, in his most patronizing Now-look-here-little-woman-don't-you-bother-your-fluffy-little-head-about-*Man*'s-stuff voice.

A crowd had collected from nowhere around Tomas and his machine – eleven strangers and Señor Arrabal. I strode across the intervening field to find out what was going on. No, they were not building a house – yet. They were flattening a small runway for a car park, *prior* to building a house. And, judging by the capacity of the car park, it was not going to be a small one. In half an hour's work with the JCB Tomas had carved out the patently impossible access. Before long, on my perfect west skyline, where the gnarled shapes of the old olive trees are beloved and familiar characters in my evening ritual, there would soon be a monstrous pile of ludicrous turrets and wiggly crenellations.

On my way to tell Spigs and Dan, I noticed an English-looking woman, accompanied by three others, showing serious interest in the ruin to the east. Double disaster. We would be overlooked from both directions, and if the 'architects' and builders had their way our view would consist of two eyesores from Bungalow Bliss. I watched with growing despair as the English woman hung around sizing up the ruin for about half an hour – quite an achievement when looking at just twenty square yards of unroofed rubble. Excited gabble from both directions was audible from our house and I foresaw a time when not just our privacy but our peace would be gone.

'Well, you can't buy a view. It was bound to happen sooner or later,' the resident nerds chorused from their respective computer games, when I rushed in to tell them the awful news. They did not even look up. I hated them both.

For the first time, this place was dust and ashes. A little tornado whipped itself into a frenzy and ripped the split cane from the pergola as I watched – the split cane that I had spent the previous day, impaled like St Sebastian with a million splinters, lurching nervously on a ladder fixing into place.

A little childhood refrain, perfect for the occasion, popped into my mind: 'Nobody loves me, everybody hates me, I'll go into the garden and eat worms.' Worms being a luxury here, I did not eat them. Instead I stomped, shouted and railed indignantly to myself. I banged unexpected things with the hammer I had planned to fix the cane with, then threw it petulantly to the ground. I cursed my fellow-residents, human and canine. I worried, worried more, and wondered for the first time how much the house was worth. I looked at the waist-high army of weeds encroaching from all sides, and wondered whether I could afford a garret in New York if I sold this place. I contemplated the delicious freedom of living on my own, in a neat and empty loft with a view of treetops and a bookshop round the corner. I pondered the pleasure of being able to hold a more than three-word discussion with the locals, of having a vocabulary that reached beyond plumbing fitments, and being able to use it. Of being able to deploy nuance, subtlety and jokes in my discourse rather than the coarse clods of brickish nouns, which are the best conversation I can aspire to here. I pictured the joy of not having to follow a hare-and-hounds trail of crusty plates and socks.

I acknowledged to myself that I was lonely, really lonely, without a single good friend here. There was not one person on whose tolerance and understanding I could count, to whom I could blub uncontrollably, and burden with profound thoughts such as 'And she just wears a thong . . . And he had the cheek to say, "Don't worry" . . . He came for a holiday and he's been here for eight months . . . There'll be years of lorries and crud and cement-mixers and two horrible houses at the end of it . . .' between sniffs.

It always feels a bit phoney, sobbing to oneself. In fact, I hardly ever cry – only in films about dogs and at the end of musicals. But even if it is not one of my talents, I believe in the therapeutic virtues of a good cry. So, feeling really, really sorry for myself, I had a bloody good shot at it.

Still sniffing I wandered down to our olive plantation, where Dan had been clearing some of the shoulder-high grasses with a scythe. Shuffling into this jungle, I came across a flattened bit where the dogs had raced and rolled, nibbling at each other in delicious high spirits. I sat down there, surrounded by susurrating barley – rye? I don't know, the tall whiskery one anyway – with the evening light gilding its whiskers and despite myself, I thought, This is heaven.

After a while Dan shouted my name from the house. I got to my feet reluctantly and scrambled up the west bank. 'Telephone. It's your brother.' Apparently my father had left us all a bit of arable land when he died, and someone now wanted to buy it for a sum that, after a four-way division with my sisters and brother, would just about pay for the completion of the house. Yet again Dan had been right. My spirits began to lift.

I rang Leo to see how they were getting on. He sounded fine, said that the baby, Chilali, had lots of brown hair and was smiling. I could hear her bubbly and imperious commentary at the other end of the line. I felt a pang, missing them all acutely. In the middle of our conversation, Leo sighed heavily, then said, 'Two and a half weeks to go. The trouble with booking to come to Spain so early is that we've been counting off the days for weeks now. Saki and me can't wait to come over, Mum.' Suddenly I couldn't wait to fatten them up with my newly discovered talent for fudge brownies. Just a couple of weeks to go. Cot, sheets, nappies – I went through a mental list of things we'd need, as excited as if Chilali were mine.

'Where's Spigs?' I asked Dan, who was glued to his computer doing drawings for his new book of filth.

'Dunno,' he said helpfully.

When I went round to the other side of the house I almost knocked Spigs off the ladder. He was manfully wrestling with the split cane, rescuing what he could and jettisoning the rest. He got down when he saw me, and accompanied me into the kitchen. Together we had a cup of tea.

'You can't own a view, Mum,' he repeated, but more kindly, 'and there is enough for everyone. Those people will gain so much from being surrounded by all this beauty. Everyone needs that.' He looked at the dead-crow effect of snivelled mascara around my eyes. 'You're being very grown-up about it.' For once, I knew he was not being ironic; nor was he putting the boot in. He was just saying that he knew how I felt and was with me.

With his uncannily accurate antenna for a fresh cup of tea, Dan ambled in a minute or so later. 'I'll make supper,' he said. Then he put his arms round me and said, 'I do really love you, you know. Not just because you're a rich capitalist. I couldn't live with anyone else, and I wouldn't do anything to jeopardize what we have. It's you I love, and only you.'

It's what I'd call a happyish ending. Or beginning. I'm not sure which. I don't believe in unflawed happiness. Anything that looks too good makes me worry, and wonder when the gods are going to do a spot of smiting. But here in Andalucía, in Casa Miranda, my family around me, is about as happy as I can be. And I think I can say confidently that the same goes for Dan and Spigs. And the dogs, come to that.

Fresh figs with Serrano ham

That's it. Heaven. If you want complications you can add slices of buffalo mozzarella, a splash of olive oil or walnut oil, juice of a lemon, and some rocket to make a salad.

Dan's pesto

You can vary quantities and ingredients according to what you have to hand. Different cheeses can be interesting, particularly grated manchego or mashed goat's cheese in olive oil, but add no more salt if you use this.

1 huge handful basil or rocket
more garlic than you think seemly, peeled
3 tbsps Parmesan cheese, finely grated
3 tbsps pine nuts, sunflower seeds, pistachios or almonds
large dollop of olive oil
salt and pepper

Put all the ingredients into a mortar and clunk them with a pestle until you have a chunky purée. Add salt and pepper, and a ladleful of hot pasta water. Heap onto hot olive-oily pasta. *Voilà.*

2001

23

HOUSE AND GARDEN

In January I wondered aloud to Dan how long it would take to finish our workrooms, and was dismayed when he said that there was no way they'd be ready before March.

'*March!*' I shrieked. 'But that's two months away.'

Of all the rooms in the house, the workrooms seemed the most vital, confirming that we are people who do more than sleep, eat, brush our teeth and watch old videos. Somehow the months have slid by, and here we are at the end of July.

Today Antonio and his son, young Antonio, are out in the shimmering white heat, putting the last touches to the courtyard, sealing a few cracks in the roof, raising the chimney so that we will no longer sit amid a black smog, coughing and weeping, trying to warm our toes in unimaginable winter. The Antonios are by far the best workmen we have had, bringing a measured perfectionism to everything they do. The workrooms are not quite finished, since Manolo *metálico* has still not put glass in the doors, but we can finally sit in our separate studios, with an undersized lemon tree between us, and hope to justify all this expensive space. Having complained vociferously for the last three years that he could not possibly paint without a studio, Dan is now convinced that he cannot possibly paint because of its overweening grandeur. He's there playing solitaire and feeling overwhelmed, waiting for a muse to drop by.

I shall be sorry to see the builders go. Young Antonio was overweight, pallid and desperately gauche when we first met them. He has become a tanned, handsome, muscular young man, still cutely mute with shyness. He is experimenting at present with a *Laughing Cavalier* beard detail, but I hope that this will pass. I have a bottle of fancy fifteen-year-old whisky for his dad, who will be very embarrassed but will have no option but to take it. The Antonios have done wonderful work, have coped patiently with our hopeless Spanish, our absurd fantasies, translating incoherent mumblings into perfect archways, octagonal fountains and a series of level terraces where we used to sit beneath Dan's yellow parasol watching our drinks slide downhill.

There are certain things that I have been unreasonably bloody-minded about. One was my categorical refusal to have an interconnecting door between the north and south houses. They are two separate buildings.

In summer Dan and I live in the north house, in cool, spacious shade and occasional privacy. This half of the house consists of three main rooms. We have a large bedroom with a rattling antique Spanish iron bed, over which hangs an improving nineteenth-century chintz patchwork with religious quotes written in sepia copperplate, of which 'Come unto ME and I will give you REST' is the most relevant to a bedroom, though I like 'Create in me a clean heart, O God, and renew a right spirit within me' too. This used to be two rooms, our old public room and a bedroom, and it has a high ceiling and the original massive walls with two small, deep windows.

'In this country, the sun will always find you,' Barbara says. And it's true, a river of sunlight floods this room first thing every morning, filtered by blue and white ticking curtains, courtesy of one of my fabric books, which blow at windows and door. The door – on the site of our old front door – opens straight onto the terrace outside where Dan and I sit secretly in a sheltered corner of morning sun and drink our coffee, him swathed fetchingly in nothing but sunlight.

There is also a door from our bedroom to the huge sitting room with its high beamed ceiling – taken by their *rustico* butchness, we decided to have rough wooden beams for all the ceilings, also favoured by house-martins. What we didn't know then was that a myriad little biting, tickling, wood-boring things would be taken by them as well and move in. They were horrible, leaving telltale piles of sawdust in their wake and planning to turn the beams into Aero bars. You could actually *hear* them eating our house, especially the bedroom beetles at four in the morning. Paco, known as Puro because of the fat cigar always in the corner of his mouth, painted the entire house inside and out, mostly using a two-inch brush, and very slow it was. He also painted the beams very slowly with his two-inch brush, using something noxious to deter the tickly things, and it has been remarkably successful. No trace of the busy tunnelling locusts remains.

In the middle of the sitting room is the chunky fireplace on whose plinth you can sit warming your bottom, and opposite is a pair of french windows opening onto a tiny balcony looking north towards El Torcal. This used to be the newer part of the house, which was drifting from its moorings and sliding down towards the peacocks. In summer this room is noticeably cooler than any of the others. A once-beautiful Bennison sofa given to me by Judy sits just inside the front door, usually embellished by a trio of dogs who have successfully reduced it to a giant knitting basket, a lamented thing of shreds and tatters. My mother's oak corner cupboard glitters with glass in here, and two of Dan's huge powerful drawings of old locomotives hang above the arch. The rough white walls are covered with his paintings.

At one end is our front door out to the courtyard and the tiny original bathroom tacked on; at the other there are two steps and an archway leading down to the big kitchen. This is dominated by a magnificent hardwood table of my parents', brought from China where they lived for thirty years and imbued with memories of family Christmas lunches and vast messy Chinese dinners served on a thick tablecloth of newspapers. Opposite the french windows onto the west terrace there is another sofa that has suffered from the excessive affection of dogs. It used to be blue and white, but is now blue and sepia and, thanks to the pungent aroma of undiluted dog, visitors tend to look for somewhere else to sit. We, unfortunately, are inured to it and probably smell like a pair of old dogs ourselves. A glass-fronted mahogany dresser, given to me by Jocasta, houses stacks of Chinese blue and white, Spanish rustic and brilliant lime-green and aquamarine Moroccan ceramics.

This is our flat, in which we live in summer, coolly facing away from the sun. It was planned to avoid the syrupy midday glare, and it does – wonderful when it's a shimmering bleached 45 degrees Celsius outside, and we can have all the doors open and a cool breeze wafting through.

High summer is when we have an influx of sun-worshippers, and they are happy to bake. Lately we have had a plethora of miscellaneous boys staying, friends of Ted and Spigs, and a handful of Doris's girl-friends. They have one common denominator: they come to stay when it's hottest, and whatever you say to them, however wisely you wag your finger, they rush out, sit in the bleaching sun all day, then feel ill. Sun craving is an addiction I can understand. We smooth cool aloe gel freshly culled from the garden over their scarlet flesh, give them aspirins and never say, 'I told you so.' It's what they come for.

They stay in the south house. At this visitors' end of the building I wanted as many bedrooms as possible – for family, friends, their friends, and complete strangers who might pay us to stay. This was the idea that my friend Sophie inspired – a painless way to make a bit of money to subsidize my writing and Dan's painting. What actually happens, of course, is that we always fill the house with friends and family, and it is a neat way of becoming quite poor and not having time to do what we meant to. But for the surprising and memorable dinners cooked by inventive visitors, because we do force them to cook at least once, the giggles, the cut-throat games of rummy played far into the night, poverty is a small price to pay. We've never had such fun, however much Dan huffs and puffs.

We did not come here for the summer sun and Dan

and I sun ourselves as often as your average slug or woodlouse. I spend the summer indoors at my computer, making brief sprints outside when it's unavoidable, and Dan ambles out from darkened rooms to the swimming-pool for a regular splosh. Only adolescents actually sit in the sun, slathering on the lowest-factor suncream they can manage without sloughing off their entire skin like barbecued snakes.

The sun is not the point, though sitting out bare-armed on Christmas Eve is something you might envy. What is absolutely wonderful is the light. Begone dull specs. I could read the *A–Z* if I had to, though thankfully I no longer do, entirely unaided. In summer the sunlight is so violent that it bleaches the flowers. The geraniums that open garnet red in the morning are a strangely striped and quite unattractive Germolene pink by evening. But in winter, when the sun comes out after rain, the air is like diamonds.

In autumn, when everyone has gone, we move into the visitors' south house to get every scrap of warmth and light, for which we are grateful. I have no intention of admitting it, certainly not to Dan, but it does seem crazy in winter to have to sprint through the pouring rain to the north house to get the rice pan, to feed the dogs, to go to bed, to make or receive a phone call. But it's my *finca*, and I'll get soaked if I want to.

The south house has three bedrooms, one of which, a secret interior one, is dominated by a resplendent carved Javanese bed. This cost more than any piece of furniture I have ever bought. I don't know what came over me, but I wrote the cheque with several noughts, and shortly afterwards the bed arrived in about thirty pieces. As Bram, a Dutch friend who kindly helped us assemble the thing, said gravely, 'I think this is a poozle.' It was an unbelievably heavy poozle too, and took all our combined strength – four of us – to carry each bit to its eventual home. A deal of head-scratching followed as we tried to guess what went where, and in what order. It took all afternoon, and made me weep with inappropriate laughter as the chaps all stood round solemnly trying to put this bit with that, standing back for a critical look, at which the whole ensemble would dismantle itself. But we finally managed it, and there it stands in all its glory, its solid carved posts supporting a huge blue and white quilt that Judy brought from India, and its serrated cross-beam liable to make a painful stripe of dents in your head, as Dan discovered on one occasion when, maddened with jealousy – he really, really wanted us to have that bed – we spent a night in its curtained splendour.

The other grand bedroom in this part of the house has a high, handsome Indian wooden bed inlaid with mirrors as its centrepiece. Its posts support a frame over which a brilliant length of scarlet and yellow turban muslin is draped to deter mosquitoes; a great idea in theory, except that the frame is apt to fall on unsuspecting sleepers if they do anything more energetic than snore quietly. We painted this room the mauve-grey of the distant hills at evening, with the result that it is always seriously dark, verging on sepulchral. The other problem with this princely boudoir is that toads are partial to its soothing gloom, and are apt to add their drone to the sleepers' snores. I was determined to have colour and loath to admit mistakes, so a gloomy toad-hostel it will remain. For a bit anyway. This room has french windows to the narrow, plant-swagged south terrace. One day it will have dappled shade from the infant fig and *Cercis siliquastrum*, known here not as the Judas tree but as the tree of love because of its heart-shaped leaves. Heavy crocheted-cotton curtains, Dutch café curtains from a Brighton car-boot sale, veil door and window for privacy, with bizarre printed-chintz ones from the calico museum in India to keep out the blinding morning light. These depict writhing mountains, trees, birds and monkeys, and if you look at them too long they guarantee nightmares.

Next door is a small, simple white bedroom with a length of bright striped blue and white Guatemalan cotton at the window. These two rooms have to be occupied by people who know each other well, since the most discreet whiffle or fart is plainly audible from each to the other.

The south kitchen is high-ceilinged with rough bright tangerine walls, embellished with Tony Daniell's shocking pink and orange fruit painting, and a luxurious marble worktop – marble is just about as cheap as Fablon here, something I wish I'd known when we made our own kitchen. There are big french windows opening onto a vine- and passionflower-covered pergola with an old grey teak table and seats for summer eating, shaded from the midday sun. Steps lead up from here to the swimming-pool. Steps also lead from the kitchen down to the west-facing sitting room. This room is roughly washed a wonderful rich yellow with a smoke-blackened pink fireplace, above which stands Dan's very fine big mirror, and brilliantly striped mostly yellow Guatemalan curtains, which featured in some book or other. I *love* the way things have found homes – all the weird junk I have hung on to for decades has found the perfect setting. It is like the solution to some algebraic equation: all the pieces suddenly fit together at last, all the colours finally make close harmony. And the answer is 5x squared.

The whole house, north and south, inside and out, has rustic terracotta-tiled floors – not a practical choice as they make clouds of pink dust, and have become swiftly but very locally patinated by grease, spilt milk, tea and wine, all of which they absorb with lightning rapidity and retain as a memorial to dinners and disasters past, not to mention things contributed by dogs. We have been told that scrubbing down with vinegar followed with a coat of olive oil is the way to seal terracotta tiles. Spaniards do it with diesel, but when we tried, apart from emanating a suffocating aroma, the tiles remained as porous as ever. In winter we lay a mosaic of rugs over the floors. There are the beautiful Moroccan rugs that Dan and I gave each other for our birthdays one year, mine pink, his blue. These were made by the wives of Berber tribesmen and are decorated with a diary of the events that took place during the nomadic absence of their menfolk. They bear an intricate narrative of camels, feasts, candles, tents, fish, goblets and dogs. Judy's beautiful Moroccan flatweave rug in indigo, ochre, cinnabar and the brown-grey of dead leaves makes the south sitting room a warm and friendly place when rain is coming down in ropes. This is the rug that Alfie has selected as the best location for chewing goat vertebrae, shoes, CDs, helmets – horse, moped and bike – dustpans, for which he has a particular fondness, and binoculars.

As soon as any tiny space is designated 'garden', I shoot out and stuff it with plants. I can't stop myself buying trees – I've always done this, with the result that all three of my minuscule English gardens have been narrow dark slug-rich tunnels, where insects and wet things would drop down the back of your neck and only the determined photophobes of the plant world flourished. Fortunately you can't achieve quite that level of damp, web-infested gloom here, but it hasn't stopped me dragging two large cherry trees, four lemons, a peach, a nectarine, an orange, a kumquat and its sad relative the limequat, an apricot and two sickly mangoes from the local nursery to cram into the courtyard, already dominated by a spreading fig – we built the high walls round the old, gnarled tree. And the tattered banana has found a less wind-raked home here, its fringed pennants arching protectively above the old gate.

The courtyard makes a large, enclosed, secret area on the east of the house, intended to have the sheltered calm of a Moorish garden. Antonio has built a hexagonal fountain in the middle and Dan's sister, Bella, is going to cover it with mosaic – I have in mind bright broken crockery, as in Gaudi's Parc Guëll, with dots of mirror to catch and reflect sunlight like the mirrored ball at the Palais. I look out from my desk

onto a frieze of fruit trees, with a gardenia on my windowsill – a gardenia, as yet not dead, that produced thirty-six cinnamon-sweet fragrant flowers and scented the air in my study. Exotic or what?

I adore the rich, gorgeous scents of Spanish flowers. One of the pleasures of driving into Málaga is the sweet fragrance of citrus blossom in March from the orange and lemon orchards that line the road. Our four lemon trees get unfair attention and extra watering because I want to have that smell all year round, contained within the courtyard walls, along with fragrant wafts of datura and *dama de noche*. We sit on the terrace outside our bedroom, with our bucket of Pimm's, and watch the sinking sun making a blaze of orange on El Torcal. We play backgammon with the aromatic inlaid thuya board we got in Marrakech (it's a moral crusade for me: I'm trying to learn to lose without spitting and sulking), and hope that someone else will cook dinner. At night we have fairy lights in the fig tree, and the cloister outside my study – in shade by day – is like a brightly lit little stage, casting fingers of light onto the fountain and lemon trees.

Gardens, for me, are either metal or candyfloss. I like them both, but they don't mix. Metal describes the yuccas, banana palms, the architectural plants whose dramatic shadows are as interesting as what cast them. Green, glaucous, the colours of verdigris and copper, bronze and aluminium, perfect for the wild, open edges of our cultivated land. Candyfloss covers all the fluffy things that Gertrude Jekyll and Marjorie Fish planted in delicate painterly swathes – impressionistic, pointillist, evanescent and sometimes scented flowers with names like baby's breath, Queen Anne's lace, love-in-a-mist. They are really too ephemeral for this violent heat and light, but I keep trying.

The cherry trees are in a shady corner outside my workroom – perfect for those Chekhov moments. I want to grow vanilla-scented *Clematis armandii* up them to flower gloriously in the clear light of early spring. This part of the courtyard will be a bit Japanese too, with smooth stones underfoot and, who knows, maybe a smattering of raked gravel? In spring I shall put on my kimono and *obi* and lie beneath the blossom as Japanese emperors used to do, and in summer I fancy sitting out and having great ripe black cherries drop into my mouth. Antonio – who has a thousand fruit trees and is a major killjoy – says that this will never happen because of the soil, and because when I planted the trees in January, digging a huge hole for each and filling it with wheelbarrow loads of the best earth we could find, I committed the fatal error of watering them in. Apparently you don't do that in Spain. He tut-tutted, saying that nothing here should be watered until June, and telling me what I already knew but chose to ignore: that small trees settle in better and catch up quickly. My trees are as big as I could transport. They certainly don't look as pert as they did when I bought them.

We should have learned this from our experience with the cypresses: we bought six giants because they were astonishingly cheap, and the following year we bought six toddler trees. We have watched five of the giants die slowly, no matter how kindly they were spoken to, how firmly guyed, how lovingly watered. The remaining one, which has assumed a peculiar and not very healthy-looking paddle shape, is no bigger than the erstwhile tiddlers.

Along the rutted track to the house I planted thirty eucalyptus from scraggy seedlings given to me by Pedro the horseman, of which two survived until they were eaten by a passing goat. He also gave me about forty seedlings of carob, umbrella pine and holm oak, which I planted with severe misgivings – they are maybe four centimetres tall, and the weeds will be ninety-four at least when they get going. Also carob and holm oak are not the trees for anyone with less than a century to hang around. Antonio scoffed at the carob, too, for good measure. 'It's much too windy for carob, anyone should know that,' he told me.

Antonio shook his head sorrowfully at our irresponsible hopelessness with our olive trees, all of our trees actually. He wrote lists of the chemicals we should be using – handling the blunt stub of pencil as warily as a rabid scorpion – the fertilizers, the herbicides, the pesticides and the fungicides, all of which we airily ignored. Then he wreaked a terrible revenge by sneaking up and pruning the trees to mere stumps.

What we have at present is our 200 little olive trees engulfed in nicely fertilized weeds, but battling gamely. Plus three fields containing a mixture of last year's wheat, the previous year's chickpeas, maybe one or two broad-bean plants from the year before that, and a rabble of weeds. Every now and then an itinerant goatherd wanders through with his flock; and Manolo goes out occasionally with a scythe and clears a patch to take home to his horse.

We sought to achieve a point of quiet stasis, but it was continually interrupted by Señor Arrabal's surprise appearances, which always drove the dogs mad. They adored everyone in the whole world except our neighbours to whom they, and Alfie in particular, took a furious dislike. Whether Señor Arrabal was on foot or horseback, he only had to bellow his unintelligible greeting and the dogs would bark their heads off and attempt to bite him. Neither party ever learned. He continued to bellow and they to bark until we decided that the noisy charade had to end. We put up a compound of two-metre-high heavy-duty chain-link fence outside the courtyard, so that the dogs could wander freely but not attack Señor Arrabal. It took Alfie five minutes to dig his way out. Dan then spent a day burying the base of the fence with earth and rocks. It delayed Alfie for ten minutes. In desperation we tied him to a tree and bought 500 metres of chicken wire from the nice lady in Villanueva. On our return, Alfie was outside waiting for us, having chewed his way through the rope. Dan spent another day attaching the chicken wire to the original fence, and burying it securely under an avalanche of rocks and earth. This stumped Alfie for a whole morning, but he managed eventually to chew his way out. Oscar and Minnie were quite happy to be fenced in and appeared to have no urge to break for freedom. We settled on chaining Alfie in their compound, and taking them all for long daily walks to try to tire them out, which very effectively tired us out.

After much nagging, Dan finally bought me the birthday present of my dreams: a gorgeous, heavy-duty strimmer. I was thrilled, and rushed outside to try it. I thought I would begin by making the dogs' new compound a more friendly place by cutting down the waist-high grass that was growing, lush and thick, under the fig and lemon trees there. After much sweating and back-ricking I managed to start the thing, at which all three dogs tried to kill it. I shut them into the courtyard, waving the whirring strings dangerously in the air above my head as I did so, thereby lopping off a lemon branch, and advanced on their compound. At first, at the top of the bank, things went swimmingly. As I proceeded down the slope, I realized that I was green from head to foot, covered in grass cuttings. No matter. I persevered until I got a face full of dog-shit. At that point, vaguely recalling something unpleasant about *Toxocara canensis*, I decided I'd had enough and put away the strimmer. I had a shower, washed my face extremely carefully, found Dan, and we retreated to a more civilized quarter of the garden for a restorative glass of something.

At the top of the west bank, overlooking the scoop of hillside where the olives will one day whisper, in the perfect watching-sunset-with-gin-and-tonic-in-hand position, I want to make a small desert, using the huge rocks that litter the fields, setting them on a base of sand. There's nothing more comforting than sitting on a hot rock as the sun goes down. Here, I intend to plant spiky yuccas and aloes for their dramatic silhouettes against a pink and scarlet sky, with a sprinkling of succulents. I have always hated succulents but they look different in Spain, more butch somehow. Below, dug into the west bank, Dan has made a secret seat from stone, where a rising feather of smoke will be the only indication that he is sitting there chilling out.

My salad

Serves 4 really, but 2 if they are likely to pick all afternoon

There is a sort of zen tranquillity about chopping and assembling a load of fresh vegetables – I never get tired of it. And this salad is just bursting with vitamins and amino acids.

Take a large, deep salad bowl. Chop and throw into it some or all of the following:

1 romaine lettuce
1 little gem
1 lollo rosso
½ well-washed oak-leaf lettuce
1 long white endive or ½ frizzy one
1 handful basil
1 handful lamb's lettuce
1 handful watercress
1 handful rocket

Then add:

1 small cucumber or courgette cut into little strips
10 or so cherry tomatoes cut in half
1 small handful sprouted alfalfa
1 handful hazelnuts
1 handful salted sunflower seeds
1 handful peeled and salted pumpkin seeds
sprinkling of sesame seeds

If you like you can add:

tiny cubes of feta
hard-boiled quail's eggs
tuna
crisply grilled bacon

Mix well and pour on a cup of olive, walnut, or hazelnut oil. Distribute this well, then squeeze 2 cloves of garlic over it and mix again. Pour on half a cup of balsamic vinegar and a generous dash of soya sauce or teriyaki marinade. Mix again.

24

STOP PRESS

Now, after our long and bumpy journey, Casa Miranda is definitely home. I find it endlessly interesting, surprising, comforting and beautiful. The things that attracted me in the first place have not palled; if anything, the more familiar they are, the better they become. I still get a thrill when I dawdle through the orange blossom on the way to Málaga, remembering what my life used to be like. Spring still shocks me with its beauty, when slanting January sunlight sweeps down the newly verdant hillsides and back-lights a frothy pink *corps de ballet* of blossoming almond trees, thick tides of petal confetti dancing on the Tarmac. It is still a privilege to pass through a majestic landscape of ragged mountains and tidy olive groves on a humble shopping trip; to join the queue collecting pure mineral water from the gushing spout at the base of El Torcal; to wade through pink, purple and mauve wild flowers when we take the dogs to the top of our hill; to toast our own almonds, pickle our own olives, gather baskets of our own figs, plums and peaches, apricots and nectarines, and gobble them warm from the tree. Our enduring love affair with the place and each other is all the sweeter for the trials that preceded it.

There have been big changes in this part of Spain since we bought the *finca*. As well as our twenty pretty magnificent street-lights, the Junta de Andalucía has erected a bouquet of signs in the village, so that the whole world knows they've found the Barriada de Pastelero, and can make their way to the bigger and better new school, village and sports' halls. These may be aspirations, blatant lies, or perhaps they are someone else's left-over signs, because we've never seen anything like a village hall or sports' hall here. The forty-two hairpin bends now have barriers to stop you tumbling down the mountain, there is a brand-new faster road to the airport, which has only five cliff-hangers, and a reservoir where a farm surrounded by beautifully tended orange groves stood just two years ago. Almogia has been designated a suburb of Málaga, and yet another more direct road to Málaga is being mooted.

Giorgio and Martina have converted their restaurant into an unbelievably smart rainbow hotel, which you will find on the Internet as arcadiaretreat.com. Dan still teaches their children on Sundays, and waddles home late and stuffed with pizza or baby lamb cooked by Martina. Paloma's latest love is an ambitious frog that likes to do lengths of the pool, and which she brings in and introduces to privileged diners.

But gaggles of goats still graze with demure fastidiousness on every hillside, never straying onto crops but picking their food from among the rocks and roadsides. Summer still means the sound of goat bells and cicadas. You drive cautiously, since around the next bend the road may be blocked by an ambling herd with udders swinging like heavy knapsacks, or littered with suicidal sleeping dogs and kamikaze scavenging chickens, their lives ever more perilous as the number of cars multiplies. When we first came here, a car coming up from the coast was something of an event. Now Pastelero is a popular day trip to the country, and the road to Villanueva is packed with bull-barred four-wheel-drive dreadnoughts. Almogia and Villanueva both have supermarkets that take credit cards, unless there has been an electricity cut, in which case the carefully made-up girl in the nylon overall is no better off than Mrs Paco, and has to undergo the public torment of complicated decimal addition with a stub of pencil on a little piece of paper with a noisy gaggle of disenchanted shoppers commenting. And the optimistic shopper has to put half the stuff back because of an embarrassing cash shortfall – since the hole-in-the-wall does not work either if there has been rain or wind.

But this is a benign place, and has revealed unexpectedly endearing qualities in everyone who has come here. Our loved and trusted A-list has been all we could have wished for and more. Friends have introduced us to strangers who have instantly become part of our lives. People about whom we had reservations – too formal, too bad-tempered, too egotistical – have turned out to be the opposite of what we feared, have cooked and laughed and listened and drunk.

I have to say that, when he came for a holiday, we did not expect Spigs to stay with us for a year – thinking that our fledglings had fledged and we had finished with hands-on parenting – but for me his presence and his growing confidence have been one of the best things to happen here. He brought youth and energy, fizzing conversation and reckless courage to our rather staid life. Dan, too, despite his occasional grumbles and rare outbursts of 'either he goes or I go', gained a real friend. They were like two naughty schoolboys most of the time, playing 'Pharaoh' together for hours on the computer, getting stoned and generally bonding. Spigs's presence healed some scar in Dan's past, and for his part, Spigs recovered bit by bit from the lack of proper loving two-parent attention that blighted his adolescence. He changed from an angry man to a humorous, positive, philosophical one, great to talk to and a fearless, willing cook. He eventually left us to do a TEFL course in Barcelona, and thence to Holland to teach Chinese and Vietnamese immigrants, and left a sizeable Spigs-shaped gap in our days.

This, after all, was why I bought this place, to try to make up to my sons for the gruesome nightmare that was living with their overworked single parent. I hoped that we could start afresh as adults, with a clean slate, in a place whose tranquillity would be healing. I wanted to make up for the parsimony of playtime we had shared during their growing up, when I was dragged down by worries, well out of my depth, and giggles were thin on the ground. I wanted my boys to come and play football, take the dogs for sprints across the mountain, splash about in the pool and generally have a wonderful and thoroughly childish time.

In his usual quietly determined fashion, Leo found his own introspective way, and made his happiness with Saki and their family. Their story was more romantic than I had gathered from his laconic sketch on the occasion of the scorpion sting: they had originally met when they were sixteen and seventeen respectively, and he had walked Saki home as the dawn rose at four a.m. after a distant party.

'At the tender age of sixteen I was rather chuffed at such a gentlemanly act, and though we were both too awkward and inexperienced to do anything about it, none of the romantic significance was lost,' Saki told me when she, Leo and their beautiful daughter first came to stay. Their paths did not cross again for ten years. 'Rhiannon, a schoolmate, had written a play that was being performed at the Southwark Playhouse,' she continued. 'On Saturday night I went to see it, bumped into Rhiannon in the audience, and we all went to the pub for drinks afterwards. We spent most of the night catching up and talking about old times, and it wasn't until the end of the evening that Rhiannon said, "Oh, by the way, this is Leo." We had had our backs to each other all night.

'We both looked at each other and said we'd met before. I'd always been sorry I'd never seen him again. For some reason I knew we'd lost out on something, and we weren't to miss out on this opportunity again.

'We started going out, and it was only the fear of what was happening to us that drove us apart later.' I have always known that Leo was incredibly circumspect in matters of the heart, and so, it appears, was Saki. 'We knew I was pregnant very early on, but we were both in denial: about the prospect of being parents, and of needing each other. We pushed each other away because we are both the kind of people who needed to get our own heads together before we could be of any use to each other. But Leo never really left. Barely a week went by that I didn't see him.

'When Leo went to Spain and made his announcement it was just after I had sent him an abrupt letter, that kept him away for about two weeks. As soon as he got back from Spain we started spending time together again. On the day Chilali was born Leo had rung me at least three times. As the day wore on I started to face the inescapable truth. I was in the early stages of labour. My mum rang me at around six thirty when she finished work, and I just broke down in tears. She said she was going to take me to the hospital. In the cab the contractions were so painful I didn't have the strength to phone Leo, but I gave Kathy his number and she rang him.

'Leo held my hand through the birth. I knew then that it was Leo and me who were in it together, and still are. Neither Leo nor I believe it was accidental that we met as we did, and our two gorgeous girls are proof of that.'

'He was made for fatherhood,' Saki's mother, Kathy, told me. 'As soon as the baby was born, he held her in his arms with all the confidence you would expect from a father of five.' And so he has continued.

They called their first daughter Chilali, a Native American name meaning 'White Dove of Peace', and her first achievement in life was an important one: to firmly unite her parents. Which she speedily followed by reconciling Leo with Brendan, his father, and subsequently Saki with her step-brother. Not bad for someone with a three-word vocabulary.

Two years on, missing Chilali, and now her little sister Maizie, sit up, acquire teeth, say their first words, take their first steps is one of my few regrets about living here.

Dan's son Ted, the Taciturn One, returned home to Sudbury, took A-level Spanish – he corrects our grammar with quiet relish – and discovered a talent for mixing music. So successful was he that his local county council awarded him a grant to make music, and various local DJs have taken an interest in Ted's opus. He now lives in London and subsidizes his music with his daytime job: he is the tall, handsome, witty guy who directs errant children at the Victoria and Albert Museum.

Doris comes to see us whenever she can take time off from becoming a serious *Übermensch*. She is still doing her art-history degree and has all the qualities necessary to rule the world. I'm very glad to be able to shine in her reflected glory.

On her most recent visit she also acted the fairy godmother – she turned up looking slim, glossy and more than usually gorgeous. So much so that Dan actually noticed and commented.

'I've just done a six-week detox,' she said breathily, 'and it's given me so much energy.'

'I think I should try that,' he said in front of witnesses. 'I've been putting on a bit of weight, and feeling a bit low.' An incredulous silence followed this announcement. Terminally depressed is how I would have described him, and it had worried me no end but he had always refused to acknowledge that anything was wrong. Doris sent us the instructions for her six-week detox, and for the first ten days or so without tea, coffee, cigarettes, alcohol, meat, dairy or wheat Dan and I were venomously toxic, hissing and spitting whenever we made the mistake of meeting.

But then palpable changes started to occur: Dan lost his tum, he awoke fresh and sparky every morning, he *ran* round the hill with the dogs and, best of all, his fathomless well of bleak nihilism dried up and a fount of pure Pollyanna took its place. It might have been the coffee – Dan was a definite caffeine addict – or bread. Possibly he had just been chronically deprived of sleep and the new blameless diet had corrected this. Perhaps he had just decided that it was time to get positive and that was why he undertook the diet in the first place. Whatever the reason, the change in Dan's demeanour has been startling. Like clouds parting to reveal sunshine and blue sky, his gloom has evaporated, leaving the benign, positive, energetic man whom we had glimpsed between cloudbursts. He is halfway through his first novel, having found his vocation. The only thing to happen to me was extra bottom.

How we would all have fared in London is anyone's guess. I think it no less than miraculous that Dan and I are genuinely fond of each other's children. Even without family complications, it is a delicate business, starting a new life. Particularly in a new language, with a new partner, and a new country. So much of life is a quiet accretion of familiar actions and behaviour, which silt imperceptibly into habits. I have been informed by everyone with whom I have ever cohabited that I am impossible and, although astonished, I have to accept that there must be some truth in this because of the consensus. But so much of who I was in London was composed of frustration at work, anxiety about money and the boys, and fury at the pitiless, dreary, bureaucratic, inhuman juggernaut that I found the city to be. I didn't know what moving to Spain would reveal, but I reasoned that I couldn't get any worse, and when my back pain was at its most acute I believed that if I did not get out I would be soon dead. And not nice dead, remembered with affection, but with thistles on my grave. Livid, indignant and unpleasantly haunting dead.

There have been brief sharp points of pain for us, as we readjusted our personalities to cope with each other and the new life, but not the endless grim, grey tunnel. And I'm not saying that sunshine and a gorgeous view cures all ills and brings guaranteed happiness, but it helps, and puts things in a much more positive perspective. No-one has to tell me to 'Cheer up, it may never happen' any more. In London, where it was a daily refrain, it had usually happened already. I believe that the best gift with which you can present your children and grandchildren, or anyone else for that matter, is to show them that happiness is possible, and what it looks like. *Carpe diem*, tomorrow may never come. Happiness is contagious. In a dodgy, whimsical world, life tends to reflect back what you give it. Anyway, true or not, it's a great excuse to be selfish and have more fun.

For myself, what I hoped for and expected from moving to Spain was that I would get bored, so bored that I would just have to sit down and write The Novel that has plagued me from Cambridge and before. It hasn't happened yet, but that I assume to be because I haven't yet managed to get properly bored. Loneliness I did not even consider, since much of the problem of London was the endless motley of people that crowded every day – I *longed* to be lonely.

I longed for time to do nothing, think nothing, slowly put down roots and produce the odd leaf and blossom in my own time, and to marvel daily at the landscape. I wondered about self-discipline, and whether, without panic and deadlines, I would become a good-for-nothing lotus-eater. At the moment my position on this question is: so what?

And yet, despite living in Paradise, when the house

calmed down over the winter we realized that we were feeling a pang of bereavement that was not just for our children and friends but for a city. We didn't know what city, only that it was not an English city. We definitely began to miss noise, chance opportunities, a changing cast, unexpected events, unpredictable outcomes. We scratched our heads and debated the notion of a flat in Paris or a house near Uzès, the allure of the Italian Marches compared with a crumbling palace in Venice. Impossible dreams, but dreams are not yet a criminal offence. Especially when an unexpected legacy came our way: a forgotten piece of woodland belonging to my mother finally sold a few years after her death, and out of the blue we were in a position to give the idea serious thought.

At that juncture we happened to visit Marrakech, where Dan fell head over heels under the spell of Morocco, and we embarked on a new adventure involving a beautiful derelict *riad* and a charismatic *marakchi*. I am intrigued to know what will come of it, but I can't bear to be away from Spain for long and crave the peace, the solitude, the comforting rhythm of life and the beauty of our house after a couple of days anywhere else.

There is something about this place, this life, that opens the heart, that nurtures security and optimism, that calms the cuticle-chewing worrywart. So what if the fridge door came off in Spigs's hand? So what if the shelves above sprang from their inadequate fixings and whirled a mélange of jam, honey, tea and cafetières to the floor? Or the pan rack crashed, with its heavy metal cargo, to the table, smashing teapots and bowls, narrowly missing diners? So what if Francisco has taken out a *denuncio* on our horrible dogs? Who cares if Spigs on his first driving lesson confused brake and accelerator, forgot completely about steering and drove Dan's van vigorously into a rock? I've forgotten how to be anxious. I've given up making lists. What will be will be. And what will be is dinner.

Hasta la vista, Gorgeous.

ACKNOWLEDGEMENTS

I want to thank the local heroes who provided the roof over our heads and entertainment too – Chris and Barbara Stallwood, Giorgio and Martina Melis (arcadiaretreat.com), Juan Romero Fernandez, and Antonio Moreno Nadales; Selina Walker and Araminta Whitley, who took a dumpy, grumpy, cussed kind of book and transformed it into something that did not bite; Deirdre McSharry and Susy Smith, who both, by very different means, propelled me along the scary path of the unpredictable.

www.marocandalucia.co.uk

OVER THE HILLS AND FAR AWAY
Candida Lycett Green

'A BRAVE, LYRICAL ACCOUNT OF CHILDHOOD, RIDING HORSES THROUGH ENGLAND, IDEAL MARRIAGE, FRIENDS – EVERYTHING THAT MATTERS – OH, AND BREAST CANCER. BUT IT'S LIFE BETJEMAN'S DAUGHTER IS CELEBRATING'
Susan Hill, *Daily Telegraph* Books of the Year

From early childhood, when her inspirational mother would take her on trips along her beloved Ridgeway in a horse-drawn cart, Candida Lycett Green has retained a love of green lanes and tracks and of moving along at a horse's pace. Her insatiable appetite for exploring unknown territory has led her to travel all over England for weeks at a time, and often these journeys have come at important turning points in her life.

In August 2000 she sets off on a 200-mile journey through Yorkshire and Northumberland to raise funds for breast cancer after her own recent fight with the disease. As she describes the ride she also dips back into past journeys by horse, her idyllic childhood in the bohemian Betjeman household, a charmed youth in the swinging sixties, her epic overland honeymoon in India, motherhood, and a marriage spanning almost forty years.

'ELOQUENT, OBSERVANT, BRACINGLY IDIOSYNCRATIC AND FILLED, LIKE A REALLY GOOD JOURNEY, WITH WORTHWHILE DETOURS'
Evening Standard

'THE SHEER VARIETY OF HER LIFE MAKES IT WORTH RECORDING . . . "ONLY WHEN FACED WITH DEATH DOES THE PURPOSE OF BEING ALIVE BECOME SO CLEAR". THAT'S WHAT THIS BOOK'S ABOUT'
The Spectator

'WE ARE NOT ONLY GIVEN NEW INSIGHTS INTO BOTH HER FATHER AND HER DAUNTING MOTHER; WE ALSO COME TO REALIZE HOW MANY OF THEIR ATTRIBUTES SHE HAS INHERITED . . . THE BOOK'S POWER, FINALLY, IS THAT IT IS FULL OF LIFE – LIFE REGAINED, LIFE REAFFIRMED'
Mail on Sunday

0 552 99983 0

NOTES FROM AN ITALIAN GARDEN
Joan Marble

'THIS DESCRIPTION OF MAKING HEAVEN ON EARTH IS AN UNLOOKED-FOR DELIGHT'
Independent on Sunday

'I fell in love with Etruria one chilly evening in January. They were having a New Year's Eve festival in a little town near Campagnano, and a group of local boys dressed in Renaissance costumes were marching in a torchlight parade down the main street. As I stood there in the cold watching the flames lurching to the sky, I realized that I felt very much at home in this ancient place. If ever we should decide to move to the country, this was the kind of place I would choose . . .'

Thirty years ago Joan Marble and her sculptor husband Robert Cook bought a piece of unpromising land in Lazio, the area north of Rome that was home to the ancient Etruscans. They built a house and, more importantly, grew a wonderful garden. The challenge was both exciting and daunting, and poor soil, an inhospitable climate and the blank incomprehension of their neighbours sometimes made it seem as though they would never realize their dream. But Joan and Robert's enthusiasm for the land, their determination and inspiration, and the unexpected friends who helped them, all served to make the landscape blossom.

'THIS BOOK IS ALL ADVENTURE. MS MARBLE DOES SOME DIZZY TRAVELLING. HER ROOF BLOWS OFF. SHE SURVIVES KILLER WASPS AND POISONOUS PINE MOTHS. MOST INSPIRING OF ALL SHE REVIVES A WILTING CLIMBER WITH TWO CUPS OF COLD RICE PUDDING AND TAKES GERMINATING SEEDS TO DINNER PARTIES. I WISH I KNEW HER. I LOVE HER BOOK'
Phyllida Law

'A STORY OF A HOME CREATED WITH LOVE AND PASSION. EVEN NON-GARDENERS WILL FIND IT ENCHANTING'
Irish News

0 552 99841 9

UNDER THE TUSCAN SUN
At Home in Italy
By Frances Mayes

'A WONDERFULLY LANGUID AND EVOCATIVE DIARY'
Independent on Sunday

Frances Mayes – widely published poet, gourmet cook and travel writer – opens the door on a wondrous new world when she buys and restores an abandoned villa in the spectacular Tuscan countryside. She finds faded frescoes beneath the whitewash in the dining room, a vineyard under wildly overgrown brambles – and even a wayward scorpion under her pillow. And from her traditional kitchen and simple garden she creates dozens of delicious seasonal recipes, all included in this book.

In the vibrant local markets and neighbouring hill towns, the author explores the nuances of the Italian landscape, history and cuisine. Each adventure yields delightful surprises – the perfect *panettone*, an unforgettable wine, or painted Etruscan tombs. Doing for Tuscany what Peter Mayle did for Provence, Mayes writes about the tastes and pleasures of a foreign country with gusto and passion. A celebration of the extraordinary quality of life in Tuscany, *Under the Tuscan Sun* is a feast for all the senses.

'A MEMOIR, TRAVELOGUE AND COOKBOOK ALL ROLLED INTO ONE'
Guardian

THE NO. 1 INTERNATIONAL BESTSELLER – NOW A MAJOR MOTION PICTURE STARRING DIANE LANE

A Bantam Paperback

0 553 81611 X

WITHOUT RESERVATIONS
The Travels of an Independent Woman
By Alice Steinbach

Each morning I am awakened by the sound of a tinkling bell. A cheerful sound, it reminds me of the bells that shopkeepers attach to their doors at Christmas time. In this case, the bell marks the opening of the hotel door. From my room, which is just off the winding staircase, I can hear it clearly. It reminds me of the bell that calls to worship the novice embarking on a new life. In a way I too am a novice, leaving, temporarily, one life for another.

'In many ways, I was an independent woman,' writes Alice Steinbach, Pulitzer Prize-winning journalist and single working mother. 'For years I'd made my own choices, paid my own bills, shovelled my own snow, and had relationships that allowed for a lot of freedom on both sides.' Slowly, however, she saw that she had become quite dependent in another way. 'I had fallen into the habit of defining myself in terms of who I was to other people and what they expected of me.' Who was she away from the things that defined her – her family, children, job, friends?

Steinbach searches for the answer on a contemporary Grand Tour that takes in some of the most exciting places in Europe. A finely crafted piece of inspirational writing, *Without Reservations* is also a personal journey about life, responsibility and being true to the inner self that will strike a chord with all women.

'ANYONE HAS WHO TRAVELLED ALONE CAN EMPATHIZE . . . THE REFLECTIVE COMMENTARY ACCOMPANYING HER VOYAGE OF SELF-DISCOVERY REVEALS A WARM AND ENTHUSIASTIC INDIVIDUAL'
Wanderlust

A Bantam Paperback

0 553 81584 9

INSTRUCTIONS FOR VISITORS
LIFE AND LOVE IN A FRENCH TOWN
Helen Stevenson

'THE MOST AUTHENTIC, ENJOYABLE AND EVOCATIVE BOOK ON FRENCH LIFE THAT I HAVE READ IN YEARS'
Joanne Harris

'WHAT BEGINS AS A SUPERIOR LYRICAL TRAVEL GUIDE TRANSFORMS INTO A TENDER LOVE STORY AND A VERY PERSONAL MEMOIR OF A DISASTROUS AFFAIR'
Good Housekeeping, Book of the Month

Le village is a small town at the southwesternmost tip of France. Here a young Englishwoman fell in love with France, the French and one Frenchman in particular. In her seductive, lyrical and witty memoir Helen Stevenson writes not as an expat but as someone adopted by villagers as one of their own. By Stefan, the Maoist tennis fanatic, who lives off his lover in solidarity with the unemployed; by Gigi, the chic boutique owner who dresses her ex-lovers' girlfriends; and by Luc, the crumpled cowboy painter and part-time dentist, who comes to embody both the joys and the difficulties of transplanting oneself into someone else's country, culture and heart.

'IN HELEN STEVENSON'S MEMOIR OF AN ILL-FATED LOVE AFFAIR . . . SEX AND GOSSIP HELP PASS THE TIME. THERE ARE AFFAIRS, BUT ALSO HISTRIONIC JEALOUSY, MELODRAMATIC BUST-UPS AND ANY AMOUNT OF UNREQUITED LUST . . . A PLAUSIBLE AND SOMETIMES AFFECTIONATE PORTRAYAL OF ONE SLICE OF FRENCH LIFE'
Independent on Sunday

'AS BEGUILING AND AS ENIGMATICALLY SEDUCTIVE A PIECE OF WRITING AS YOU COULD ASK FOR . . . A BEAUTIFULLY TACTILE AND REFLECTIVE MEDITATION ON THE OUTSIDER'S EXPERIENCE OF A COMMUNITY'
The Times

'A STARTLINGLY ORIGINAL WORK'
Harpers & Queen, Book of the Month

'CLEVER, GRIPPING AND ELEGANTLY WRITTEN'
Independent

0 552 99928 8

BLACK SWAN

PERFUME FROM PROVENCE
Lady Fortescue

'HAS CHARM AND PERIOD FRAGRANCE'
Adam Ruck, *Daily Telegraph*

In the early 1930s, Winifred Fortescue and her husband, Sir John Fortescue, left England and settled in Provence, in a small stone house amid olive groves, on the border of Grasse. Almost at once they were bewitched, by the scenery, by their garden – an incredible terraced landscape of vines, wild flowers, roses and lavender – and above all by the charming, infuriating, warm-hearted and wily Provençals. The house was delightful but tiny, and at once plans were put in hand to extend it over the mountain terrace. Winifred Fortescue's witty and warm account of life with stonemasons, craftsmen, gardeners, and above all her total involvement with the everyday events of a Provençal village made *Perfume From Provence* an instant bestseller.

'Lady Fortescue bursts upon the unsuspecting village with unaffected delight, torpedoing the siesta'd somnolence of small-town bureaucrats . . . regally chauffeuring neighbours' wedding guests in the Fortescue fiat . . . her world centres on house and garden . . . on her bald, fanatical but devoted gardener. The perfume of this Provence may belong to a forgotten age, but thanks to her own undisguised enjoyment, its fragrance charms and lingers still'
City Limits

0 552 99479 0

BLACK SWAN